D1376140

SPANISH
Grammar
& Verb Tables

Collins Gem

SPANISH
Grammar
& Verb Tables

CollinsGem

An Imprint of HarperCollins*Publishers*

third edition 2001

© William Collins Sons & Co. Ltd. 1985
© HarperCollins Publishers 1995, 2001

latest reprint 2001

ISBN 0-00-710202-X

Collins Gem® is a registered trademark of
HarperCollins Publishers Limited

The Collins Gem website address is
www.**collins-gem**.com

The HarperCollins USA website address is
www.harpercollins.com

A de Benito de Harland • I F Ariza

editor
Jeremy Butterfield

editorial staff
Linda Chestnutt, Enrique González Sardinero

editorial management
Vivian Marr

Typeset by Ruth Noble, Peebles
Printed and bound in Italy by Amadeus S.p.A.

INTRODUCTION

Your **Collins Gem Spanish Verb Tables and Grammar** is designed to offer students of Spanish of all ages and at all levels an uncluttered, step-by-step guide to the grammar of the language. For beginners, the book provides a clear introduction to all the basic rules and structures, and more advanced learners will find it an invaluable guide for reference and revision.

For ease of use, each part of speech (nouns, verbs, adjectives etc) has been treated separately (see the list of contents on the next page).

A special feature of this book is the clear demarcation of grammatical points, each treated on a left-hand page, and illustrated by examples in up-to-date Spanish on the opposite right-hand page. The appropriate example is clearly indicated by a system of boxed numbers e.g. → 1, → 2 etc, corresponding to an example number on the facing page.

Special attention has been paid throughout to areas in which Spanish and English usage differ, thus helping the user to avoid the mistake of trying to translate English structures by identical structures in Spanish.

The tables of irregular verbs complement the extensive treatment of regular verbs in the grammar section of the book. In them 80 major irregular verbs are conjugated in their simple tenses so you can see where they differ from regular verbs. In addition, the verb index, in which all verbs are cross-referred to the appropriate conjugation model, enables you to check how over 2,800 Spanish verbs are conjugated.

A comprehensive index, containing key words in both Spanish and English, as well as subject references, completes the grammar.

ABBREVIATIONS

algn	alguien	**masc**	masculine	**sing**	singular
cond	conditional	**p(p)**	page(s)	**sth**	something
fem	feminine	**plur**	plural	**subj**	subjunctive
ff	and following pages	**sb**	somebody		

CONTENTS

4

		Page
VERBS	Simple Tenses: formation	6
	: First conjugation	8
	: Second conjugation	10
	: Third conjugation	12
	The imperative	14
	Compound tenses: formation	18
	Reflexive verbs	24
	The passive	32
	Impersonal verbs	40
	The infinitive	46
	The gerund	52
	The present participle	52
	Use of tenses	54
	The subjunctive: when to use it	58
	Verbs governing *a, de, con, en,*	
	para and *por*	66
	Ser and *estar*	74
	Verbal idioms	78
VERB TABLES: IRREGULAR VERBS		80
VERB INDEX		162
NOUNS	The gender of nouns	188
	Formation of feminines	192
	Formation of plurals	194
ARTICLES	The definite article	196
	The indefinite article	200
	The article *lo*	202
ADJECTIVES	Formation of feminines and plurals	204
	Invariable adjectives; shortened forms	206
	Comparatives and superlatives	208
	Demonstrative adjectives	212
	Interrogative and exclamatory adjectives	214
	Possessive adjectives	216
	Indefinite adjectives	220
	Position of adjectives	224

CONTENTS

		Page
PRONOUNS	Personal pronouns	226
	Indefinite pronouns	236
	Relative pronouns	238
	Interrogative pronouns	244
	Possessive pronouns	246
	Demonstrative pronouns	248
ADVERBS	Formation; position; irregular adverbs	250
	Comparatives; superlatives	252
	Common adverbs and their usage	254
PREPOSITIONS		256
CONJUNCTIONS		266
SUFFIXES		268
SENTENCE STRUCTURE	Word order	270
	Negatives	272
	Question forms	276
TRANSLATION PROBLEMS		278
PRONUNCIATION		284
SPELLING	Accents	292
	Spelling changes	296
ALPHABET		298
PUNCTUATION		299
USE OF NUMBERS	Cardinal numbers	300
	Ordinal numbers	302
	The time	304
	Calendar	306
INDEX		308

❐ Simple Tenses: Formation

In Spanish the simple tenses are:

Present	→ 1
Imperfect	→ 2
Future	→ 3
Conditional	→ 4
Preterite	→ 5
Present Subjunctive	→ 6
Imperfect Subjunctive	→ 7

They are formed by adding endings to a verb stem. The endings show the number and person of the subject of the verb → 8

The stem and endings of regular verbs are totally predictable. The following sections show all the patterns for regular verbs. For irregular verbs see pp 80 ff.

Regular Verbs

There are three regular verb patterns (called conjugations), each identifiable by the ending of the infinitive:

- First conjugation verbs end in **-ar** e.g. **hablar** to speak.

- Second conjugation verbs end in **-er** e.g. **comer** to eat.

- Third conjugation verbs end in **-ir** e.g. **vivir** to live.

These three conjugations are treated in order on the following pages. The subject pronouns will appear in brackets because they are not always necessary in Spanish (see p 226).

Grammar

1	**(yo) hablo**	I speak I am speaking I do speak
2	**(yo) hablaba**	I spoke I was speaking I used to speak
3	**(yo) hablaré**	I shall speak I shall be speaking
4	**(yo) hablaría**	I should/would speak I should/would be speaking
5	**(yo) hablé**	I spoke
6	**(que) (yo) hable**	(that) I speak
7	**(que) (yo) hablara** or **hablase**	(that) I speak
8	**(yo) hablo** **(nosotros) hablamos** **(yo) hablaría** **(nosotros) hablaríamos**	I speak we speak I would speak we would speak

◻ Simple Tenses: First Conjugation

- The stem is formed as follows:

TENSE	FORMATION	EXAMPLE
Present Imperfect Preterite Present Subjunctive Imperfect Subjunctive*	infinitive minus **-ar** * For irregular verbs see p 80	**habl-**
Future Conditional	infinitive	**hablar-**

- To the appropriate stem add the following endings:

		PRESENT → ①	IMPERFECT → ②	PRETERITE → ③
sing	1st person	**-o**	**-aba**	**-é**
	2nd person	**-as**	**-abas**	**-aste**
	3rd person	**-a**	**-aba**	**-ó**
plur	1st person	**-amos**	**-ábamos**	**-amos**
	2nd person	**-áis**	**-abais**	**-asteis**
	3rd person	**-an**	**-aban**	**-aron**

		PRESENT SUBJUNCTIVE → ④	IMPERFECT SUBJUNCTIVE → ⑤
sing	1st person	**-e**	**-ara** *or* **-ase**
	2nd person	**-es**	**-aras** *or* **-ases**
	3rd person	**-e**	**-ara** *or* **-ase**
plur	1st person	**-emos**	**-áramos** *or* **-ásemos**
	2nd person	**-éis**	**-arais** *or* **-aseis**
	3rd person	**-en**	**-aran** *or* **-asen**

		FUTURE → ⑥	CONDITIONAL → ⑦
sing	1st person	**-é**	**-ía**
	2nd person	**-ás**	**-ías**
	3rd person	**-á**	**-ía**
plur	1st person	**-emos**	**-íamos**
	2nd person	**-éis**	**-íais**
	3rd person	**-án**	**-ían**

Examples

① PRESENT

(yo)	hablo
(tú)	hablas
(él/ella/Vd)	habla
(nosotros/as)	hablamos
(vosotros/as)	habláis
(ellos/as/Vds)	hablan

② IMPERFECT

hablaba
hablabas
hablaba
hablábamos
hablabais
hablaban

③ PRETERITE

hablé
hablaste
habló
hablamos
hablasteis
hablaron

④ PRESENT SUBJUNCTIVE

(yo)	hable
(tú)	hables
(él/ella/Vd)	hable
(nosotros/as)	hablemos
(vosotros/as)	habléis
(ellos/as/Vds)	hablen

⑤ IMPERFECT SUBJUNCTIVE

hablara *or* hablase
hablaras *or* hablases
hablara *or* hablase
habláramos *or* hablásemos
hablarais *or* hablaseis
hablaran *or* hablasen

⑥ FUTURE

(yo)	hablaré
(tú)	hablarás
(él/ella/Vd)	hablará
(nosotros/as)	hablaremos
(vosotros/as)	hablaréis
(ellos/as/Vds)	hablarán

⑦ CONDITIONAL

hablaría
hablarías
hablaría
hablaríamos
hablaríais
hablarían

☐ Simple Tenses: Second Conjugation

• The stem is formed as follows:

TENSE	FORMATION	EXAMPLE
Present		
Imperfect		
Preterite	infinitive minus **-er**	**com-**
Present Subjunctive		
Imperfect Subjunctive*	*For irregular verbs see p80	
Future	infinitive	**comer-**
Conditional		

• To the appropriate stem add the following endings:

		PRESENT → ①	IMPERFECT → ②	PRETERITE → ③
sing	1st person	**-o**	**-ía**	**-í**
	2nd person	**-es**	**-ías**	**-iste**
	3rd person	**-e**	**-ía**	**-ió**
plur	1st person	**-emos**	**-íamos**	**-imos**
	2nd person	**-éis**	**-íais**	**-isteis**
	3rd person	**-en**	**-ían**	**-ieron**

		PRESENT SUBJUNCTIVE → ④	IMPERFECT SUBJUNCTIVE → ⑤
sing	1st person	**-a**	**-iera** or **-iese**
	2nd person	**-as**	**-ieras** or **-ieses**
	3rd person	**-a**	**-iera** or **-iese**
plur	1st person	**-amos**	**-iéramos** or **-iésemos**
	2nd person	**-áis**	**-ierais** or **-ieseis**
	3rd person	**-an**	**-ieran** or **-iesen**

		FUTURE → ⑥	CONDITIONAL → ⑦
sing	1st person	**-é**	**-ía**
	2nd person	**-ás**	**-ías**
	3rd person	**-á**	**-ía**
plur	1st person	**-emos**	**-íamos**
	2nd person	**-éis**	**-íais**
	3rd person	**-án**	**-ían**

Examples

1 PRESENT

(yo)	como
(tú)	comes
(él/ella/Vd)	come
(nosotros/as)	comemos
(vosotros/as)	coméis
(ellos/as/Vds)	comen

2 IMPERFECT

comía
comías
comía
comíamos
comíais
comían

3 PRETERITE

comí
comiste
comió
comimos
comisteis
comieron

4 PRESENT SUBJUNCTIVE

(yo)	coma
(tú)	comas
(él/ella/Vd)	coma
(nosotros/as)	comamos
(vosotros/as)	comáis
(ellos/as/Vds)	coman

5 IMPERFECT SUBJUNCTIVE

comiera or comiese
comieras or comieses
comiera or comiese
comiéramos or comiésemos
comierais or comieseis
comieran or comiesen

6 FUTURE

(yo)	comeré
(tú)	comerás
(él/ella/Vd)	comerá
(nosotros/as)	comeremos
(vosotros/as)	comeréis
(ellos/as/Vds)	comerán

7 CONDITIONAL

comería
comerías
comería
comeríamos
comeríais
comerían

◻ Simple Tenses: Third Conjugation

- The stem is formed as follows:

TENSE	FORMATION	EXAMPLE
Present Imperfect Preterite Present Subjunctive Imperfect Subjunctive*	} infinitive minus **-ir**	**viv-**
	*For irregular verbs see p80	
Future Conditional	} infinitive	**vivir-**

- To the appropriate stem add the following endings:

		PRESENT → ①	IMPERFECT → ②	PRETERITE → ③
sing	1st person	**-o**	**-ía**	**-í**
	2nd person	**-es**	**-ías**	**-iste**
	3rd person	**-e**	**-ía**	**-ió**
plur	1st person	**-imos**	**-íamos**	**-imos**
	2nd person	**-ís**	**-íais**	**-isteis**
	3rd person	**-en**	**-ían**	**-ieron**

		PRESENT SUBJUNCTIVE → ④	IMPERFECT SUBJUNCTIVE → ⑤
sing	1st person	**-a**	**-iera** or **-iese**
	2nd person	**-as**	**-ieras** or **-ieses**
	3rd person	**-a**	**-iera** or **-iese**
plur	1st person	**-amos**	**-iéramos** or **-iésemos**
	2nd person	**-áis**	**-ierais** or **-ieseis**
	3rd person	**-an**	**-ieran** or **-iesen**

		FUTURE → ⑥	CONDITIONAL → ⑦
sing	1st person	**-é**	**-ía**
	2nd person	**-ás**	**-ías**
	3rd person	**-á**	**-ía**
plur	1st person	**-emos**	**-íamos**
	2nd person	**-éis**	**-íais**
	3rd person	**-án**	**-ían**

Examples

Grammar

1 PRESENT		2 IMPERFECT	3 PRETERITE
(yo)	viv**o**	viv**ía**	viv**í**
(tú)	viv**es**	viv**ías**	viv**iste**
(él/ella/Vd)	viv**e**	viv**ía**	viv**ió**
(nosotros/as)	viv**imos**	viv**íamos**	viv**imos**
(vosotros/as)	viv**ís**	viv**íais**	viv**isteis**
(ellos/as/Vds)	viv**en**	viv**ían**	viv**ieron**

4 PRESENT SUBJUNCTIVE		5 IMPERFECT SUBJUNCTIVE
(yo)	viv**a**	viv**iera** or viv**iese**
(tú)	viv**as**	viv**ieras** or viv**ieses**
(él/ella/Vd)	viv**a**	viv**iera** or viv**iese**
(nosotros/as)	viv**amos**	viv**iéramos** or viv**iésemos**
(vosotros/as)	viv**áis**	viv**ierais** or viv**ieseis**
(ellos/as/Vds)	viv**an**	viv**ieran** or viv**iesen**

6 FUTURE		7 CONDITIONAL
(yo)	vivir**é**	vivir**ía**
(tú)	vivir**ás**	vivir**ías**
(él/ella/Vd)	vivir**á**	vivir**ía**
(nosotros/as)	vivir**emos**	vivir**íamos**
(vosotros/as)	vivir**éis**	vivir**íais**
(ellos/as/Vds)	vivir**án**	vivir**ían**

❐ The Imperative

The imperative is the form of the verb used to give commands or orders. It can be used politely, as in English 'Shut the door, please'.

In POSITIVE commands, the imperative forms for **Vd**, **Vds** and **nosotros** are the same as the subjunctive. The other forms are as follows:

> **tú** (same as 3rd person singular present indicative)
> **vosotros** (final **-r** of infinitive changes to **-d**) → ①

(tú)	**habla**	**come**	**vive**
	speak	*eat*	*live*
(Vd)	**hable**	**coma**	**viva**
	speak	*eat*	*live*
(nosotros)	**hablemos**	**comamos**	**vivamos**
	let's speak	*let's eat*	*let's live*
(vosotros)	**hablad**	**comed**	**vivid**
	speak	*eat*	*live*
(Vds)	**hablen**	**coman**	**vivan**
	speak	*eat*	*live*

In NEGATIVE commands, all the imperative forms are exactly the same as the present subjunctive.

◆ The imperative of irregular verbs is given in the verb tables, pp 82 ff.

Position of object pronouns with the imperative

In POSITIVE commands: they follow the verb and are attached to it. An accent is needed to show the correct position for stress (see p 292) → ②

In NEGATIVE commands: they precede the verb and are not attached to it → ③

◆ For the order of object pronouns, see page 232.

1   **cantar**   **cantad**
to sing   sing

2   **Perdóneme**   **Enviémoselos**
Excuse me   Let's send them to him/her/them
Elíjanos   **Explíquemelo**
Choose us   Explain it to me
Esperémosla   **Devuélvaselo**
Let's wait for her/it   Give it back to him/her/them

3   **No me molestes**   **No se la devolvamos**
Don't disturb me   Let's not give it back to him/
                                    her/them

No les castiguemos   **No me lo mandes**
Let's not punish them   Don't send it to me
No las conteste   **No nos lo hagan**
Don't answer them   Don't do it to us

❏ The Imperative *(Continued)*

* For reflexive verbs – e.g. **levantarse** *to get up* – the object pronoun is the reflexive pronoun. It should be noted that the imperative forms need an accent to show the correct position for stress (see p 292). The forms **nosotros** and **vosotros** also drop the final **-s** and **-d** respectively before the pronoun → 1

  BUT: **idos (vosotros)** *go*

  ⚠ NOTE: For general instructions, the infinitive is used instead of the imperative → 2, but when it is preceded by **vamos a** it often translates *let's …* → 3

☐ **Levántate**
Get up
No te levantes
Don't get up

Levántese (Vd)
Get up
No se levante (Vd)
Don't get up

Levantémonos
Let's get up
No nos levantemos
Let's not get up

Levantaos
Get up
No os levantéis
Don't get up

Levántense (Vds)
Get up
No se levanten (Vds)
Don't get up

② **Ver pág …**
See page
No pasar
Do not pass …

③ **Vamos a ver**
Let's see
Vamos a empezar
Let's start

❑ Compound Tenses: Formation

In Spanish the compound tenses are:

Perfect	→ ①
Pluperfect	→ ②
Future Perfect	→ ③
Conditional Perfect	→ ④
Past Anterior	→ ⑤
Perfect Subjunctive	→ ⑥
Pluperfect Subjunctive	→ ⑦

They consist of the past participle of the verb together with the auxiliary verb **haber**.

Compound tenses are formed in exactly the same way for both regular and irregular verbs, the only difference being that irregular verbs may have an irregular past participle.

The Past Participle

For all compound tenses you need to know how to form the past participle of the verb. For regular verbs this is as follows:

◆ 1st conjugation: replace the **-ar** of the infinitive by **-ado** → ⑧

◆ 2nd conjugation: replace the **-er** of the infinitive by **-ido** → ⑨

◆ 3rd conjugation: replace the **-ir** of the infinitive by **-ido** → ⑩

1   **(yo) he hablado**
I have spoken

2   **(yo) había hablado**
I had spoken

3   **(yo) habré hablado**
I shall have spoken

4   **(yo) habría hablado**
I should/would have spoken

5   **(yo) hube hablado**
I had spoken

6   **(que) (yo) haya hablado**
(that) I spoke, have spoken

7   **(que) (yo) hubiera/hubiese hablado**
(that) I had spoken

8   **cantar**   →   **cantado**
to sing   sung

9   **comer**   →   **comido**
to eat   eaten

10   **vivir**   →   **vivido**
to live   lived

◻ **Compound Tenses: Formation** (Continued)

Perfect tense: the present tense of **haber** plus the past participle
→ 1

Pluperfect tense: the imperfect tense of **haber** plus the past
participle → 2

Future Perfect: the future tense of **haber** plus the past participle
→ 3

Conditional Perfect: the conditional of **haber** plus the past participle
→ 4

Examples

grammar

① PERFECT		
	(yo)	**he** hablado
	(tú)	**has** hablado
	(él/ella/Vd)	**ha** hablado
	(nosotros/as)	**hemos** hablado
	(vosotros/as)	**habéis** hablado
	(ellos/as/Vds)	**han** hablado

② PLUPERFECT		
	(yo)	**había** hablado
	(tú)	**habías** hablado
	(él/ella/Vd)	**había** hablado
	(nosotros/as)	**habíamos** hablado
	(vosotros/as)	**habíais** hablado
	(ellos/as/Vds)	**habían** hablado

③ FUTURE PERFECT		
	(yo)	**habré** hablado
	(tú)	**habrás** hablado
	(él/ella/Vd)	**habrá** hablado
	(nosotros/as)	**habremos** hablado
	(vosotros/as)	**habréis** hablado
	(ellos/as/Vds)	**habrán** hablado

④ CONDITIONAL PERFECT		
	(yo)	**habría** hablado
	(tú)	**habrías** hablado
	(él/ella/Vd)	**habría** hablado
	(nosotros/as)	**habríamos** hablado
	(vosotros/as)	**habríais** hablado
	(ellos/as/Vds)	**habrían** hablado

❐ Compound Tenses: Formation *(Continued)*

Past Anterior: the preterite of **haber** plus the past
                                  participle → [1]

Perfect Subjunctive: the present subjunctive of **haber** plus
                                  the past participle → [2]

Pluperfect Subjunctive: the imperfect subjunctive of **haber** plus
                                  the past participle → [3]

- For how to form the past participle of regular verbs see p 18. The
  past participle of irregular verbs is given for each verb in the verb
  tables, pp 82 to 161.

Examples

①	PAST ANTERIOR	(yo)	**hube** hablado
		(tú)	**hubiste** hablado
		(él/ella/Vd)	**hubo** hablado
		(nosotros/as)	**hubimos** hablado
		(vosotros/as)	**hubisteis** hablado
		(ellos/as/Vds)	**hubieron** hablado

②	PRESENT SUBJUNCTIVE	(yo)	**haya** hablado
		(tú)	**hayas** hablado
		(él/ella/Vd)	**haya** hablado
		(nosotros/as)	**hayamos** hablado
		(vosotros/as)	**hayáis** hablado
		(ellos/as/Vds)	**hayan** hablado

③	PLUPERFECT SUBJUNCTIVE	(yo)	**hubiera** or **hubiese** hablado
		(tú)	**hubieras** or **hubieses** hablado
		(él/ella/Vd)	**hubiera** or **hubiese** hablado
		(nosotros/as)	**hubiéramos** or **hubiésemos** hablado
		(vosotros/as)	**hubierais** or **hubieseis** hablado
		(ellos/as/Vds)	**hubieran** or **hubiesen** hablado

❏ Reflexive Verbs

A reflexive verb is one accompanied by a reflexive pronoun. The infinitive of a reflexive verb ends with the pronoun **se**, which is added to the verb form e.g.

levantarse *to get up;* **lavarse** *to wash (oneself)*

The reflexive pronouns are:

PERSON	SINGULAR	PLURAL
1st	**me**	**nos**
2nd	**te**	**os**
3rd	**se**	**se**

- The reflexive pronoun 'reflects back' to the subject, but it is not always translated in English → ①

The plural pronouns are sometimes translated as *one another, each other* (the 'reciprocal' meaning) → ②

The reciprocal meaning may be emphasized by **el uno al otro/la una a la otra (los unos a los otros/las unas a las otras)** → ③

- Both simple and compound tenses of reflexive verbs are conjugated in exactly the same way as those of non-reflexive verbs, except that the reflexive pronoun is always used.

The only irregularity is in the 1st and 2nd person plural of the affirmative imperative (see p 16). A sample reflexive verb is conjugated in full on pp 28 to 31.

Position of reflexive pronouns

- Except with the infinitive, gerund and positive commands, the pronoun comes before the verb → ④
- In the infinitive, gerund and positive commands, the pronoun follows the verb and is attached to it (but see also p 228) → ⑤

1. **Me visto**
I'm dressing (myself)

   Nos lavamos
We're washing (ourselves)

   Se levanta
He gets up

2. **Nos queremos**
We love each other

   Se parecen
They resemble one another

3. **Se miraban el uno al otro**
They were looking at each other

4. **Me acuesto temprano**
I go to bed early

   No se ha despertado
He hasn't woken up

   ¿Cómo se llama Vd?
What is your name?

   No te levantes
Don't get up

5. **Quiero irme**
I want to go away

   Siéntense
Sit down

   Estoy levantándome
I am getting up

   Vámonos
Let's go

❐ **Reflexive Verbs** (Continued)

Some verbs have both a reflexive and non-reflexive form. When used reflexively, they have a different but closely related meaning, as shown in the following examples.

NON-REFLEXIVE	REFLEXIVE
acostar to put to bed	**acostarse** to go to bed
casar to marry (off)	**casarse** to get married
detener to stop	**detenerse** to come to a halt
dormir to sleep	**dormirse** to go to sleep
enfadar to annoy	**enfadarse** to get annoyed
hacer to make	**hacerse** to become
ir to go	**irse** to leave, go away
lavar to wash	**lavarse** to get washed
levantar to raise	**levantarse** to get up
llamar to call	**llamarse** to be called
poner to put	**ponerse** to put on (clothing), to become
sentir to feel (something)	**sentirse** to feel (sick, tired, etc)
vestir to dress (someone)	**vestirse** to get dressed
volver to return	**volverse** to turn round

+ Some other verbs exist only in the reflexive:

> **arrepentirse** to repent   **jactarse** to boast
> **atreverse** to dare   **quejarse** to complain

+ Some verbs acquire a different nuance when used reflexively:

> **caer** to fall → 1   **caerse** to fall down (by accident) → 2
> **morir** to die, be killed (by accident or on purpose) → 3   **morirse** to die (from natural causes) → 4

+ Often a reflexive verb can be used:
  — to avoid the passive (see p 34) → 5
  — in impersonal expressions (see p 40) → 6

1. **El agua caía desde las rocas**
Water fell from the rocks

2. **Me caí y me rompí el brazo**
I fell and broke my arm

3. **Tres personas han muerto en un accidente/atentado terrorista**
Three people were killed in an accident/a terrorist attack

4. **Mi abuelo se murió a los ochenta años**
My grandfather died at the age of eighty

5. **Se perdió la batalla**
The battle was lost

   No se veían las casas
The houses could not be seen

6. **Se dice que ...**
It is said that ..., People say that ...

   No se puede entrar
You/One can't go in

   No se permite
It is not allowed

☐ **Reflexive Verbs** (Continued)

Conjugation of: **lavarse** to wash oneself

I SIMPLE TENSES

PRESENT	
(yo)	**me** lavo
(tú)	**te** lavas
(él/ella/Vd)	**se** lava
(nosotros/as)	**nos** lavamos
(vosotros/as)	**os** laváis
(ellos/as/Vds)	**se** lavan

IMPERFECT	
(yo)	**me** lavaba
(tú)	**te** lavabas
(él/ella/Vd)	**se** lavaba
(nosotros/as)	**nos** lavábamos
(vosotros/as)	**os** lavabais
(ellos/as/Vds)	**se** lavaban

FUTURE	
(yo)	**me** lavaré
(tú)	**te** lavarás
(él/ella/Vd)	**se** lavará
(nosotros/as)	**nos** lavaremos
(vosotros/as)	**os** lavaréis
(ellos/as/Vds)	**se** lavarán

CONDITIONAL	
(yo)	**me** lavaría
(tú)	**te** lavarías
(él/ella/Vd)	**se** lavaría
(nosotros/as)	**nos** lavaríamos
(vosotros/as)	**os** lavaríais
(ellos/as/Vds)	**se** lavarían

◻ **Reflexive Verbs** *(Continued)*

Conjugation of: **lavarse** *to wash oneself*

I SIMPLE TENSES

PRETERITE

(yo)	**me** lav**é**
(tú)	**te** lav**aste**
(él/ella/Vd)	**se** lav**ó**
(nosotros/as)	**nos** lav**amos**
(vosotros/as)	**os** lav**asteis**
(ellos/as/Vds)	**se** lav**aron**

PRESENT SUBJUNCTIVE

(yo)	**me** lav**e**
(tú)	**te** lav**es**
(él/ella/Vd)	**se** lav**e**
(nosotros/as)	**nos** lav**emos**
(vosotros/as)	**os** lav**éis**
(ellos/as/Vds)	**se** lav**en**

IMPERFECT SUBJUNCTIVE

(yo)	**me** lav**ara** *or* lav**ase**
(tú)	**te** lav**aras** *or* lav**ases**
(él/ella/Vd)	**se** lav**ara** *or* lav**ase**
(nosotros/as)	**nos** lav**áramos** *or* lav**ásemos**
(vosotros/as)	**os** lav**arais** *or* lav**aseis**
(ellos/as/Vds)	**se** lav**aran** *or* lav**asen**

❐ **Reflexive Verbs** *(Continued)*

Conjugation of: **lavarse** *to wash oneself*

II COMPOUND TENSES

PERFECT	
(yo)	**me he** lavado
(tú)	**te has** lavado
(él/ella/Vd)	**se ha** lavado
(nosotros/as)	**nos hemos** lavado
(vosotros/as)	**os habéis** lavado
(ellos/as/Vds)	**se han** lavado

PLUPERFECT	
(yo)	**me había** lavado
(tú)	**te habías** lavado
(él/ella/Vd)	**se había** lavado
(nosotros/as)	**nos habíamos** lavado
(vosotros/as)	**os habíais** lavado
(ellos/as/Vds)	**se habían** lavado

FUTURE PERFECT	
(yo)	**me habré** lavado
(tú)	**te habrás** lavado
(él/ella/Vd)	**se habrá** lavado
(nosotros/as)	**nos habremos** lavado
(vosotros/as)	**os habréis** lavado
(ellos/as/Vds)	**se habrán** lavado

Examples

□ **Reflexive Verbs** *(Continued)*

Conjugation of: **lavarse** *to wash oneself*

II COMPOUND TENSES

PAST ANTERIOR

(yo)	**me hube** lavado
(tú)	**te hubiste** lavado
(él/ella/Vd)	**se hubo** lavado
(nosotros/as)	**nos hubimos** lavado
(vosotros/as)	**os hubisteis** lavado
(ellos/as/Vds)	**se hubieron** lavado

PERFECT SUBJUNCTIVE

(yo)	**me haya** lavado
(tú)	**te hayas** lavado
(él/ella/Vd)	**se haya** lavado
(nosotros/as)	**nos hayamos** lavado
(vosotros/as)	**os hayáis** lavado
(ellos/as/Vds)	**se hayan** lavado

PLUPERFECT SUBJUNCTIVE

(yo)	**me hubiera** *or* **hubiese** lavado
(tú)	**te hubieras** *or* **hubieses** lavado
(él/ella/Vd)	**se hubiera** *or* **hubiese** lavado
(nosotros/as)	**nos hubiéramos** *or* **hubiésemos** lavado
(vosotros/as)	**os hubierais** *or* **hubieseis** lavado
(ellos/as/Vds)	**se hubieran** *or* **hubiesen** lavado

☐ The Passive

In active sentences, the subject of a verb carries out the action of that verb, but in passive sentences the subject receives the action. Compare the following:

> *The car hit Jane* (subject: *the car*)
> *Jane was hit by the car* (subject: *Jane*)

♦ English uses the verb *'to be'* with the past participle to form passive sentences. Spanish forms them in the same way, i.e.:

> a tense of **ser** + past participle

The past participle agrees in number and gender with the subject → ①

A sample verb is conjugated in the passive voice on pp 36 to 39.

♦ In English, the word *'by'* usually introduces the agent through which the action of a passive sentence is performed. In Spanish this agent is preceded by **por** → ②

♦ The passive voice is used much less frequently in Spanish than English. It is, however, often used in expressions where the identity of the agent is unknown or unimportant → ③

1   **Pablo ha sido despedido**
Paul has been sacked

    Su madre era muy admirada
His mother was greatly admired

    El palacio será vendido
The palace will be sold

    Las puertas habían sido cerradas
The doors had been closed

2   **La casa fue diseñada por mi hermano**
The house was designed by my brother

3   **La ciudad fue conquistada tras un largo asedio**
The city was conquered after a long siege

    Ha sido declarado el estado de excepción
A state of emergency has been declared

❐ **The Passive** (Continued)

In English the indirect object in an active sentence can become the subject of the related passive sentence, e.g.

> *His mother gave him the book* (indirect object: *him*)
> He was given the book by his mother

This is not possible in Spanish. The indirect object remains as such, while the object of the active sentence becomes the subject of the passive sentence → 1

Other ways to express a passive meaning

Since modern Spanish tends to avoid the passive, it uses various other constructions to replace it:

- If the agent (person or object performing the action) is known, the active is often preferred where English might prefer the passive → 2

- The 3rd person plural of the active voice can be used. The meaning is equivalent to *they* + verb → 3

- When the action of the sentence is performed on a person, the reflexive form of the verb can be used in the 3rd person singular, and the person becomes the object → 4

- When the action is performed on a thing, this becomes the subject of the sentence and the verb is made reflexive, agreeing in number with the subject → 5

1. **Su madre le regaló el libro**
His mother gave him the book

   becomes

   El libro le fue regalado por su madre
The book was given to him by his mother

2. **La policía interrogó al sospechoso**
The police questioned the suspect

   rather than

   El sospechoso fue interrogado por la policía

3. **Usan demasiada publicidad en la televisión**
Too much advertising is used on television

4. **Últimamente no se le/les ha visto mucho en público**
He has/they have not been seen much in public recently

5. **Esta palabra ya no se usa**
This word is no longer used
Todos los libros se han vendido
All the books have been sold

☐ **The Passive** (Continued)

Conjugation of: **ser amado** to be loved

PRESENT	
(yo)	**soy** amado(a)
(tú)	**eres** amado(a)
(él/ella/Vd)	**es** amado(a)
(nosotros/as)	**somos** amado(a)s
(vosotros/as)	**sois** amado(a)s
(ellos/as/Vds)	**son** amado(a)s

IMPERFECT	
(yo)	**era** amado(a)
(tú)	**eras** amado(a)
(él/ella/Vd)	**era** amado(a)
(nosotros/as)	**éramos** amado(a)s
(vosotros/as)	**erais** amado(a)s
(ellos/as/Vds)	**eran** amado(a)s

FUTURE	
(yo)	**seré** amado(a)
(tú)	**serás** amado(a)
(él/ella/Vd)	**será** amado(a)
(nosotros/as)	**seremos** amado(a)s
(vosotros/as)	**seréis** amado(a)s
(ellos/as/Vds)	**serán** amado(a)s

CONDITIONAL	
(yo)	**sería** amado(a)
(tú)	**serías** amado(a)
(él/ella/Vd)	**sería** amado(a)
(nosotros/as)	**seríamos** amado(a)s
(vosotros/as)	**seríais** amado(a)s
(ellos/as/Vds)	**serían** amado(a)s

◻ **The Passive** *(Continued)*

Conjugation of: **ser amado** *to be loved*

PRETERITE

(yo)	**fui** am**ado(a)**
(tú)	**fuiste** am**ado(a)**
(él/ella/Vd)	**fue** am**ado(a)**
(nosotros/as)	**fuimos** am**ado(a)s**
(vosotros/as)	**fuisteis** am**ado(a)s**
(ellos/as/Vds)	**fueron** am**ado(a)s**

PRESENT SUBJUNCTIVE

(yo)	**sea** am**ado(a)**
(tú)	**seas** am**ado(a)**
(él/ella/Vd)	**sea** am**ado(a)**
(nosotros/as)	**seamos** am**ado(a)s**
(vosotros/as)	**seáis** am**ado(a)s**
(ellos/as/Vds)	**sean** am**ado(a)s**

IMPERFECT SUBJUNCTIVE

(yo)	**fuera** *or* **fuese** am**ado(a)**
(tú)	**fueras** *or* **fueses** am**ado(a)**
(él/ella/Vd)	**fuera** *or* **fuese** am**ado(a)**
(nosotros/as)	**fuéramos** *or* **fuésemos** am**ado(a)s**
(vosotros/as)	**fuerais** *or* **fueseis** am**ado(a)s**
(ellos/as/Vds)	**fueran** *or* **fuesen** am**ado(a)s**

❑ The Passive *(Continued)*

Conjugation of: **ser amado** *to be loved*

PERFECT	
(yo)	**he sido** am**ado(a)**
(tú)	**has sido** am**ado(a)**
(él/ella/Vd)	**ha sido** am**ado(a)**
(nosotros/as)	**hemos sido** am**ado(a)s**
(vosotros/as)	**habéis sido** am**ado(a)s**
(ellos/as/Vds)	**han sido** am**ado(a)s**

PLUPERFECT	
(yo)	**había sido** am**ado(a)**
(tú)	**habías sido** am**ado(a)**
(él/ella/Vd)	**había sido** am**ado(a)**
(nosotros/as)	**habíamos sido** am**ado(a)s**
(vosotros/as)	**habíais sido** am**ado(a)s**
(ellos/as/Vds)	**habían sido** am**ado(a)s**

FUTURE PERFECT	
(yo)	**habré sido** am**ado(a)**
(tú)	**habrás sido** am**ado(a)**
(él/ella/Vd)	**habrá sido** am**ado(a)**
(nosotros/as)	**habremos sido** am**ado(a)s**
(vosotros/as)	**habréis sido** am**ado(a)s**
(ellos/as/Vds)	**habrán sido** am**ado(a)s**

CONDITIONAL PERFECT	
(yo)	**habría sido** am**ado(a)**
(tú)	**habrías sido** am**ado(a)**
(él/ella/Vd)	**habría sido** am**ado(a)**
(nosotros/as)	**habríamos sido** am**ado(a)s**
(vosotros/as)	**habríais sido** am**ado(a)s**
(ellos/as/Vds)	**habrían sido** am**ado(a)s**

□ **The Passive** *(Continued)*

Conjugation of: **ser amado** *to be loved*

PAST ANTERIOR

(yo)	**hube sido** amado(a)
(tú)	**hubiste sido** amado(a)
(él/ella/Vd)	**hubo sido** amado(a)
(nosotros/as)	**hubimos sido** amado(a)s
(vosotros/as)	**hubisteis sido** amado(a)s
(ellos/as/Vds)	**hubieron sido** amado(a)s

PERFECT SUBJUNCTIVE

(yo)	**haya sido** amado(a)
(tú)	**hayas sido** amado(a)
(él/ella/Vd)	**haya sido** amado(a)
(nosotros/as)	**hayamos sido** amado(a)s
(vosotros/as)	**hayáis sido** amado(a)s
(ellos/as/Vds)	**hayan sido** amado(a)s

PLUPERFECT SUBJUNCTIVE

(yo)	**hubiera/-se sido** amado(a)
(tú)	**hubieras/-ses sido** amado(a)
(él/ella/Vd)	**hubiera/-se sido** amado(a)
(nosotros/as)	**hubiéramos/-semos sido** amado(a)s
(vosotros/as)	**hubierais/-seis sido** amado(a)s
(ellos/as/Vds)	**hubieran/-sen sido** amado(a)s

◻ Impersonal Verbs

Impersonal verbs are used only in the infinitive, the gerund, and in the 3rd person (usually singular); unlike English, Spanish does not use the subject pronoun with impersonal verbs, e.g.

> **llueve**
> *it's raining*
>
> **es fácil decir que ...**
> *it's easy to say that ...*

The most common impersonal verbs are:

INFINITIVE	CONSTRUCTION	
amanecer	**amanece/está amaneciendo** *it's daybreak*	
anochecer	**anochece/está anocheciendo** *it's getting dark*	
granizar	**graniza/está granizando** *it's hailing*	
llover	**llueve/está lloviendo** *it's raining*	→ 1
lloviznar	**llovizna/está lloviznando** *it's drizzling*	
nevar	**nieva/está nevando** *it's snowing*	
tronar	**truena/está tronando** *it's thundering*	

Some reflexive verbs are also used impersonally.
The most common are:

INFINITIVE	CONSTRUCTION
creerse	**se cree que*** + indicative → 2 *it is thought that; people think that*
decirse	**se dice que*** + indicative → 3 *it is said that; people say that*

1. **Llovía a cántaros**
   It was raining cats and dogs
   Estaba nevando cuando salieron
   It was snowing when they left

2. **Se cree que llegarán mañana**
   It is thought they will arrive tomorrow

3. **Se dice que ha sido el peor invierno en 50 años**
   People say it's been the worst winter in 50 years

◻ Impersonal Verbs *(Continued)*

INFINITIVE	CONSTRUCTION
poderse	**se puede** + infinitive → 1
	one/people can, it is possible to
tratarse de	**se trata de** + noun → 2
	it's a question/matter of something
	it's about something
	se trata de + infinitive → 3
	it's a question/matter of doing;
	somebody must do
venderse	**se vende*** + noun → 4
	to be sold; for sale

* This impersonal construction conveys the same meaning as the 3rd person plural of these verbs; **creen que, dicen que, venden**

The following verbs are also commonly used in impersonal constructions:

INFINITIVE	CONSTRUCTION
bastar	**basta con** + infinitive → 5
	it is enough to do
	basta con + noun → 6
	something is enough, it only takes something
faltar	**falta** + infinitive → 7
	we still have to/one still has to
haber	**hay** + noun → 8
	there is/are
	hay que + infinitive → 9
	one has to/we have to
hacer	**hace** + noun/adjective depicting weather/ dark/light etc → 10
	it is
	hace + time expression + **que** + indicative → 11
	somebody has done OR *been doing something since …*
	hace + time expression + **que** + negative indicative → 12
	it is … since

① **Aquí se puede aparcar**
One can park here

② **No se trata de dinero**
It isn't a question/matter of money

③ **Se trata de poner fin al asunto**
We must put an end to the matter

④ **Se vende coche**
Car for sale

⑤ **Basta con telefonear para reservar un asiento**
You need only phone to reserve a seat

⑥ **Basta con un error para que todo se estropee**
One single error is enough to ruin everything

⑦ **Aún falta cerrar las maletas**
We/One still have/has to close the suitcases

⑧ **Hay una habitación libre**
There is one spare room

No había cartas esta mañana
There were no letters this morning

⑨ **Hay que cerrar las puertas**
We have/One has to shut the doors

⑩ **Hace calor/viento/sol**
It is hot/windy/sunny

Mañana hará bueno
It'll be nice (weather) tomorrow

⑪ **Hace seis meses que vivo/vivimos aquí**
I/We have lived or been living here for six months

⑫ **Hace tres años que no le veo**
It is three years since I last saw him

◻ **Impersonal Verbs** *(Continued)*

INFINITIVE	CONSTRUCTION
hacer falta	**hace falta** + noun object (+ indirect object) → ① *(somebody) needs something, something is necessary (to somebody)* **hace falta** + infinitive (+ indirect object) → ② *it is necessary to do* **hace falta que** + subjunctive → ③ *it is necessary to do, somebody must do*
parecer	**parece que** (+ indirect object) + indicative → ④ *it seems/appears that*
ser	**es/son** + time expression → ⑤ *it is* **es** + **de día/noche** → ⑥ *it is* **es** + adjective + infinitive → ⑦ *it is*
ser mejor	**es mejor** + infinitive → ⑧ *it's better to do* **es mejor que** + subjunctive → ⑨ *it's better if/that*
valer más	**más vale** + infinitive → ⑩ *it's better to do* **más vale que** + subjunctive → ⑪ *it's better to do/that somebody does*

1. **Hace falta valor para hacer eso**
   One needs courage to do that, Courage
   is needed to do that

   Me hace falta otro vaso más
   I need an extra glass

2. **Hace falta volver**
   It is necessary to return, We/I/You must return*

   Me hacía falta volver
   I had to return

3. **Hace falta que Vd se vaya**
   You have to/must leave

4. **(Me) parece que estás equivocado**
   It seems (to me) you are wrong

5. **Son las tres y media**
   It is half past three

   Ya es primavera
   It is spring now

6. **Era de noche cuando llegamos**
   It was night when we arrived

7. **Era inútil protestar**
   It was useless to complain

8. **Es mejor no decir nada**
   It's better to keep quiet

9. **Es mejor que lo pongas aquí**
   It's better if/that you put it here

10. **Más vale prevenir que curar**
    Prevention is better than cure

11. **Más valdría que no fuéramos**
    It would be better if we didn't go/We'd better not go

---

* The translation here obviously depends on context

◻ The Infinitive

The infinitive is the form of the verb found in dictionary entries meaning
'to …', e.g. **hablar** to speak, **vivir** to live.

The infinitive is used in the following ways:

- After a preposition → 1

- As a verbal noun → 2
  In this use the article may precede the infinitive, especially when the
  infinitive is the subject and begins the sentence → 3

- As a dependent infinitive, in the following verbal constructions:

  — with no linking preposition → 4

  — with the linking preposition **a** → 5
    (see also p 66)

  — with the linking preposition **de** → 6
    (see also p 66)

  — with the linking preposition **en** → 7
    (see also p 66)

  — with the linking preposition **con** → 8
    (see also p 66)

  — with the linking preposition **por** → 9
    (see also p 66)

- The following construction should also be noted: indefinite pronoun
  + **que** + infinitive → 10

- The object pronouns generally follow the infinitive and are attached
  to it. For exceptions see p 228.

1   **Después de acabar el desayuno, salió de casa**
After finishing her breakfast she went out

    Al enterarse de lo ocurrido se puso furiosa
When she found out what had happened she was furious

    Me hizo daño sin saberlo
She hurt me without her knowing

2   **Su deporte preferido es montar a caballo**
Her favourite sport is horse riding

    Ver es creer
Seeing is believing

3   **El viajar tanto me resulta cansado**
I find so much travelling tiring

4   **¿Quiere Vd esperar?**
Would you like to wait?

5   **Aprenderán pronto a nadar**
They will soon learn to swim

6   **Pronto dejará de llover**
It'll stop raining soon

7   **La comida tarda en hacerse**
The meal is taking a long time to cook

8   **Amenazó con denunciarles**
He threatened to report them (to the police)

9   **Comience Vd por decirme su nombre**
Please start by giving me your name

10   **Tengo algo que decirte**
I have something to tell you

❒ **The Infinitive** *(Continued)*

The verbs set out below are followed by the infinitive with no linking preposition.

- **deber, poder, saber, querer** and **tener que** (**hay que** in impersonal constructions) → ①
- **valer más, hacer falta:** see Impersonal Verbs, p 44.
- verbs of seeing or hearing, e.g. **ver** to see, **oír** to hear → ②
- **hacer** → ③
- **dejar** to let, allow → ③
- The following common verbs:

aconsejar	to advise	→ ④
conseguir	to manage to	→ ⑤
decidir	to decide	
desear	to wish, want	→ ⑥
esperar	to hope	→ ⑦
evitar	to avoid	→ ⑧
impedir	to prevent	→ ⑨
intentar	to try	→ ⑩
lograr	to manage to	→ ⑤
necesitar	to need	→ ⑪
odiar	to hate	
olvidar	to forget	→ ⑫
pensar	to think	→ ⑬
preferir	to prefer	→ ⑭
procurar	to try	→ ⑩
prohibir	to forbid	→ ⑮
prometer	to promise	→ ⑯
proponer	to propose	→ ⑰

1. **¿Quiere Vd esperar?**
   Would you like to wait?
   No puede venir
   She can't come

2. **Nos ha visto llegar**
   She saw us arriving
   Se les oye cantar
   You can hear them singing

3. **No me hagas reír**
   Don't make me laugh
   Déjeme pasar
   Let me past

4. **Le aconsejamos dejarlo para mañana**
   We advise you to leave it until tomorrow

5. **Aún no he conseguido/logrado entenderlo**
   I still haven't managed to understand it

6. **No desea tener más hijos**
   She doesn't want to have any more children

7. **Esperamos ir de vacaciones este verano**
   We are hoping to go on holiday this summer

8. **Evite beber cuando conduzca**
   Avoid drinking and driving

9. **No pudo impedirle hablar**
   He couldn't prevent him from speaking

10. **Intentamos/procuramos pasar desapercibidos**
    We tried not to be noticed

11. **Necesitaba salir a la calle**
    I/he/she needed to go out

12. **Olvidó dejar su dirección**
    He/she forgot to leave his/her address

13. **¿Piensan venir por Navidad?**
    Are you thinking of coming for Christmas?

14. **Preferiría elegirlo yo mismo**
    I'd rather choose it myself

15. **Prohibió fumar a los alumnos**
    He forbade the pupils to smoke

16. **Prometieron volver pronto**
    They promised to come back soon

17. **Propongo salir cuanto antes**
    I propose to leave as soon as possible

☐ The Infinitive: Set Expressions

The following are set in Spanish with the meaning shown:

dejar caer	*to drop* → ①
hacer entrar	*to show in* → ②
hacer saber	*to let know, make known* → ③
hacer salir	*to let out* → ④
hacer venir	*to send for* → ⑤
ir(se) a buscar	*to go for, go and get* → ⑥
mandar hacer	*to order* → ⑦
mandar llamar	*to send for* → ⑧
oír decir que	*to hear it said that* → ⑨
oír hablar de	*to hear of/about* → ⑩
querer decir	*to mean* → ⑪

The Perfect Infinitive

- The perfect infinitive is formed using the auxiliary verb **haber** with the past participle of the verb → ⑫

- The perfect infinitive is found:
  — following certain prepositions, especially **después de** *after* → ⑬
  — following certain verbal constructions → ⑭

Examples

1. **Al verlo, dejó caer lo que llevaba en las manos**
When he saw him he dropped what he was carrying

2. **Haz entrar a nuestros invitados**
Show our guests in

3. **Quiero hacerles saber que no serán bien recibidos**
I want to let them know that they won't be welcome

4. **Hágale salir, por favor**
Please let him out

5. **Le he hecho venir a Vd porque ...**
I sent for you because ...

6. **Vete a buscar los guantes**
Go and get your gloves

7. **Me he mandado hacer un traje**
I have ordered a suit

8. **Mandaron llamar al médico**
They sent for the doctor

9. **He oído decir que está enfermo**
I've heard it said that he's ill

10. **No he oído hablar más de él**
I haven't heard anything more (said) of him

11. **¿Qué quiere decir eso?**
What does that mean?

12. **haber terminado**   **haberse vestido**
to have finished   to have got dressed

13. **Después de haber comprado el regalo, volvió a casa**
After buying/having bought the present, he went back home
Después de haber madrugado tanto, el taxi se retrasó
After she got up so early, the taxi arrived late

14. **perdonar a alguien por haber hecho**
to forgive somebody for doing/having done
dar las gracias a alguien por haber hecho
to thank somebody for doing/having done
pedir perdón por haber hecho
to be sorry for doing/having done

❑ The Gerund

Formation

- 1st conjugation

  Replace the **-ar** of the infinitive by **-ando** → [1]
- 2nd conjugation

  Replace the **-er** of the infinitive by **-iendo** → [2]
- 3rd conjugation

  Replace the **-ir** of the infinitive by **-iendo** → [3]
- For irregular gerunds, see irregular verbs, p 80 ff.

Uses

- After the verb **estar**, to form the continuous tenses → [4]
- After the verbs **seguir** and **continuar** *to continue*, and **ir** when meaning *to happen gradually* → [5]
- In time constructions, after **llevar** → [6]
- When the action in the main clause needs to be complemented by another action → [7]
- The position of object pronouns is the same as for the infinitive (see p 46).
- The gerund is invariable and strictly verbal in sense.

❑ The Present Participle

- It is formed by replacing the **-ar** of the infinitive of 1st conjugation verbs by **-ante**, and the **-er** and **-ir** of the 2nd and 3rd conjugations by **-iente** → [8]
- A very limited number of verbs have a present participle, which is either used as an adjective or a noun → [9]/[10]

Examples

1. **cantar** → **cantando**
   to sing   singing

2. **temer** → **temiendo**
   to fear   fearing

3. **partir** → **partiendo**
   to leave   leaving

4. **Estoy escribiendo una carta**
   I am writing a letter
   Estaban esperándonos
   They were waiting for us

5. **Sigue viniendo todos los días**
   He/she is still coming every day
   Continuarán subiendo los precios
   Prices will continue to go up
   El ejército iba avanzando poco a poco
   The army was gradually advancing

6. **Lleva dos años estudiando inglés**
   He/she has been studying English for two years

7. **Pasamos el día tomando el sol en la playa**
   We spent the day sunbathing on the beach
   Iba cojeando
   He/she/I was limping
   Salieron corriendo
   They ran out

8. **cantar** → **cantante**
   to sing   singing/singer
   pender → **pendiente**
   to hang   hanging
   seguir → **siguiente**
   to follow   following

9. **agua corriente**
   running water

10. **un estudiante**
    a student

❑ Use of Tenses

The Present

- Unlike English, Spanish often uses the same verb form for the simple present (e.g. *I smoke, he reads, we live*) and the continuous present (e.g. *I am smoking, he is reading, we are living*) → ①

- Normally, however, the continuous present is used to translate the English:

  to be doing **estar haciendo** → ②

- Spanish uses the present tense where English uses the perfect in the following cases:

  — with certain prepositions of time – notably **desde** *for/since* – when an action begun in the past is continued in the present → ③

  ⚠ NOTE: The perfect can be used as in English when the verb is negative → ④

  — in the construction **acabar de hacer** *to have just done* → ⑤

- Like English, Spanish often uses the present where a future action is implied → ⑥

The Future

The future is generally used as in English → ⑦, but note the following:

- Immediate future time is often expressed by means of the present tense of **ir** + **a** + infinitive → ⑧

- When '*will*' or '*shall*' mean '*wish to*', '*are willing to*', **querer** is used → ⑨

The Future Perfect

- Used as in English *shall/will have done* → ⑩

- It can also express conjecture, usually about things in the recent past → ⑪

1. **Fumo** I smoke OR: I am smoking
   Lee He reads OR: He is reading
   Vivimos We live OR: We are living

2. **Está fumando**
   He is smoking

3. **Linda estudia español desde hace seis meses**
   Linda's been learning Spanish for six months (*and still is*)
   Estoy de pie desde las siete
   I've been up since seven
   ¿Hace mucho que esperan?
   Have you been waiting long?
   Ya hace dos semanas que estamos aquí
   That's two weeks we've been here (now)

4. **No se han visto desde hace meses**
   They haven't seen each other for months

5. **Isabel acaba de salir**
   Isabel has just left

6. **Mañana voy a Madrid**
   I am going to Madrid tomorrow

7. **Lo haré mañana**
   I'll do it tomorrow

8. **Te vas a caer si no tienes cuidado**
   You'll fall if you're not careful
   Va a perder el tren
   He's going to miss the train
   Va a llevar una media hora
   It'll take about half an hour

9. **¿Me quieres esperar un momento, por favor?**
   Will you wait for me a second, please?

10. **Lo habré acabado para mañana**
    I will have finished it for tomorrow

11. **Ya habrán llegado a casa**
    They must have arrived home by now

❏ Use of Tenses *(Continued)*

The Imperfect

- The imperfect describes:
  - an action or state in the past without definite limits in time → ①
  - habitual action(s) in the past (often expressed in English by means of *would* or *used to*) → ②
- Spanish uses the imperfect tense where English uses the pluperfect in the following cases:
  - with certain prepositions of time – notably **desde** *for/since* – when an action begun in the remoter past was continued in the more recent past → ③

  ⚠ NOTE: The pluperfect is used as in English when the verb is negative or the action has been completed → ④

  - in the construction **acabar de hacer** *to have just done* → ⑤
- Both the continuous and simple forms in English can be translated by the Spanish simple imperfect, but the continuous imperfect is used when the emphasis is on the fact that an action was going on at a precise moment in the past → ⑥

The Perfect

- The perfect is generally used as in English → ⑦

The Preterite

- The preterite generally corresponds to the English simple past in both written and spoken Spanish → ⑧

However, while English can use the simple past to describe habitual actions or settings, Spanish uses the imperfect (see above) → ⑨

The Past Anterior

- This tense is only ever used in written, literary Spanish, to replace the pluperfect in time clauses where the verb in the main clause is in the preterite → ⑩

1. **Todos mirábamos en silencio**
   We were all watching in silence
   Nuestras habitaciones daban a la playa
   Our rooms overlooked the beach

2. **En su juventud se levantaba de madrugada**
   In his youth he got up at dawn
   Hablábamos sin parar durante horas
   We would talk non-stop for hours on end
   Mi hermano siempre me tomaba el pelo
   My brother always used to tease me

3. **Hacía dos años que vivíamos en Irlanda**
   We had been living in Ireland for two years
   Estaba enfermo desde 1990
   He had been ill since 1990
   Hacía mucho tiempo que salían juntos
   They had been going out together for a long time

4. **Hacía un año que no le había visto**
   I hadn't seen him for a year
   Hacía una hora que había llegado
   She had arrived an hour before

5. **Acababa de encontrármelos**
   I had just met them

6. **Cuando llegué, todos estaban fumando**
   When I arrived, they were all smoking

7. **Todavía no han salido**
   They haven't come out yet

8. **Me desperté y salté de la cama**
   I woke up and jumped out of bed

9. **Siempre iban en coche al trabajo**
   They always travelled to work by car

10. **Apenas hubo acabado, se oyeron unos golpes en la puerta**
    She had scarcely finished when there was a knock at the door

❐ The Subjunctive: when to use it

(For how to form the subjunctive see pp 6 ff.)

◆ After verbs of:

— 'wishing'

querer que
desear que } to wish that, want → 1

— 'emotion' (e.g. regret, surprise, shame, pleasure, etc)

sentir que to be sorry that → 2
sorprender que to be surprised that → 3
alegrarse de que to be pleased that → 4

— 'asking' and 'advising'

pedir que to ask that → 5
aconsejar que to advise that → 6

In all the above constructions, when the subject of the verbs in the main and subordinate clause is the same, the infinitive is used, and the conjunction **que** omitted → 7

— 'ordering', 'forbidding', 'allowing'

mandar que*
ordenar que } to order that → 8

permitir que*
dejar que* } to allow that → 9

prohibir que* to forbid that → 10
impedir que* to prevent that → 11

* With these verbs either the subjunctive or the infinitive is used when the object of the main verb is the subject of the subordinate verb → 12

◆ Always after verbs expressing doubt or uncertainty, and verbs of opinion used negatively

dudar que to doubt that → 13

no creer que
no pensar que } not to think that → 14

1. **Queremos que esté contenta**
   We want her to be happy (literally: We want that she is happy)
   ¿Desea Vd que lo haga yo?
   Do you want me to do it?

2. **Sentí mucho que no vinieran**
   I was very sorry that they didn't come

3. **Nos sorprendió que no les vieran Vds**
   We were surprised you didn't see them

4. **Me alegro de que te gusten**
   I'm pleased that you like them

5. **Solo les pedimos que tengan cuidado**
   We're only asking you to take care

6. **Le aconsejé que no llegara tarde**
   I advised him not to be late

7. **Quiero que lo termines pronto**
   I want you to finish it soon
   ⚠ BUT: **Quiero terminarlo pronto**
   I want to finish it soon

8. **Ha mandado que vuelvan**
   He has ordered them to come back
   Ordenó que fueran castigados
   He ordered them to be punished

9. **No permitas que te tomen el pelo**
   Don't let them pull your leg
   No me dejó que la llevara a casa
   She didn't allow me to take her home

10. **Te prohíbo que digas eso**
    I forbid you to say that

11. **No les impido que vengan**
    I am not preventing them from coming

12. **Les ordenó que salieran** OR: **Les ordenó salir**
    She ordered them to go out

13. **Dudo que lo sepan hacer**
    I doubt they can do it

14. **No creo que sean tan listos**
    I don't think they are as clever as that

❏ The Subjunctive: when to use it *(Continued)*

• In impersonal constructions which express necessity, possibility, etc:

hace falta que } es necesario que	*it is necessary that* → 1
es posible que	*it is possible that* → 2
más vale que	*it is better that* → 3
es una lástima que	*it is a pity that* → 4

⚠ NOTE: In impersonal constructions which state a fact or express certainty the indicative is used when the impersonal verb is affirmative. When it is negative, the subjunctive is used → 5

• After certain conjunctions

para que } a fin de que*	*so that* → 6
como si sin que*	*as if* → 7 *without* → 8
a condición de que* } con tal (de) que* siempre que	*provided that,* *on condition that* → 9
a menos que } a no ser que	*unless* → 10
antes (de) que*	*before* → 11
no sea que	*lest/in case* → 12
mientras (que) } siempre que	*as long as* → 13
(el) que	*the fact that* → 14

* When the subject of both verbs is the same, the infinitive is used, and the final **que** is omitted → 8

1. **¿Hace falta que vaya Jaime?**
   Does James have to go?

2. **Es posible que tengan razón**
   It's possible that they are right

3. **Más vale que se quede Vd en su casa**
   It's better that you stay at home

4. **Es una lástima que haya perdido su perrito**
   It's a shame/pity that she has lost her puppy

5. **Es verdad que va a venir**
   It's true that he's coming

   ⚠ BUT: **No es verdad que vayan a hacerlo**
            It's not true that they are going to do it

6. **Átalas bien para que no se caigan**
   Tie them up tightly so that they won't fall

7. **Hablaba como si no creyera en sus propias palabras**
   He talked as if he didn't believe in his own words

8. **Salimos sin que nos vieran**
   We left without them seeing us

   ⚠ BUT: **Me fui sin esperarla**
            I went without waiting for her

9. **Lo haré con tal de que me cuentes todo lo que pasó**
   I'll do it provided you tell me all that happened

10. **Saldremos de paseo a menos que esté lloviendo**
    We'll go for a walk unless it's raining

11. **Avísale antes de que sea demasiado tarde**
    Warn him before it's too late

12. **Habla en voz baja, no sea que alguien nos oiga**
    Speak softly in case anyone hears us

13. **Eso no pasará mientras yo sea el jefe aquí**
    That won't happen as long as I am the boss here

14. **El que no me escribiera no me importaba demasiado**
    The fact that he didn't write didn't matter to me too much

❏ **The Subjunctive: when to use it** *(Continued)*

• After the conjunctions

> **de modo que**
> **de forma que** } *so that* (indicating a purpose) → ①
> **de manera que**

⚠ NOTE: When these conjunctions introduce a result and not a purpose the subjunctive is not used → ②

• In relative clauses with an antecedent which is:

— negative → ③

— indefinite → ④

— non-specific → ⑤

• In main clauses, to express a wish or exhortation. The verb may be preceded by expressions like **ojalá** or **que** → ⑥

• In the **si** clause of conditions where the English sentence contains a conditional tense → ⑦

• In set expressions → ⑧

• In the following constructions which translate *however*:

— **por** + adjective + subjunctive → ⑨

— **por** + adverb + subjunctive → ⑩

— **por** + **mucho** + subjunctive → ⑪

Examples

1. **Vuélvanse de manera que les vea bien**
Turn round so that I can see you properly

2. **No quieren hacerlo, de manera que tendré que hacerlo yo**
They won't do it, so I'll have to do it myself

3. **No he encontrado a nadie que la conociera**
I haven't met anyone who knows her
No dijo nada que no supiéramos ya
He/she didn't say anything we didn't already know

4. **Necesito alguien que sepa conducir**
I need someone who can drive
Busco algo que me distraiga
I'm looking for something to take my mind off it

5. **Busca una casa que tenga calefacción central**
He/she's looking for a house which has central heating
(*subjunctive used since such a house may or may not exist*)
El que lo haya visto tiene que decírmelo
Anyone who has seen it must tell me
(*subjunctive used since it is not known who has seen it*)

6. **¡Ojalá haga buen tiempo!**
Let's hope the weather will be good!
¡Que te diviertas!
Have a good time!

7. **Si fuéramos en coche llegaríamos a tiempo**
If we went by car we'd be there in time

8. **Diga lo que diga ...**   **Sea lo que sea ...**
Whatever he may say ...   Be that as it may ...
Pase lo que pase ...   **Sea como sea ...**
Come what may ...   One way or another ...

9. **Por cansado que esté, seguirá trabajando**
No matter how/however tired he may be, he'll go on working

10. **Por lejos que viva, iremos a buscarle**
No matter how/however far away he lives, we'll go and look for him

11. **Por mucho que lo intente, nunca lo conseguirá**
No matter how/however hard he tries, he'll never succeed

❑ The Subjunctive: when to use it *(Continued)*

Clauses taking either a subjunctive or an indicative

In certain constructions, a subjunctive is needed when the action refers to future events or hypothetical situations, whereas an indicative is used when stating a fact or experience → ①

The commonest of these are:

- The conjunctions

cuando	*when* → ①
en cuanto **tan pronto como** }	*as soon as* → ②
después (de) que*	*after* → ③
hasta que	*until* → ④
mientras	*while* → ⑤
siempre que	*whenever* → ⑥
aunque	*even though* → ⑦

All conjunctions and pronouns ending in **-quiera** (*-ever*) → ⑧

* ⚠ NOTE: If the subject of both verbs is the same, the subjunctive introduced by **después (de) que** may be replaced by **después de** + infinitive → ⑨

Sequence of tenses in Subordinate Clauses

- If the verb in the main clause is in the present, future or imperative, the verb in the dependent clause will be in the present or perfect subjunctive → ⑩

- If the verb in the main clause is in the conditional or any past tense, the verb in the dependent clause will be in the imperfect or pluperfect subjunctive → ⑪

1 **Le aconsejé que oyera música cuando estuviera nervioso**
I advised him to listen to music when he felt nervous
Me gusta nadar cuando hace calor
I like to swim when it is warm

2 **Te devolveré el libro tan pronto como lo haya leído**
I'll give you back the book as soon as I have read it

3 **Te lo diré después de que te hayas sentado**
I'll tell you after you've sat down

4 **Quédate aquí hasta que volvamos**
Stay here until we come back

5 **No hablen en voz alta mientras estén ellos aquí**
Don't speak loudly while they are here

6 **Vuelvan por aquí siempre que quieran**
Come back whenever you wish to

7 **No le creeré aunque diga la verdad**
I won't believe him even if he tells the truth

8 **La encontraré dondequiera que esté**
I will find her wherever she might be

9 **Después de cenar nos fuimos al cine**
After dinner we went to the cinema

10 **Quiero que lo hagas** (*pres + pres subj*)
I want you to do it
Temo que no haya venido (*pres + perf subj*)
I fear he hasn't come (might not have come)
Iremos por aquí para que no nos vean
(*future + pres subj*)
We'll go this way so that they won't see us

11 **Me gustaría que llegaras temprano**
(*cond + imperf subj*)
I'd like you to arrive early
Les pedí que me esperaran (*preterite + imperf subj*)
I asked them to wait for me
Sentiría mucho que hubiese muerto
(*cond + pluperf subj*)
I would be very sorry if he were dead

❐ **Verbs governing a, de, con, en, por and para**

The following lists (pp 66 to 73) contain common verbal constructions using the prepositions **a, de, con, en, por** and **para**.

Note the following abbreviations:

infin	infinitive
perf infin	perfect infinitive*
algn	alguien
sb	somebody
sth	something

* For formation see p 50

aburrirse de + infin	to get bored with doing → 1
acabar con algo/algn	to put an end to sth/finish with sb → 2
acabar de* + infin	to have just done → 3
acabar por + infin	to end up doing → 4
acercarse a algo/algn	to approach sth/sb
acordarse de algo/algn/de + infin	to remember sth/sb/doing → 5
acostumbrarse a algo/algn/a + infin	to get used to sth/sb/to doing → 6
acusar a algn de algo/de + perf infin	to accuse sb of sth/of doing, having done → 7
advertir a algn de algo	to notify, warn sb about sth → 8
aficionarse a algo/a + infin	to grow fond of sth/of doing → 9
alegrarse de algo/de + perf infin	to be glad about sth/of doing, having done → 10
alejarse de algn/algo	to move away from sb/sth
amenazar a algn con algo/ con + infin	to threaten sb with sth/to do → 11
animar a algn a + infin	to encourage sb to do
apresurarse a + infin	to hurry to do → 12

* See also Use of Tenses, pp 54 and 56

Examples

1. **Me aburría de no poder salir de casa**
   I used to get bored with not being able to leave the house

2. **Quiso acabar con su vida**
   He wanted to put an end to his life

3. **Acababan de llegar cuando ...**
   They had just arrived when ...

4. **El acusado acabó por confesarlo todo**
   The accused ended up by confessing everything

5. **Nos acordamos muy bien de aquellas vacaciones**
   We remember that holiday very well

6. **Me he acostumbrado a levantarme temprano**
   I've got used to getting up early

7. **Le acusó de haber mentido**
   She accused him of lying

8. **Advertí a mi amigo del peligro que corría**
   I warned my friend about the danger he was in

9. **Nos hemos aficionado a la música clásica**
   We've grown fond of classical music

10. **Me alegro de haberle conocido**
    I'm glad I met him

11. **Amenazó con denunciarles**
    He threatened to report them

12. **Se apresuraron a coger sitio**
    They hurried to find a seat

❐ **Verbs governing a, de, con, en, por and para** (Continued)

aprender a + infin	*to learn to do* → 1
aprovecharse de algo/algn	*to take advantage of sth/sb*
aproximarse a algn/algo	*to approach sb/sth*
asistir a algo	*to attend sth, be at sth*
asomarse a/por	*to lean out of* → 2
asombrarse de + infin	*to be surprised at doing* → 3
atreverse a + infin	*to dare to do*
avergonzarse de algo/algn/de + perf infin	*to be ashamed of sth/sb/of doing, having done* → 4
ayudar a algn a + infin	*to help sb to do* → 5
bajarse de (+ place/vehicle)	*to get off/out of* → 6
burlarse de algn	*to make fun of sb*
cansarse de algo/algn/de + infin	*to tire of sth/sb/of doing*
carecer de algo	*to lack sth* → 7
cargar de algo	*to load with sth* → 8
casarse con algn	*to get married to sb* → 9
cesar de + infin	*to stop doing*
chocar con algo	*to crash/bump into sth* → 10
comenzar a + infin	*to begin to do*
comparar con algn/algo	*to compare with sb/sth*
consentir en + infin	*to agree to do*
consistir en + infin	*to consist of doing* → 11
constar de algo	*to consist of sth* → 12
contar con algn/algo	*to rely on sb/sth* → 13
convenir en + infin	*to agree to do* → 14
darse cuenta de algo	*to realize sth*
dejar de + infin	*to stop doing* → 15
depender de algo/algn	*to depend on sth/sb* → 16
despedirse de algn	*to say goodbye to sb*
dirigirse a + place/**a algn**	*to head for/address sb*
disponerse a + infin	*to get ready to do*
empezar a + infin	*to begin to do*
empezar por + infin	*to begin by doing* → 17

1. **Me gustaría aprender a nadar**
   I'd like to learn to swim

2. **No te asomes a la ventana**
   Don't lean out of the window

3. **Nos asombramos mucho de verles ahí**
   We were very surprised at seeing them there

4. **No me avergüenzo de haberlo hecho**
   I'm not ashamed of having done it

5. **Ayúdeme a llevar estas maletas**
   Help me to carry these cases

6. **Se bajó del coche**
   He got out of the car

7. **La casa carecía de jardín**
   The house lacked (did not have) a garden

8. **El carro iba cargado de paja**
   The cart was loaded with straw

9. **Se casó con Andrés**
   She married Andrew

10. **Enciende la luz, o chocarás con la puerta**
    Turn the light on, or you'll bump into the door

11. **Mi plan consistía en vigilarles de cerca**
    My plan consisted of keeping a close eye on them

12. **El examen consta de tres partes**
    The exam consists of three parts

13. **Cuento contigo para que me ayudes a hacerlo**
    I rely on you to help me do it

14. **Convinieron en reunirse al día siguiente**
    They agreed to meet the following day

15. **¿Quieres dejar de hablar?**
    Will you stop talking?

16. **No depende de mí**
    It doesn't depend on me

17. **Empieza por enterarte de lo que se trata**
    Begin by finding out what it is about

◻ **Verbs governing a, de, con, en, por and para** *(Continued)*

encontrarse con algn	*to meet sb (by chance)* → 1
enfadarse con algn	*to get annoyed with sb*
enseñar a algn a + infin	*to teach sb to* → 2
enterarse de algo	*to find out about sth* → 3
entrar en (+ place)	*to enter, go into*
esperar a + infin	*to wait until* → 4
estar de acuerdo con algn/algo	*to agree with sb/sth*
fiarse de algn/algo	*to trust sb/sth*
fijarse en algo/algn	*to notice sth/sb* → 5
hablar con algn	*to talk to sb* → 6
hacer caso a algn	*to pay attention to sb*
hartarse de algo/algn/de + infin	*to get fed up with sth/sb/with doing* → 7
interesarse por algo/algn	*to be interested in sth/sb* → 8
invitar a algn a + infin	*to invite sb to do*
jugar a (+ sports, games)	*to play*
luchar por algo/por + infin	*to fight, strive for/to do* → 9
llegar a (+ place)/a + infin	*to reach/to manage to do* → 10
llenar de algo	*to fill with sth*
negarse a + infin	*to refuse to do* → 11
obligar a algn a + infin	*to make sb do* → 12
ocuparse de algn/algo	*to take care of sb/attend to sth*
oler a algo	*to smell of sth* → 13
olvidarse de algo/algn/de + infin	*to forget sth/sb/to do* → 14
oponerse a algo/a + infin	*to be opposed to sth/to doing*
parecerse a algn/algo	*to resemble sb/sth*
pensar en algo/algn/en + infin	*to think about sth/sb/about doing* → 15
preguntar por algn	*to ask for/about sb*
preocuparse de or por algo/algn	*to worry about sth/sb* → 16

Examples

1 **Me encontré con ella al entrar en el banco**
I met her as I was entering the bank

2 **Le estoy enseñando a nadar**
I am teaching him to swim

3 **¿Te has enterado del sitio adonde hay que ir?**
Have you found out where we have to go?

4 **Espera a saber lo que quiere antes de comprar el regalo**
Wait until you know what he wants before buying the present

5 **Me fijé en él cuando subía a su coche**
I noticed him when he was getting into his car

6 **¿Puedo hablar con Vd un momento?**
May I talk to you for a moment?

7 **Me he hartado de escribirle**
I've got fed up with writing to him

8 **Me interesaba mucho por la arqueología**
I was very interested in archaeology

9 **Hay que luchar por mantener la paz**
One must strive to preserve peace

10 **Lo intenté sin llegar a conseguirlo**
I tried without managing to do it

11 **Se negó a hacerlo**
He refused to do it

12 **Le obligó a sentarse**
He made him sit down

13 **Este perfume huele a jazmín**
This perfume smells of jasmine

14 **Siempre me olvido de cerrar la puerta**
I always forget to shut the door

15 **No quiero pensar en eso**
I don't want to think about that

16 **Se preocupa mucho de/por su apariencia**
He worries a lot about his appearance

◻ **Verbs governing a, de, con, en, por and para** *(Continued)*

prepararse a + infin	*to prepare to do*
probar a + infin	*to try to do*
quedar en + infin	*to agree to do* → 1
quedar por + infin	*to remain to be done* → 2
quejarse de algo	*to complain of sth*
referirse a algo	*to refer to sth*
reírse de algo/algn	*to laugh at sth/sb*
rodear de	*to surround with* → 3
romper a + infin	*to (suddenly) start to do* → 4
salir de (+ place)	*to leave*
sentarse a (+ table etc)	*to sit down at*
subir(se) a (+ vehicle/place)	*to get on, into/to climb* → 5
servir de algo a algn	*to be useful to/serve sb as sth* → 6
servir para algo/para + infin	*to be good as sth/for doing* → 7
servirse de algo	*to use sth* → 8
soñar con algn/algo/con + infin	*to dream about/of sb/sth/of doing*
sorprenderse de algo	*to be surprised at sth*
tardar en + infin	*to take time to do* → 9
tener ganas de algo/de + infin	*to want sth/to do* → 10
tener miedo de algo	*to be afraid of sth* → 11
tener miedo a algn	*to be afraid of sb* → 12
terminar por + infin	*to end by doing*
tirar de algo/algn	*to pull sth/sb*
trabajar de (+ occupation)	*to work as* → 13
trabajar en (+ place of work)	*to work at/in* → 14
traducir a (+ language)	*to translate into*
tratar de algo	*to try to do* → 15
tratarse de algo/algn/de + infin	*to be a question of sth/about sb/about doing* → 16
vacilar en + infin	*to hesitate to do* → 17
volver a + infin	*to do again* → 18

1. **Habíamos quedado en encontrarnos a las 8**
   We had agreed to meet at 8

2. **Queda por averiguar dónde se ocultan**
   It remains to be discovered where they are hiding

3. **Habían rodeado el jardín de un seto de cipreses**
   They had surrounded the garden with a hedge of cypress trees

4. **Al apagarse la luz, el niño rompió a llorar**
   When the lights went out, the little boy suddenly started to cry

5. **¡De prisa, sube al coche!**   Get into the car, quick!

6. **Esto me servirá de bastón**
   This will serve me as a walking stick

7. **No sirvo para (ser) jardinero**
   I'm no good as a gardener

8. **Se sirvió de un destornillador para abrirlo**
   She used a screwdriver to open it

9. **Tardaron mucho en salir**
   They took a long time to come out

10. **Tengo ganas de volver a España**
    I want to go back to Spain

11. **Mi hija tiene miedo de la oscuridad**
    My daughter is afraid of the dark

12. **Nunca tuvieron miedo a su padre**
    They were never afraid of their father

13. **Pedro trabaja de camarero en Londres**
    Peter works as a waiter in London

14. **Trabajaba en una oficina**
    I used to work in an office

15. **No trates de engañarme**
    Don't try to fool me

16. **Se trata de nuestro nuevo vecino**
    It's about our new neighbour

17. **Nunca vacilaban en pedir dinero**
    They never hesitated to borrow money

18. **No vuelvas a hacerlo nunca más**
    Don't ever do it again

▫ Ser and Estar

Spanish has two verbs – **ser** and **estar** – for *to be*.

They are not interchangeable and each one is used in defined contexts.

ser is used:

• With an adjective, to express a permanent or inherent quality → **1**

• To express occupation or nationality → **2**

• To express possession → **3**

• To express origin or the material from which something is made → **4**

• With a noun, pronoun or infinitive following the verb → **5**

• To express the time and date → **6**

• To form the passive, with the past participle (see p 32).

⚠ NOTE: This use emphasizes the action of the verb. If, however, the resultant state or condition needs to be emphasized, **estar** is used. The past participle then functions as an adjective (see p 204) and has to agree in gender and in number with the noun → **7**

estar is used:

• Always, to indicate place or location → **8**

• With an adjective or adjectival phrase, to express a quality or state seen by the speaker as subject to change or different from expected → **9**

• When speaking of a person's state of health → **10**

• To form the continuous tenses, used with the gerund (see p 52) → **11**

• With **de** + noun, to indicate a temporary occupation → **12**

Grammar

1	**Mi hermano es alto**	**María es inteligente**
	My brother is tall	Mary is intelligent
2	**Javier es aviador**	**Sus padres son italianos**
	Javier is an airman	His parents are Italian
3	**La casa es de Miguel**	
	The house belongs to Michael	
4	**Mi hermana es de Granada**	**Las paredes son de ladrillo**
	My sister is from Granada	The walls are made of brick
5	**Andrés es un niño travieso**	
	Andrew is a naughty boy	
	Soy yo, Enrique	
	It's me, Henry	
	Todo es proponérselo	
	It's all a question of putting your mind to it	
6	**Son las tres y media**	**Mañana es sábado**
	It's half past three	Tomorrow is Saturday
7	**Las puertas eran cerradas sigilosamente**	
	The doors were being silently closed	
	Las puertas estaban cerradas	
	The doors were closed (*resultant action*)	
8	**La comida está en la mesa**	
	The meal is on the table	
9	**Su amigo está enfermo**	**El lavabo está ocupado**
	Her friend is ill	The toilet is engaged
	Hoy estoy de mal humor	**Las tiendas están cerradas**
	I'm in a bad mood today	The shops are closed
10	**¿Cómo están Vds?**	**Estamos todos bien**
	How are you?	We are all well
11	**Estamos aprendiendo mucho**	
	We are learning a great deal	
12	**Mi primo está de médico en un pueblo**	
	My cousin works as a doctor in a village	

❑ Ser and Estar (Continued)

With certain adjectives, both **ser** and **estar** can be used, although they are not interchangeable when used in this way:

— **ser** will express a permanent or inherent quality → ①

— **estar** will express a temporary state or quality → ②

Both **ser** and **estar** may also be used in set expressions.

The commonest of these are:

- With ser

Sea como sea	*Be that as it may*
Es igual/Es lo mismo	*It's all the same*
llegar a ser	*to become*
¿Cómo fue eso?	*How did that happen?*
¿Qué ha sido de él?	*What has become of him?*
ser para (with the idea of purpose)	*to be for* → ③

- With estar

estar de pie/de rodillas	*to be standing/kneeling*
estar de viaje	*to be travelling*
estar de vacaciones	*to be on holiday*
estar de vuelta	*to be back*
estar de moda	*to be in fashion*
Está bien	*It's all right*
estar para	*to be about to do sth/to be in a mood for* → ④
estar por	*to be inclined to/to be (all) for* → ⑤
estar a punto de	*to be just about to do sth* → ⑥

1. **Su hermana es muy joven/vieja**
   His sister is very young/old
   Son muy ricos/pobres
   They are very rich/poor
   Su amigo era un enfermo
   His friend was an invalid
   Es un borracho
   He is a drunkard
   Mi hijo es bueno/malo
   My son is good/naughty
   Viajar es cansado
   Travelling is tiring

2. **Está muy joven/vieja con ese vestido**
   She looks very young/old in that dress
   Ahora están muy ricos/pobres
   They have become very rich/poor lately
   Estaba enfermo
   He was ill
   Está borracho
   He is drunk
   Está bueno/malo
   He is well/ill
   Hoy estoy cansada
   I am tired today

3. **Este paquete es para Vd**
   This parcel is for you
   Esta caja es para guardar semillas
   This box is for keeping seeds in

4. **Están para llegar**
   They're about to arrive

5. **Estoy por irme a vivir a España**
   I'm inclined to go and live in Spain

6. **Las rosas están a punto de salir**
   The roses are about to come out

☐ Verbal Idioms

Special Intransitive Verbs

With the following verbs the Spanish construction is the opposite of the English. The subject in English becomes the indirect object of the Spanish verb, while the object in English becomes the subject of the Spanish verb.

Compare the following:

> *I like that house* (subject: *I*, object: *that house*)
> **Esa casa me gusta** (subject: **esa casa**, indirect object: **me**)

The commonest of these verbs are:

gustar	*to like* →	1
gustar más	*to prefer* →	2
encantar	(colloquial) *to love* →	3
faltar	*to need/to be short of/to have missing* →	4
quedar	*to be/have left* →	5
doler	*to have a pain in/to hurt, ache* →	6
interesar	*to be interested in* →	7
importar	*to mind* →	8

1   **Me gusta este vestido**
I like this dress (This dress pleases me)

2   **Me gustan más éstas**
I prefer these

3   **Nos encanta hacer deporte**
We love sport

4   **Me faltaban 100 pesetas**
I was short of 100 pesetas

     Sólo le falta el toque final
It just needs the finishing touch

     Le faltaban tres dientes
He/she had three teeth missing

5   **Sólo nos quedan dos kilómetros**
We only have two kilometres (left) to go

6   **Me duele la cabeza**
I have a headache

7   **Nos interesa mucho la política**
We are very interested in politics

8   **No me importa la lluvia**
I don't mind the rain

☐ Irregular Verbs

The verbs listed opposite and conjugated on pp 82 to 161 provide the main patterns for irregular verbs. The verbs are grouped opposite according to their infinitive ending and are shown in the following tables in alphabetical order.

In the tables, the most important irregular verbs are given in their most common simple tenses, together with the imperative and the gerund.

The past participle is also shown for each verb, to enable you to form all the compound tenses, as on pp 18 to 23.

The pronouns **ella** and **Vd** take the same verb endings as **él**, while **ellas** and **Vds** take the same endings as **ellos**.

- All the verbs included in the tables differ from the three conjugations set out on pp 8 to 13. Many – e.g. **contar** – serve as models for groups of verbs, while others – e.g. **ir** – are unique. On pp 162 to 186 you will find over 2,800 commonly used verbs listed alphabetically and cross-referred either to the relevant basic conjugation or to the appropriate model in the verb tables.

Imperfect Subjunctive of Irregular Verbs

For verbs with an irregular root form in the preterite tense – e.g. **andar** → **anduvieron** – the imperfect subjunctive is formed by using the root form of the 3rd person plural of the preterite tense, and adding the imperfect subjunctive endings **-iera/-iese** etc where the verb has an 'i' in the preterite ending – e.g. anduv**ieron** → anduv**iera/iese**. Where the verb has no 'i' in the preterite ending, add **-era/-ese** etc – e.g. produj**eron** → produj**era/ese**.

Grammar

'-ar':

actuar
almorzar
andar
aunar
avergonzar
averiguar
contar
cruzar
dar
empezar
enviar
errar
estar
jugar
negar
pagar
pensar
rehusar
rogar
sacar
volcar

'-er':

caber
caer
cocer
coger
crecer

'-er':

entender
haber
hacer
hay
leer
llover
mover
nacer
oler
poder
poner
querer
resolver
romper
saber
satisfacer
ser
tener
torcer
traer
valer
vencer
ver
volver

'-ir':

abolir
abrir

'-ir':

adquirir
bendecir
conducir
construir
cubrir
decir
dirigir
distinguir
dormir
elegir
erguir
escribir
freír
gruñir
ir
lucir
morir
oír
pedir
prohibir
reír
reñir
reunir
salir
seguir
sentir
venir
zurcir

abolir *to abolish*

PAST PARTICIPLE	IMPERATIVE
abol**ido**	abol**id**
GERUND	
abol**iendo**	

PRESENT*	PRESENT SUBJUNCTIVE
nosotros abol**imos**	*not used*
vosotros abol**ís**	
* Present tense only used in persons shown	

FUTURE		CONDITIONAL	
yo	aboliré	yo	aboliría
tú	abolirás	tú	abolirías
él	abolirá	él	aboliría
nosotros	aboliremos	nosotros	aboliríamos
vosotros	aboliréis	vosotros	aboliríais
ellos	abolirán	ellos	abolirían

IMPERFECT		PRETERITE	
yo	abolía	yo	abolí
tú	abolías	tú	aboliste
él	abolía	él	abolió
nosotros	abolíamos	nosotros	abolimos
vosotros	abolíais	vosotros	abolisteis
ellos	abolían	ellos	abolieron

VERB TABLE

abrir to open

PAST PARTICIPLE	IMPERATIVE
abierto	abre
	abrid
GERUND	
abri**endo**	

PRESENT		PRESENT SUBJUNCTIVE	
yo	abro	yo	abra
tú	abres	tú	abras
él	abre	él	abra
nosotros	abrimos	nosotros	abramos
vosotros	abrís	vosotros	abráis
ellos	abren	ellos	abran

FUTURE		CONDITIONAL	
yo	abriré	yo	abriría
tú	abrirás	tú	abrirías
él	abrirá	él	abriría
nosotros	abriremos	nosotros	abriríamos
vosotros	abriréis	vosotros	abriríais
ellos	abrirán	ellos	abrirían

IMPERFECT		PRETERITE	
yo	abría	yo	abrí
tú	abrías	tú	abriste
él	abría	él	abrió
nosotros	abríamos	nosotros	abrimos
vosotros	abríais	vosotros	abristeis
ellos	abrían	ellos	abrieron

actuar to act

PAST PARTICIPLE	IMPERATIVE
actuado	actúa
	actuad
GERUND	
actuando	

PRESENT		PRESENT SUBJUNCTIVE	
yo	actúo	yo	actúe
tú	actúas	tú	actúes
él	actúa	él	actúe
nosotros	actuamos	nosotros	actuemos
vosotros	actuáis	vosotros	actuéis
ellos	actúan	ellos	actúen

FUTURE		CONDITIONAL	
yo	actuaré	yo	actuaría
tú	actuarás	tú	actuarías
él	actuará	él	actuaría
nosotros	actuaremos	nosotros	actuaríamos
vosotros	actuaréis	vosotros	actuaríais
ellos	actuarán	ellos	actuarían

IMPERFECT		PRETERITE	
yo	actuaba	yo	actué
tú	actuabas	tú	actuaste
él	actuaba	él	actuó
nosotros	actuábamos	nosotros	actuamos
vosotros	actuabais	vosotros	actuasteis
ellos	actuaban	ellos	actuaron

---

adquirir *to acquire*

PAST PARTICIPLE	IMPERATIVE
adquir**ido**	**adquiere**
	adquir**id**
GERUND	
adquir**iendo**	

PRESENT		PRESENT SUBJUNCTIVE	
yo	adqu**iero**	yo	adqu**iera**
tú	adqu**ieres**	tú	adqu**ieras**
él	adqu**iere**	él	adqu**iera**
nosotros	adquirimos	nosotros	adquir**amos**
vosotros	adquirís	vosotros	adquir**áis**
ellos	adqu**ieren**	ellos	adqu**ieran**

FUTURE		CONDITIONAL	
yo	adquirir**é**	yo	adquirir**ía**
tú	adquirir**ás**	tú	adquirir**ías**
él	adquirir**á**	él	adquirir**ía**
nosotros	adquirir**emos**	nosotros	adquirir**íamos**
vosotros	adquirir**éis**	vosotros	adquirir**íais**
ellos	adquirir**án**	ellos	adquirir**ían**

IMPERFECT		PRETERITE	
yo	adquir**ía**	yo	adquir**í**
tú	adquir**ías**	tú	adquir**iste**
él	adquir**ía**	él	adquir**ió**
nosotros	adquir**íamos**	nosotros	adquir**imos**
vosotros	adquir**íais**	vosotros	adquir**isteis**
ellos	adquir**ían**	ellos	adquir**ieron**

almorzar *to have lunch*

PAST PARTICIPLE	IMPERATIVE
almorz**ado**	**almuerza**
	almorz**ad**
GERUND	
almorz**ando**	

PRESENT		PRESENT SUBJUNCTIVE	
yo	**almuerzo**	yo	**almuerce**
tú	**almuerzas**	tú	**almuerces**
él	**almuerza**	él	**almuerce**
nosotros	almorz**amos**	nosotros	almorc**emos**
vosotros	almorz**áis**	vosotros	almorc**éis**
ellos	**almuerzan**	ellos	**almuercen**

FUTURE		CONDITIONAL	
yo	almorzar**é**	yo	almorzar**ía**
tú	almorzar**ás**	tú	almorzar**ías**
él	almorzar**á**	él	almorzar**ía**
nosotros	almorzar**emos**	nosotros	almorzar**íamos**
vosotros	almorzar**éis**	vosotros	almorzar**íais**
ellos	almorzar**án**	ellos	almorzar**ían**

IMPERFECT		PRETERITE	
yo	almorz**aba**	yo	almor**cé**
tú	almorz**abas**	tú	almorz**aste**
él	almorz**aba**	él	almorz**ó**
nosotros	almorz**ábamos**	nosotros	almorz**amos**
vosotros	almorz**abais**	vosotros	almorz**asteis**
ellos	almorz**aban**	ellos	almorz**aron**

andar *to walk*

PAST PARTICIPLE	IMPERATIVE
and**ado**	and**a**
	and**ad**
GERUND	
and**ando**	

PRESENT		PRESENT SUBJUNCTIVE	
yo	ando	yo	ande
tú	andas	tú	andes
él	anda	él	ande
nosotros	and**amos**	nosotros	and**emos**
vosotros	and**áis**	vosotros	and**éis**
ellos	andan	ellos	anden

FUTURE		CONDITIONAL	
yo	andar**é**	yo	andar**ía**
tú	andar**ás**	tú	andar**ías**
él	andar**á**	él	andar**ía**
nosotros	andar**emos**	nosotros	andar**íamos**
vosotros	andar**éis**	vosotros	andar**íais**
ellos	andar**án**	ellos	andar**ían**

IMPERFECT		PRETERITE	
yo	and**aba**	yo	anduve
tú	and**abas**	tú	anduviste
él	and**aba**	él	anduvo
nosotros	and**ábamos**	nosotros	anduvimos
vosotros	and**abais**	vosotros	anduvisteis
ellos	and**aban**	ellos	anduvieron

aunar *to join together*

PAST PARTICIPLE	IMPERATIVE
aun**ado**	aúna
GERUND	aunad
aun**ando**	

PRESENT		PRESENT SUBJUNCTIVE	
yo	aúno	yo	aúne
tú	aúnas	tú	aúnes
él	aúna	él	aúne
nosotros	aunamos	nosotros	aunemos
vosotros	aunáis	vosotros	aunéis
ellos	aúnan	ellos	aúnen

FUTURE		CONDITIONAL	
yo	aunaré	yo	aunaría
tú	aunarás	tú	aunarías
él	aunará	él	aunaría
nosotros	aunaremos	nosotros	aunaríamos
vosotros	aunaréis	vosotros	aunaríais
ellos	aunarán	ellos	aunarían

IMPERFECT		PRETERITE	
yo	aunaba	yo	auné
tú	aunabas	tú	aunaste
él	aunaba	él	aunó
nosotros	aunábamos	nosotros	aunamos
vosotros	aunabais	vosotros	aunasteis
ellos	aunaban	ellos	aunaron

VERB TABLE

Grammar

---

avergonzar *to shame*

PAST PARTICIPLE	IMPERATIVE
avergonz**ado**	avergü**enza**
GERUND	avergonz**ad**
avergonz**ando**	

PRESENT		PRESENT SUBJUNCTIVE	
yo	avergü**enzo**	yo	avergü**ence**
tú	avergü**enzas**	tú	avergü**ences**
él	avergü**enza**	él	avergü**ence**
nosotros	avergonz**amos**	nosotros	avergonc**emos**
vosotros	avergonz**áis**	vosotros	avergonc**éis**
ellos	avergü**enzan**	ellos	avergü**encen**

FUTURE		CONDITIONAL	
yo	avergonzar**é**	yo	avergonzar**ía**
tú	avergonzar**ás**	tú	avergonzar**ías**
él	avergonzar**á**	él	avergonzar**ía**
nosotros	avergonzar**emos**	nosotros	avergonzar**íamos**
vosotros	avergonzar**éis**	vosotros	avergonzar**íais**
ellos	avergonzar**án**	ellos	avergonzar**ían**

IMPERFECT		PRETERITE	
yo	avergonz**aba**	yo	avergonc**é**
tú	avergonz**abas**	tú	avergonz**aste**
él	avergonz**aba**	él	avergonz**ó**
nosotros	avergonz**ábamos**	nosotros	avergonz**amos**
vosotros	avergonz**abais**	vosotros	avergonz**asteis**
ellos	avergonz**aban**	ellos	avergonz**aron**

averiguar *to find out*

PAST PARTICIPLE	IMPERATIVE
averigu**ado**	averigu**a**
GERUND	averigu**ad**
averigu**ando**	

PRESENT		PRESENT SUBJUNCTIVE	
yo	averigu**o**	yo	averig**üe**
tú	averigu**as**	tú	averig**ües**
él	averigu**a**	él	averig**üe**
nosotros	averigu**amos**	nosotros	averig**üemos**
vosotros	averigu**áis**	vosotros	averig**üéis**
ellos	averigu**an**	ellos	averig**üen**

FUTURE		CONDITIONAL	
yo	averiguar**é**	yo	averiguar**ía**
tú	averiguar**ás**	tú	averiguar**ías**
él	averiguar**á**	él	averiguar**ía**
nosotros	averiguar**emos**	nosotros	averiguar**íamos**
vosotros	averiguar**éis**	vosotros	averiguar**íais**
ellos	averiguar**án**	ellos	averiguar**ían**

IMPERFECT		PRETERITE	
yo	averigu**aba**	yo	averig**üé**
tú	averigu**abas**	tú	averigu**aste**
él	averigu**aba**	él	averigu**ó**
nosotros	averigu**ábamos**	nosotros	averigu**amos**
vosotros	averigu**abais**	vosotros	averigu**asteis**
ellos	averigu**aban**	ellos	averigu**aron**

VERB TABLE

bendecir *to bless*

PAST PARTICIPLE

bende**cido**

GERUND

bendiciendo

IMPERATIVE

bendice
bendec**id**

PRESENT		PRESENT SUBJUNCTIVE	
yo	bendigo	yo	bendiga
tú	bendices	tú	bendigas
él	bendice	él	bendiga
nosotros	bendecimos	nosotros	bendigamos
vosotros	bendecís	vosotros	bendigáis
ellos	bendicen	ellos	bendigan

FUTURE		CONDITIONAL	
yo	bendeciré	yo	bendeciría
tú	bendecirás	tú	bendecirías
él	bendecirá	él	bendeciría
nosotros	bendeciremos	nosotros	bendeciríamos
vosotros	bendeciréis	vosotros	bendeciríais
ellos	bendecirán	ellos	bendecirían

IMPERFECT		PRETERITE	
yo	bendecía	yo	bendije
tú	bendecías	tú	bendijiste
él	bendecía	él	bendijo
nosotros	bendecíamos	nosotros	bendijimos
vosotros	bendecíais	vosotros	bendijisteis
ellos	bendecían	ellos	bendijeron

caber to fit	
PAST PARTICIPLE	IMPERATIVE
cabido	cabe
	cabed
GERUND	
cabiendo	

PRESENT		PRESENT SUBJUNCTIVE	
yo	quepo	yo	quepa
tú	cabes	tú	quepas
él	cabe	él	quepa
nosotros	cabemos	nosotros	quepamos
vosotros	cabéis	vosotros	quepáis
ellos	caben	ellos	quepan

FUTURE		CONDITIONAL	
yo	cabré	yo	cabría
tú	cabrás	tú	cabrías
él	cabrá	él	cabría
nosotros	cabremos	nosotros	cabríamos
vosotros	cabréis	vosotros	cabríais
ellos	cabrán	ellos	cabrían

IMPERFECT		PRETERITE	
yo	cabía	yo	cupe
tú	cabías	tú	cupiste
él	cabía	él	cupo
nosotros	cabíamos	nosotros	cupimos
vosotros	cabíais	vosotros	cupisteis
ellos	cabían	ellos	cupieron

caer *to fall*

PAST PARTICIPLE	IMPERATIVE
caído	cae
	caed
GERUND	
cayendo	

PRESENT		PRESENT SUBJUNCTIVE	
yo	caigo	yo	caiga
tú	caes	tú	caigas
él	cae	él	caiga
nosotros	caemos	nosotros	caigamos
vosotros	caéis	vosotros	caigáis
ellos	caen	ellos	caigan

FUTURE		CONDITIONAL	
yo	caeré	yo	caería
tú	caerás	tú	caerías
él	caerá	él	caería
nosotros	caeremos	nosotros	caeríamos
vosotros	caeréis	vosotros	caeríais
ellos	caerán	ellos	caerían

IMPERFECT		PRETERITE	
yo	caía	yo	caí
tú	caías	tú	caíste
él	caía	él	cayó
nosotros	caíamos	nosotros	caímos
vosotros	caíais	vosotros	caísteis
ellos	caían	ellos	cayeron

cocer *to boil*

PAST PARTICIPLE	IMPERATIVE
cocido	cuece
	coced
GERUND	
cociendo	

PRESENT		PRESENT SUBJUNCTIVE	
yo	cuezo	yo	cueza
tú	cueces	tú	cuezas
él	cuece	él	cueza
nosotros	cocemos	nosotros	cozamos
vosotros	cocéis	vosotros	cozáis
ellos	cuecen	ellos	cuezan

FUTURE		CONDITIONAL	
yo	coceré	yo	cocería
tú	cocerás	tú	cocerías
él	cocerá	él	cocería
nosotros	coceremos	nosotros	coceríamos
vosotros	coceréis	vosotros	coceríais
ellos	cocerán	ellos	cocerían

IMPERFECT		PRETERITE	
yo	cocía	yo	cocí
tú	cocías	tú	cociste
él	cocía	él	coció
nosotros	cocíamos	nosotros	cocimos
vosotros	cocíais	vosotros	cocisteis
ellos	cocían	ellos	cocieron

VERB TABLE

coger *to catch*

PAST PARTICIPLE	IMPERATIVE
cog**ido**	coge
	coged
GERUND	
cog**iendo**	

PRESENT		PRESENT SUBJUNCTIVE	
yo	cojo	yo	coja
tú	coges	tú	cojas
él	coge	él	coja
nosotros	cogemos	nosotros	cojamos
vosotros	cogéis	vosotros	cojáis
ellos	cogen	ellos	cojan

FUTURE		CONDITIONAL	
yo	cogeré	yo	cogería
tú	cogerás	tú	cogerías
él	cogerá	él	cogería
nosotros	cogeremos	nosotros	cogeríamos
vosotros	cogeréis	vosotros	cogeríais
ellos	cogerán	ellos	cogerían

IMPERFECT		PRETERITE	
yo	cogía	yo	cogí
tú	cogías	tú	cogiste
él	cogía	él	cogió
nosotros	cogíamos	nosotros	cogimos
vosotros	cogíais	vosotros	cogisteis
ellos	cogían	ellos	cogieron

conducir *to drive, to lead*

PAST PARTICIPLE	IMPERATIVE
conduci**do**	conduce
	conducid
GERUND	
conduci**endo**	

PRESENT		PRESENT SUBJUNCTIVE	
yo	conduzco	yo	conduzca
tú	conduces	tú	conduzcas
él	conduce	él	conduzca
nosotros	conducimos	nosotros	conduzcamos
vosotros	conducís	vosotros	conduzcáis
ellos	conducen	ellos	conduzcan

FUTURE		CONDITIONAL	
yo	conduciré	yo	conduciría
tú	conducirás	tú	conducirías
él	conducirá	él	conduciría
nosotros	conduciremos	nosotros	conduciríamos
vosotros	conduciréis	vosotros	conduciríais
ellos	conducirán	ellos	conducirían

IMPERFECT		PRETERITE	
yo	conducía	yo	conduje
tú	conducías	tú	condujiste
él	conducía	él	condujo
nosotros	conducíamos	nosotros	condujimos
vosotros	conducíais	vosotros	condujisteis
ellos	conducían	ellos	condujeron

construir *to build*

PAST PARTICIPLE	IMPERATIVE
construi**do**	constru**ye**
GERUND	construi**d**
constru**yendo**	

PRESENT		PRESENT SUBJUNCTIVE	
yo	construy**o**	yo	construy**a**
tú	construy**es**	tú	construy**as**
él	construy**e**	él	construy**a**
nosotros	constru**imos**	nosotros	construy**amos**
vosotros	constru**ís**	vosotros	construy**áis**
ellos	construy**en**	ellos	construy**an**

FUTURE		CONDITIONAL	
yo	construir**é**	yo	construir**ía**
tú	construir**ás**	tú	construir**ías**
él	construir**á**	él	construir**ía**
nosotros	construir**emos**	nosotros	construir**íamos**
vosotros	construir**éis**	vosotros	construir**íais**
ellos	construir**án**	ellos	construir**ían**

IMPERFECT		PRETERITE	
yo	constru**ía**	yo	constru**í**
tú	constru**ías**	tú	constru**iste**
él	constru**ía**	él	constru**yó**
nosotros	constru**íamos**	nosotros	constru**imos**
vosotros	constru**íais**	vosotros	constru**isteis**
ellos	constru**ían**	ellos	constru**yeron**

contar *to tell, to count*

PAST PARTICIPLE	IMPERATIVE
contado	**cuenta**
	contad
GERUND	
contando	

PRESENT		PRESENT SUBJUNCTIVE	
yo	cuento	yo	cuente
tú	cuentas	tú	cuentes
él	cuenta	él	cuente
nosotros	contamos	nosotros	contemos
vosotros	contáis	vosotros	contéis
ellos	cuentan	ellos	cuenten

FUTURE		CONDITIONAL	
yo	contaré	yo	contaría
tú	contarás	tú	contarías
él	contará	él	contaría
nosotros	contaremos	nosotros	contaríamos
vosotros	contaréis	vosotros	contaríais
ellos	contarán	ellos	contarían

IMPERFECT		PRETERITE	
yo	contaba	yo	conté
tú	contabas	tú	contaste
él	contaba	él	contó
nosotros	contábamos	nosotros	contamos
vosotros	contabais	vosotros	contasteis
ellos	contaban	ellos	contaron

crecer *to grow*

PAST PARTICIPLE	IMPERATIVE
crecido	crece
	creced
GERUND	
creciendo	

PRESENT		PRESENT SUBJUNCTIVE	
yo	crezco	yo	crezca
tú	creces	tú	crezcas
él	crece	él	crezca
nosotros	crecemos	nosotros	crezcamos
vosotros	crecéis	vosotros	crezcáis
ellos	crecen	ellos	crezcan

FUTURE		CONDITIONAL	
yo	creceré	yo	crecería
tú	crecerás	tú	crecerías
él	crecerá	él	crecería
nosotros	creceremos	nosotros	creceríamos
vosotros	creceréis	vosotros	creceríais
ellos	crecerán	ellos	crecerían

IMPERFECT		PRETERITE	
yo	crecía	yo	crecí
tú	crecías	tú	creciste
él	crecía	él	creció
nosotros	crecíamos	nosotros	crecimos
vosotros	crecíais	vosotros	crecisteis
ellos	crecían	ellos	crecieron

cruzar *to cross*

PAST PARTICIPLE	IMPERATIVE
cruzado	cruza
	cruzad
GERUND	
cruzando	

PRESENT		PRESENT SUBJUNCTIVE	
yo	cruzo	yo	cruce
tú	cruzas	tú	cruces
él	cruza	él	cruce
nosotros	cruzamos	nosotros	crucemos
vosotros	cruzáis	vosotros	crucéis
ellos	cruzan	ellos	crucen

FUTURE		CONDITIONAL	
yo	cruzaré	yo	cruzaría
tú	cruzarás	tú	cruzarías
él	cruzará	él	cruzaría
nosotros	cruzaremos	nosotros	cruzaríamos
vosotros	cruzaréis	vosotros	cruzaríais
ellos	cruzarán	ellos	cruzarían

IMPERFECT		PRETERITE	
yo	cruzaba	yo	crucé
tú	cruzabas	tú	cruzaste
él	cruzaba	él	cruzó
nosotros	cruzábamos	nosotros	cruzamos
vosotros	cruzabais	vosotros	cruzasteis
ellos	cruzaban	ellos	cruzaron

cubrir *to cover*

PAST PARTICIPLE	IMPERATIVE
cubierto	cubre
GERUND	cubrid
cubr**iendo**	

PRESENT		PRESENT SUBJUNCTIVE	
yo	cubro	yo	cubra
tú	cubres	tú	cubras
él	cubre	él	cubra
nosotros	cubrimos	nosotros	cubramos
vosotros	cubrís	vosotros	cubráis
ellos	cubren	ellos	cubran

FUTURE		CONDITIONAL	
yo	cubriré	yo	cubriría
tú	cubrirás	tú	cubrirías
él	cubrirá	él	cubriría
nosotros	cubriremos	nosotros	cubriríamos
vosotros	cubriréis	vosotros	cubriríais
ellos	cubrirán	ellos	cubrirían

IMPERFECT		PRETERITE	
yo	cubría	yo	cubrí
tú	cubrías	tú	cubriste
él	cubría	él	cubrió
nosotros	cubríamos	nosotros	cubrimos
vosotros	cubríais	vosotros	cubristeis
ellos	cubrían	ellos	cubrieron

dar *to give*

PAST PARTICIPLE	IMPERATIVE
dado	da
	dad
GERUND	
dando	

PRESENT		PRESENT SUBJUNCTIVE	
yo	doy	yo	dé
tú	das	tú	des
él	da	él	dé
nosotros	damos	nosotros	demos
vosotros	dais	vosotros	deis
ellos	dan	ellos	den

FUTURE		CONDITIONAL	
yo	daré	yo	daría
tú	darás	tú	darías
él	dará	él	daría
nosotros	daremos	nosotros	daríamos
vosotros	daréis	vosotros	daríais
ellos	darán	ellos	darían

IMPERFECT		PRETERITE	
yo	daba	yo	di
tú	dabas	tú	diste
él	daba	él	dio
nosotros	dábamos	nosotros	dimos
vosotros	dabais	vosotros	disteis
ellos	daban	ellos	dieron

VERB TABLE

decir *to say*

PAST PARTICIPLE	IMPERATIVE
dicho	**di**
GERUND	**decid**
diciendo	

PRESENT		PRESENT SUBJUNCTIVE	
yo	digo	yo	diga
tú	dices	tú	digas
él	dice	él	diga
nosotros	decimos	nosotros	digamos
vosotros	decís	vosotros	digáis
ellos	dicen	ellos	digan

FUTURE		CONDITIONAL	
yo	diré	yo	diría
tú	dirás	tú	dirías
él	dirá	él	diría
nosotros	diremos	nosotros	diríamos
vosotros	diréis	vosotros	diríais
ellos	dirán	ellos	dirían

IMPERFECT		PRETERITE	
yo	decía	yo	dije
tú	decías	tú	dijiste
él	decía	él	dijo
nosotros	decíamos	nosotros	dijimos
vosotros	decíais	vosotros	dijisteis
ellos	decían	ellos	dijeron

dirigir *to direct*

PAST PARTICIPLE	IMPERATIVE
dirig**ido**	dirig**e**
	dirig**id**
GERUND	
dirig**iendo**	

PRESENT		PRESENT SUBJUNCTIVE	
yo	diri**jo**	yo	diri**ja**
tú	dirig**es**	tú	diri**jas**
él	dirig**e**	él	diri**ja**
nosotros	dirig**imos**	nosotros	diri**jamos**
vosotros	dirig**ís**	vosotros	diri**jáis**
ellos	dirig**en**	ellos	diri**jan**

FUTURE		CONDITIONAL	
yo	dirigir**é**	yo	dirigir**ía**
tú	dirigir**ás**	tú	dirigir**ías**
él	dirigir**á**	él	dirigir**ía**
nosotros	dirigir**emos**	nosotros	dirigir**íamos**
vosotros	dirigir**éis**	vosotros	dirigir**íais**
ellos	dirigir**án**	ellos	dirigir**ían**

IMPERFECT		PRETERITE	
yo	dirig**ía**	yo	dirig**í**
tú	dirig**ías**	tú	dirig**iste**
él	dirig**ía**	él	dirig**ió**
nosotros	dirig**íamos**	nosotros	dirig**imos**
vosotros	dirig**íais**	vosotros	dirig**isteis**
ellos	dirig**ían**	ellos	dirig**ieron**

distinguir *to distinguish*

PAST PARTICIPLE	IMPERATIVE
distinguido	
	distingue
	distinguid
GERUND	
distinguiendo	

PRESENT		PRESENT SUBJUNCTIVE	
yo	distingo	yo	distinga
tú	distingues	tú	distingas
él	distingue	él	distinga
nosotros	distinguimos	nosotros	distingamos
vosotros	distinguís	vosotros	distingáis
ellos	distinguen	ellos	distingan

FUTURE		CONDITIONAL	
yo	distinguiré	yo	distinguiría
tú	distinguirás	tú	distinguirías
él	distinguirá	él	distinguiría
nosotros	distinguiremos	nosotros	distinguiríamos
vosotros	distinguiréis	vosotros	distinguiríais
ellos	distinguirán	ellos	distinguirían

IMPERFECT		PRETERITE	
yo	distinguía	yo	distinguí
tú	distinguías	tú	distinguiste
él	distinguía	él	distinguió
nosotros	distinguíamos	nosotros	distinguimos
vosotros	distinguíais	vosotros	distinguisteis
ellos	distinguían	ellos	distinguieron

dormir *to sleep*

PAST PARTICIPLE	IMPERATIVE
dormido	duerme
	dormid
GERUND	
durmiendo	

PRESENT		PRESENT SUBJUNCTIVE	
yo	duermo	yo	duerma
tú	duermes	tú	duermas
él	duerme	él	duerma
nosotros	dormimos	nosotros	durmamos
vosotros	dormís	vosotros	durmáis
ellos	duermen	ellos	duerman

FUTURE		CONDITIONAL	
yo	dormiré	yo	dormiría
tú	dormirás	tú	dormirías
él	dormirá	él	dormiría
nosotros	dormiremos	nosotros	dormiríamos
vosotros	dormiréis	vosotros	dormiríais
ellos	dormirán	ellos	dormirían

IMPERFECT		PRETERITE	
yo	dormía	yo	dormí
tú	dormías	tú	dormiste
él	dormía	él	durmió
nosotros	dormíamos	nosotros	dormimos
vosotros	dormíais	vosotros	dormisteis
ellos	dormían	ellos	durmieron

Grammar

elegir *to choose*	
PAST PARTICIPLE	IMPERATIVE
elegido	elige
	elegid
GERUND	
eligiendo	

PRESENT		PRESENT SUBJUNCTIVE	
yo	elijo	yo	elija
tú	eliges	tú	elijas
él	elige	él	elija
nosotros	elegimos	nosotros	elijamos
vosotros	elegís	vosotros	elijáis
ellos	eligen	ellos	elijan

FUTURE		CONDITIONAL	
yo	elegiré	yo	elegiría
tú	elegirás	tú	elegirías
él	elegirá	él	elegiría
nosotros	elegiremos	nosotros	elegiríamos
vosotros	elegiréis	vosotros	elegiríais
ellos	elegirán	ellos	elegirían

IMPERFECT		PRETERITE	
yo	elegía	yo	elegí
tú	elegías	tú	elegiste
él	elegía	él	eligió
nosotros	elegíamos	nosotros	elegimos
vosotros	elegíais	vosotros	elegisteis
ellos	elegían	ellos	eligieron

empezar *to begin*

PAST PARTICIPLE	IMPERATIVE
empez**ado**	**empieza**
	empez**ad**
GERUND	
empez**ando**	

PRESENT		PRESENT SUBJUNCTIVE	
yo	**empiezo**	yo	**empiece**
tú	**empiezas**	tú	**empieces**
él	**empieza**	él	**empiece**
nosotros	empez**amos**	nosotros	**empecemos**
vosotros	empez**áis**	vosotros	**empecéis**
ellos	**empiezan**	ellos	**empiecen**

FUTURE		CONDITIONAL	
yo	empezar**é**	yo	empezar**ía**
tú	empezar**ás**	tú	empezar**ías**
él	empezar**á**	él	empezar**ía**
nosotros	empezar**emos**	nosotros	empezar**íamos**
vosotros	empezar**éis**	vosotros	empezar**íais**
ellos	empezar**án**	ellos	empezar**ían**

IMPERFECT		PRETERITE	
yo	empez**aba**	yo	**empecé**
tú	empez**abas**	tú	empez**aste**
él	empez**aba**	él	empez**ó**
nosotros	empez**ábamos**	nosotros	empez**amos**
vosotros	empez**abais**	vosotros	empez**asteis**
ellos	empez**aban**	ellos	empez**aron**

entender *to understand*

PAST PARTICIPLE	IMPERATIVE
entend**ido**	entiend**e**
GERUND	entend**ed**
entend**iendo**	

PRESENT		PRESENT SUBJUNCTIVE	
yo	entiendo	yo	entienda
tú	entiendes	tú	entiendas
él	entiende	él	entienda
nosotros	entendemos	nosotros	entendamos
vosotros	entendéis	vosotros	entendáis
ellos	entienden	ellos	entiendan

FUTURE		CONDITIONAL	
yo	entenderé	yo	entendería
tú	entenderás	tú	entenderías
él	entenderá	él	entendería
nosotros	entenderemos	nosotros	entenderíamos
vosotros	entenderéis	vosotros	entenderíais
ellos	entenderán	ellos	entenderían

IMPERFECT		PRETERITE	
yo	entendía	yo	entendí
tú	entendías	tú	entendiste
él	entendía	él	entendió
nosotros	entendíamos	nosotros	entendimos
vosotros	entendíais	vosotros	entendisteis
ellos	entendían	ellos	entendieron

enviar *to send*

PAST PARTICIPLE	IMPERATIVE
enviado	envía
	enviad
GERUND	
enviando	

PRESENT		PRESENT SUBJUNCTIVE	
yo	envío	yo	envíe
tú	envías	tú	envíes
él	envía	él	envíe
nosotros	enviamos	nosotros	enviemos
vosotros	enviáis	vosotros	enviéis
ellos	envían	ellos	envíen

FUTURE		CONDITIONAL	
yo	enviaré	yo	enviaría
tú	enviarás	tú	enviarías
él	enviará	él	enviaría
nosotros	enviaremos	nosotros	enviaríamos
vosotros	enviaréis	vosotros	enviaríais
ellos	enviarán	ellos	enviarían

IMPERFECT		PRETERITE	
yo	enviaba	yo	envié
tú	enviabas	tú	enviaste
él	enviaba	él	envió
nosotros	enviábamos	nosotros	enviamos
vosotros	enviabais	vosotros	enviasteis
ellos	enviaban	ellos	enviaron

VERB TABLE

---

erguir *to erect*

PAST PARTICIPLE

ergu**ido**

IMPERATIVE

yergue
ergu**id**

GERUND

irguiendo

PRESENT		PRESENT SUBJUNCTIVE	
yo	**yergo**	yo	**yerga**
tú	**yergues**	tú	**yergas**
él	**yergue**	él	**yerga**
nosotros	ergu**imos**	nosotros	**irgamos**
vosotros	ergu**ís**	vosotros	**irgáis**
ellos	**yerguen**	ellos	**yergan**

FUTURE		CONDITIONAL	
yo	erguir**é**	yo	erguir**ía**
tú	erguir**ás**	tú	erguir**ías**
él	erguir**á**	él	erguir**ía**
nosotros	erguir**emos**	nosotros	erguir**íamos**
vosotros	erguir**éis**	vosotros	erguir**íais**
ellos	erguir**án**	ellos	erguir**ían**

IMPERFECT		PRETERITE	
yo	ergu**ía**	yo	ergu**í**
tú	ergu**ías**	tú	ergu**iste**
él	ergu**ía**	él	**irguió**
nosotros	ergu**íamos**	nosotros	ergu**imos**
vosotros	ergu**íais**	vosotros	ergu**isteis**
ellos	ergu**ían**	ellos	**irguieron**

errar *to err*

PAST PARTICIPLE	IMPERATIVE
errado	
	yerra
	errad
GERUND	
errando	

PRESENT		PRESENT SUBJUNCTIVE	
yo	yerro	yo	yerre
tú	yerras	tú	yerres
él	yerra	él	yerre
nosotros	erramos	nosotros	erremos
vosotros	erráis	vosotros	erréis
ellos	yerran	ellos	yerren

FUTURE		CONDITIONAL	
yo	erraré	yo	erraría
tú	errarás	tú	errarías
él	errará	él	erraría
nosotros	erraremos	nosotros	erraríamos
vosotros	erraréis	vosotros	erraríais
ellos	errarán	ellos	errarían

IMPERFECT		PRETERITE	
yo	erraba	yo	erré
tú	errabas	tú	erraste
él	erraba	él	erró
nosotros	errábamos	nosotros	erramos
vosotros	errabais	vosotros	errasteis
ellos	erraban	ellos	erraron

Grammar

escribir *to write*

PAST PARTICIPLE	IMPERATIVE
escrito	escribe
	escribid
GERUND	
escribiendo	

PRESENT		PRESENT SUBJUNCTIVE	
yo	escribo	yo	escriba
tú	escribes	tú	escribas
él	escribe	él	escriba
nosotros	escribimos	nosotros	escribamos
vosotros	escribís	vosotros	escribáis
ellos	escriben	ellos	escriban

FUTURE		CONDITIONAL	
yo	escribiré	yo	escribiría
tú	escribirás	tú	escribirías
él	escribirá	él	escribiría
nosotros	escribiremos	nosotros	escribiríamos
vosotros	escribiréis	vosotros	escribiríais
ellos	escribirán	ellos	escribirían

IMPERFECT		PRETERITE	
yo	escribía	yo	escribí
tú	escribías	tú	escribiste
él	escribía	él	escribió
nosotros	escribíamos	nosotros	escribimos
vosotros	escribíais	vosotros	escribisteis
ellos	escribían	ellos	escribieron

estar *to be*

PAST PARTICIPLE	IMPERATIVE
estado	**está**
GERUND	estad
estando	

PRESENT		PRESENT SUBJUNCTIVE	
yo	**estoy**	yo	**esté**
tú	**estás**	tú	**estés**
él	**está**	él	**esté**
nosotros	**estamos**	nosotros	**estemos**
vosotros	**estáis**	vosotros	**estéis**
ellos	**están**	ellos	**estén**

FUTURE		CONDITIONAL	
yo	estaré	yo	estaría
tú	estarás	tú	estarías
él	estará	él	estaría
nosotros	estaremos	nosotros	estaríamos
vosotros	estaréis	vosotros	estaríais
ellos	estarán	ellos	estarían

IMPERFECT		PRETERITE	
yo	estaba	yo	**estuve**
tú	estabas	tú	**estuviste**
él	estaba	él	**estuvo**
nosotros	estábamos	nosotros	**estuvimos**
vosotros	estabais	vosotros	**estuvisteis**
ellos	estaban	ellos	**estuvieron**

freír *to fry*

PAST PARTICIPLE	IMPERATIVE
frito	**fríe**
GERUND	**freíd**
friendo	

PRESENT		PRESENT SUBJUNCTIVE	
yo	frío	yo	fría
tú	fríes	tú	frías
él	fríe	él	fría
nosotros	freímos	nosotros	friamos
vosotros	freís	vosotros	friáis
ellos	fríen	ellos	frían

FUTURE		CONDITIONAL	
yo	freiré	yo	freiría
tú	freirás	tú	freirías
él	freirá	él	freiría
nosotros	freiremos	nosotros	freiríamos
vosotros	freiréis	vosotros	freiríais
ellos	freirán	ellos	freirían

IMPERFECT		PRETERITE	
yo	freía	yo	freí
tú	freías	tú	freíste
él	freía	él	frió
nosotros	freíamos	nosotros	freímos
vosotros	freíais	vosotros	freísteis
ellos	freían	ellos	frieron

gruñir *to grunt*

PAST PARTICIPLE	IMPERATIVE
gruñ**ido**	gruñe
	gruñ**id**
GERUND	
gruñ**endo**	

PRESENT		PRESENT SUBJUNCTIVE	
yo	gruño	yo	gruña
tú	gruñes	tú	gruñas
él	gruñe	él	gruña
nosotros	gruñimos	nosotros	gruñ**amos**
vosotros	gruñís	vosotros	gruñ**áis**
ellos	gruñen	ellos	gruñan

FUTURE		CONDITIONAL	
yo	gruñiré	yo	gruñiría
tú	gruñirás	tú	gruñirías
él	gruñirá	él	gruñiría
nosotros	gruñi**remos**	nosotros	gruñi**ríamos**
vosotros	gruñi**réis**	vosotros	gruñi**ríais**
ellos	gruñirán	ellos	gruñirían

IMPERFECT		PRETERITE	
yo	gruñía	yo	gruñí
tú	gruñías	tú	gruñiste
él	gruñía	él	gruñó
nosotros	gruñíamos	nosotros	gruñimos
vosotros	gruñíais	vosotros	gruñisteis
ellos	gruñían	ellos	gruñeron

haber *to have (auxiliary)*

PAST PARTICIPLE	IMPERATIVE
hab**ido**	*not used*

GERUND

hab**iendo**

PRESENT		PRESENT SUBJUNCTIVE
yo	he	yo	haya
tú	has	tú	hayas
él	ha	él	haya
nosotros	hemos	nosotros	hayamos
vosotros	habéis	vosotros	hayáis
ellos	han	ellos	hayan

FUTURE		CONDITIONAL	
yo	habré	yo	habría
tú	habrás	tú	habrías
él	habrá	él	habría
nosotros	habremos	nosotros	habríamos
vosotros	habréis	vosotros	habríais
ellos	habrán	ellos	habrían

IMPERFECT		PRETERITE	
yo	había	yo	hube
tú	habías	tú	hubiste
él	había	él	hubo
nosotros	habíamos	nosotros	hubimos
vosotros	habíais	vosotros	hubisteis
ellos	habían	ellos	hubieron

hacer *to do, to make*

PAST PARTICIPLE	IMPERATIVE
hecho	**haz**
GERUND	**haced**
hac**iendo**	

PRESENT		PRESENT SUBJUNCTIVE	
yo	hago	yo	haga
tú	haces	tú	hagas
él	hace	él	haga
nosotros	hacemos	nosotros	hagamos
vosotros	hacéis	vosotros	hagáis
ellos	hacen	ellos	hagan

FUTURE		CONDITIONAL	
yo	haré	yo	haría
tú	harás	tú	harías
él	hará	él	haría
nosotros	haremos	nosotros	haríamos
vosotros	haréis	vosotros	haríais
ellos	harán	ellos	harían

IMPERFECT		PRETERITE	
yo	hacía	yo	hice
tú	hacías	tú	hiciste
él	hacía	él	hizo
nosotros	hacíamos	nosotros	hicimos
vosotros	hacíais	vosotros	hicisteis
ellos	hacían	ellos	hicieron

VERB TABLE

hay *there is, there are*	
PAST PARTICIPLE	IMPERATIVE
hab**ido**	*not used*
GERUND	
hab**iendo**	

PRESENT	PRESENT SUBJUNCTIVE
hay	**haya**

FUTURE	CONDITIONAL
habrá	**habría**

IMPERFECT	PRETERITE
hab**ía**	**hubo**

ir *to go*	
PAST PARTICIPLE	IMPERATIVE
ido	**ve**
GERUND	**id**
yendo	

PRESENT		PRESENT SUBJUNCTIVE	
yo	**voy**	yo	**vaya**
tú	**vas**	tú	**vayas**
él	**va**	él	**vaya**
nosotros	**vamos**	nosotros	**vayamos**
vosotros	**vais**	vosotros	**vayáis**
ellos	**van**	ellos	**vayan**

FUTURE		CONDITIONAL	
yo	**iré**	yo	**iría**
tú	**irás**	tú	**irías**
él	**irá**	él	**iría**
nosotros	**iremos**	nosotros	**iríamos**
vosotros	**iréis**	vosotros	**iríais**
ellos	**irán**	ellos	**irían**

IMPERFECT		PRETERITE	
yo	**iba**	yo	**fui**
tú	**ibas**	tú	**fuiste**
él	**iba**	él	**fue**
nosotros	**íbamos**	nosotros	**fuimos**
vosotros	**ibais**	vosotros	**fuisteis**
ellos	**iban**	ellos	**fueron**

jugar *to play*

PAST PARTICIPLE	IMPERATIVE
jug**ado**	**juega**
	jug**ad**
GERUND	
jug**ando**	

PRESENT		PRESENT SUBJUNCTIVE	
yo	**juego**	yo	**juegue**
tú	**juegas**	tú	**juegues**
él	**juega**	él	**juegue**
nosotros	jug**amos**	nosotros	jug**uemos**
vosotros	jug**áis**	vosotros	jug**uéis**
ellos	**juegan**	ellos	**jueguen**

FUTURE		CONDITIONAL	
yo	jugar**é**	yo	jugar**ía**
tú	jugar**ás**	tú	jugar**ías**
él	jugar**á**	él	jugar**ía**
nosotros	jugar**emos**	nosotros	jugar**íamos**
vosotros	jugar**éis**	vosotros	jugar**íais**
ellos	jugar**án**	ellos	jugar**ían**

IMPERFECT		PRETERITE	
yo	jug**aba**	yo	jug**ué**
tú	jug**abas**	tú	jug**aste**
él	jug**aba**	él	jug**ó**
nosotros	jug**ábamos**	nosotros	jug**amos**
vosotros	jug**abais**	vosotros	jug**asteis**
ellos	jug**aban**	ellos	jug**aron**

leer *to read*

PAST PARTICIPLE	IMPERATIVE
leído	lee
GERUND	leed
leyendo	

PRESENT		PRESENT SUBJUNCTIVE	
yo	leo	yo	lea
tú	lees	tú	leas
él	lee	él	lea
nosotros	leemos	nosotros	leamos
vosotros	leéis	vosotros	leáis
ellos	leen	ellos	lean

FUTURE		CONDITIONAL	
yo	leeré	yo	leería
tú	leerás	tú	leerías
él	leerá	él	leería
nosotros	leeremos	nosotros	leeríamos
vosotros	leeréis	vosotros	leeríais
ellos	leerán	ellos	leerían

IMPERFECT		PRETERITE	
yo	leía	yo	leí
tú	leías	tú	leíste
él	leía	él	leyó
nosotros	leíamos	nosotros	leímos
vosotros	leíais	vosotros	leísteis
ellos	leían	ellos	leyeron

lucir to shine

PAST PARTICIPLE	IMPERATIVE
lucido	luce
	lucid
GERUND	
luciendo	

PRESENT		PRESENT SUBJUNCTIVE	
yo	luzco	yo	luzca
tú	luces	tú	luzcas
él	luce	él	luzca
nosotros	lucimos	nosotros	luzcamos
vosotros	lucís	vosotros	luzcáis
ellos	lucen	ellos	luzcan

FUTURE		CONDITIONAL	
yo	luciré	yo	luciría
tú	lucirás	tú	lucirías
él	lucirá	él	luciría
nosotros	luciremos	nosotros	luciríamos
vosotros	luciréis	vosotros	luciríais
ellos	lucirán	ellos	lucirían

IMPERFECT		PRETERITE	
yo	lucía	yo	lucí
tú	lucías	tú	luciste
él	lucía	él	lució
nosotros	lucíamos	nosotros	lucimos
vosotros	lucíais	vosotros	lucisteis
ellos	lucían	ellos	lucieron

llover to rain

PAST PARTICIPLE	IMPERATIVE
llo**vido**	*not used*
GERUND	
llo**viendo**	

PRESENT	PRESENT SUBJUNCTIVE
llueve	**llueva**

FUTURE	CONDITIONAL
llover**á**	llover**ía**

IMPERFECT	PRETERITE
llov**ía**	llov**ió**

morir *to die*

PAST PARTICIPLE	IMPERATIVE
muerto	**muere**
	morid
GERUND	
muriendo	

PRESENT		PRESENT SUBJUNCTIVE	
yo	**muero**	yo	**muera**
tú	**mueres**	tú	**mueras**
él	**muere**	él	**muera**
nosotros	morimos	nosotros	**muramos**
vosotros	morís	vosotros	**muráis**
ellos	**mueren**	ellos	**mueran**

FUTURE		CONDITIONAL	
yo	moriré	yo	moriría
tú	morirás	tú	morirías
él	morirá	él	moriría
nosotros	moriremos	nosotros	moriríamos
vosotros	moriréis	vosotros	moriríais
ellos	morirán	ellos	morirían

IMPERFECT		PRETERITE	
yo	moría	yo	morí
tú	morías	tú	moriste
él	moría	él	murió
nosotros	moríamos	nosotros	morimos
vosotros	moríais	vosotros	moristeis
ellos	morían	ellos	murieron

mover *to move*

PAST PARTICIPLE	IMPERATIVE
movido	**mueve**
	moved
GERUND	
moviendo	

PRESENT		PRESENT SUBJUNCTIVE	
yo	muevo	yo	mueva
tú	mueves	tú	muevas
él	mueve	él	mueva
nosotros	movemos	nosotros	movamos
vosotros	movéis	vosotros	mováis
ellos	mueven	ellos	muevan

FUTURE		CONDITIONAL	
yo	moveré	yo	movería
tú	moverás	tú	moverías
él	moverá	él	movería
nosotros	moveremos	nosotros	moveríamos
vosotros	moveréis	vosotros	moveríais
ellos	moverán	ellos	moverían

IMPERFECT		PRETERITE	
yo	movía	yo	moví
tú	movías	tú	moviste
él	movía	él	movió
nosotros	movíamos	nosotros	movimos
vosotros	movíais	vosotros	movisteis
ellos	movían	ellos	movieron

VERB TABLE

Grammar

---

nacer *to be born*

PAST PARTICIPLE	IMPERATIVE
nacido	
	nace
GERUND	naced
naciendo	

PRESENT		PRESENT SUBJUNCTIVE	
yo	nazco	yo	nazca
tú	naces	tú	nazcas
él	nace	él	nazca
nosotros	nacemos	nosotros	nazcamos
vosotros	nacéis	vosotros	nazcáis
ellos	nacen	ellos	nazcan

FUTURE		CONDITIONAL	
yo	naceré	yo	nacería
tú	nacerás	tú	nacerías
él	nacerá	él	nacería
nosotros	naceremos	nosotros	naceríamos
vosotros	naceréis	vosotros	naceríais
ellos	nacerán	ellos	nacerían

IMPERFECT		PRETERITE	
yo	nacía	yo	nací
tú	nacías	tú	naciste
él	nacía	él	nació
nosotros	nacíamos	nosotros	nacimos
vosotros	nacíais	vosotros	nacisteis
ellos	nacían	ellos	nacieron

negar *to deny*

PAST PARTICIPLE	IMPERATIVE
negado	niega
	negad
GERUND	
negando	

PRESENT		PRESENT SUBJUNCTIVE	
yo	niego	yo	niegue
tú	niegas	tú	niegues
él	niega	él	niegue
nosotros	negamos	nosotros	neguemos
vosotros	negáis	vosotros	neguéis
ellos	niegan	ellos	nieguen

FUTURE		CONDITIONAL	
yo	negaré	yo	negaría
tú	negarás	tú	negarías
él	negará	él	negaría
nosotros	negaremos	nosotros	negaríamos
vosotros	negaréis	vosotros	negaríais
ellos	negarán	ellos	negarían

IMPERFECT		PRETERITE	
yo	negaba	yo	negué
tú	negabas	tú	negaste
él	negaba	él	negó
nosotros	negábamos	nosotros	negamos
vosotros	negabais	vosotros	negasteis
ellos	negaban	ellos	negaron

oír *to hear*

PAST PARTICIPLE	IMPERATIVE
oído	oye
	oíd
GERUND	
oyendo	

PRESENT		PRESENT SUBJUNCTIVE	
yo	oigo	yo	oiga
tú	oyes	tú	oigas
él	oye	él	oiga
nosotros	oímos	nosotros	oigamos
vosotros	oís	vosotros	oigáis
ellos	oyen	ellos	oigan

FUTURE		CONDITIONAL	
yo	oiré	yo	oiría
tú	oirás	tú	oirías
él	oirá	él	oiría
nosotros	oiremos	nosotros	oiríamos
vosotros	oiréis	vosotros	oiríais
ellos	oirán	ellos	oirían

IMPERFECT		PRETERITE	
yo	oía	yo	oí
tú	oías	tú	oíste
él	oía	él	oyó
nosotros	oíamos	nosotros	oímos
vosotros	oíais	vosotros	oísteis
ellos	oían	ellos	oyeron

oler *to smell*

PAST PARTICIPLE	IMPERATIVE
olido	huele
	oled
GERUND	
oliendo	

PRESENT		PRESENT SUBJUNCTIVE	
yo	huelo	yo	huela
tú	hueles	tú	huelas
él	huele	él	huela
nosotros	olemos	nosotros	olamos
vosotros	oléis	vosotros	oláis
ellos	huelen	ellos	huelan

FUTURE		CONDITIONAL	
yo	oleré	yo	olería
tú	olerás	tú	olerías
él	olerá	él	olería
nosotros	oleremos	nosotros	oleríamos
vosotros	oleréis	vosotros	oleríais
ellos	olerán	ellos	olerían

IMPERFECT		PRETERITE	
yo	olía	yo	olí
tú	olías	tú	oliste
él	olía	él	olió
nosotros	olíamos	nosotros	olimos
vosotros	olíais	vosotros	olisteis
ellos	olían	ellos	olieron

Grammar

---

pagar *to pay*

PAST PARTICIPLE	IMPERATIVE
pagado	paga
GERUND	pagad
pagando	

PRESENT		PRESENT SUBJUNCTIVE	
yo	pago	yo	pague
tú	pagas	tú	pagues
él	paga	él	pague
nosotros	pagamos	nosotros	paguemos
vosotros	pagáis	vosotros	paguéis
ellos	pagan	ellos	paguen

FUTURE		CONDITIONAL	
yo	pagaré	yo	pagaría
tú	pagarás	tú	pagarías
él	pagará	él	pagaría
nosotros	pagaremos	nosotros	pagaríamos
vosotros	pagaréis	vosotros	pagaríais
ellos	pagarán	ellos	pagarían

IMPERFECT		PRETERITE	
yo	pagaba	yo	pagué
tú	pagabas	tú	pagaste
él	pagaba	él	pagó
nosotros	pagábamos	nosotros	pagamos
vosotros	pagabais	vosotros	pagasteis
ellos	pagaban	ellos	pagaron

pedir *to ask for*

PAST PARTICIPLE	IMPERATIVE
ped**ido**	**pide**
	pedi**d**
GERUND	
pidi**endo**	

PRESENT		PRESENT SUBJUNCTIVE	
yo	pido	yo	pida
tú	pides	tú	pidas
él	pide	él	pida
nosotros	pedimos	nosotros	pidamos
vosotros	pedís	vosotros	pidáis
ellos	piden	ellos	pidan

FUTURE		CONDITIONAL	
yo	pediré	yo	pediría
tú	pedirás	tú	pedirías
él	pedirá	él	pediría
nosotros	pediremos	nosotros	pediríamos
vosotros	pediréis	vosotros	pediríais
ellos	pedirán	ellos	pedirían

IMPERFECT		PRETERITE	
yo	pedía	yo	pedí
tú	pedías	tú	pediste
él	pedía	él	pidió
nosotros	pedíamos	nosotros	pedimos
vosotros	pedíais	vosotros	pedisteis
ellos	pedían	ellos	pidieron

pensar *to think*

PAST PARTICIPLE	IMPERATIVE
pensado	
	piensa
GERUND	pensad
pensando	

PRESENT		PRESENT SUBJUNCTIVE	
yo	**pienso**	yo	**piense**
tú	**piensas**	tú	**pienses**
él	**piensa**	él	**piense**
nosotros	pensamos	nosotros	pensemos
vosotros	pensáis	vosotros	penséis
ellos	**piensan**	ellos	**piensen**

FUTURE		CONDITIONAL	
yo	pensaré	yo	pensaría
tú	pensarás	tú	pensarías
él	pensará	él	pensaría
nosotros	pensaremos	nosotros	pensaríamos
vosotros	pensaréis	vosotros	pensaríais
ellos	pensarán	ellos	pensarían

IMPERFECT		PRETERITE	
yo	pensaba	yo	pensé
tú	pensabas	tú	pensaste
él	pensaba	él	pensó
nosotros	pensábamos	nosotros	pensamos
vosotros	pensabais	vosotros	pensasteis
ellos	pensaban	ellos	pensaron

poder *to be able*

PAST PARTICIPLE	IMPERATIVE
pod**ido**	pued**e**
	pod**ed**
GERUND	
pud**iendo**	

PRESENT		PRESENT SUBJUNCTIVE	
yo	puedo	yo	pueda
tú	puedes	tú	puedas
él	puede	él	pueda
nosotros	podemos	nosotros	podamos
vosotros	podéis	vosotros	podáis
ellos	pueden	ellos	puedan

FUTURE		CONDITIONAL	
yo	podré	yo	podría
tú	podrás	tú	podrías
él	podrá	él	podría
nosotros	podremos	nosotros	podríamos
vosotros	podréis	vosotros	podríais
ellos	podrán	ellos	podrían

IMPERFECT		PRETERITE	
yo	podía	yo	pude
tú	podías	tú	pudiste
él	podía	él	pudo
nosotros	podíamos	nosotros	pudimos
vosotros	podíais	vosotros	pudisteis
ellos	podían	ellos	pudieron

poner *to put*

PAST PARTICIPLE	IMPERATIVE
puesto	**pon**
GERUND	**poned**
pon**iendo**	

PRESENT		PRESENT SUBJUNCTIVE	
yo	pon**go**	yo	ponga
tú	pones	tú	pongas
él	pone	él	ponga
nosotros	ponemos	nosotros	pongamos
vosotros	ponéis	vosotros	pongáis
ellos	ponen	ellos	pongan

FUTURE		CONDITIONAL	
yo	pondré	yo	pondría
tú	pondrás	tú	pondrías
él	pondrá	él	pondría
nosotros	pondremos	nosotros	pondríamos
vosotros	pondréis	vosotros	pondríais
ellos	pondrán	ellos	pondrían

IMPERFECT		PRETERITE	
yo	ponía	yo	puse
tú	ponías	tú	pusiste
él	ponía	él	puso
nosotros	poníamos	nosotros	pusimos
vosotros	poníais	vosotros	pusisteis
ellos	ponían	ellos	pusieron

prohibir *to forbid*

PAST PARTICIPLE	IMPERATIVE
prohib**ido**	
	prohíbe
GERUND	prohib**id**
prohib**iendo**	

PRESENT		PRESENT SUBJUNCTIVE	
yo	**prohíbo**	yo	**prohíba**
tú	**prohíbes**	tú	**prohíbas**
él	**prohíbe**	él	**prohíba**
nosotros	prohib**imos**	nosotros	prohib**amos**
vosotros	prohib**ís**	vosotros	prohib**áis**
ellos	**prohíben**	ellos	**prohíban**

FUTURE		CONDITIONAL	
yo	prohibir**é**	yo	prohibir**ía**
tú	prohibir**ás**	tú	prohibir**ías**
él	prohibir**á**	él	prohibir**ía**
nosotros	prohibir**emos**	nosotros	prohibir**íamos**
vosotros	prohibir**éis**	vosotros	prohibir**íais**
ellos	prohibir**án**	ellos	prohibir**ían**

IMPERFECT		PRETERITE	
yo	prohib**ía**	yo	prohib**í**
tú	prohib**ías**	tú	prohib**iste**
él	prohib**ía**	él	prohib**ió**
nosotros	prohib**íamos**	nosotros	prohib**imos**
vosotros	prohib**íais**	vosotros	prohib**isteis**
ellos	prohib**ían**	ellos	prohib**ieron**

querer *to want*

PAST PARTICIPLE	IMPERATIVE
quer**ido**	
	quiere
GERUND	quer**ed**
quer**iendo**	

PRESENT		PRESENT SUBJUNCTIVE	
yo	quiero	yo	quiera
tú	quieres	tú	quieras
él	quiere	él	quiera
nosotros	queremos	nosotros	queramos
vosotros	queréis	vosotros	queráis
ellos	quieren	ellos	quieran

FUTURE		CONDITIONAL	
yo	querré	yo	querría
tú	querrás	tú	querrías
él	querrá	él	querría
nosotros	querremos	nosotros	querríamos
vosotros	querréis	vosotros	querríais
ellos	querrán	ellos	querrían

IMPERFECT		PRETERITE	
yo	quería	yo	quise
tú	querías	tú	quisiste
él	quería	él	quiso
nosotros	queríamos	nosotros	quisimos
vosotros	queríais	vosotros	quisisteis
ellos	querían	ellos	quisieron

rehusar *to refuse*

PAST PARTICIPLE	IMPERATIVE
rehus**ado**	rehús**a**
	rehusa**d**
GERUND	
rehus**ando**	

PRESENT		PRESENT SUBJUNCTIVE	
yo	rehúso	yo	rehúse
tú	rehúsas	tú	rehúses
él	rehúsa	él	rehúse
nosotros	rehusamos	nosotros	rehusemos
vosotros	rehusáis	vosotros	rehuséis
ellos	rehúsan	ellos	rehúsen

FUTURE		CONDITIONAL	
yo	rehusaré	yo	rehusaría
tú	rehusarás	tú	rehusarías
él	rehusará	él	rehusaría
nosotros	rehusaremos	nosotros	rehusaríamos
vosotros	rehusaréis	vosotros	rehusaríais
ellos	rehusarán	ellos	rehusarían

IMPERFECT		PRETERITE	
yo	rehusaba	yo	rehusé
tú	rehusabas	tú	rehusaste
él	rehusaba	él	rehusó
nosotros	rehusábamos	nosotros	rehusamos
vosotros	rehusabais	vosotros	rehusasteis
ellos	rehusaban	ellos	rehusaron

reír *to laugh*

PAST PARTICIPLE	IMPERATIVE
reído	ríe
GERUND	reíd
riendo	

PRESENT		PRESENT SUBJUNCTIVE	
yo	río	yo	ría
tú	ríes	tú	rías
él	ríe	él	ría
nosotros	reímos	nosotros	riamos
vosotros	reís	vosotros	riáis
ellos	ríen	ellos	rían

FUTURE		CONDITIONAL	
yo	reiré	yo	reiría
tú	reirás	tú	reirías
él	reirá	él	reiría
nosotros	reiremos	nosotros	reiríamos
vosotros	reiréis	vosotros	reiríais
ellos	reirán	ellos	reirían

IMPERFECT		PRETERITE	
yo	reía	yo	reí
tú	reías	tú	reíste
él	reía	él	rió
nosotros	reíamos	nosotros	reímos
vosotros	reíais	vosotros	reísteis
ellos	reían	ellos	rieron

reñir *to scold*

PAST PARTICIPLE	IMPERATIVE
reñ**ido**	ri**ñe**
	reñ**id**
GERUND	
ri**ñendo**	

PRESENT		PRESENT SUBJUNCTIVE	
yo	ri**ño**	yo	ri**ña**
tú	ri**ñes**	tú	ri**ñas**
él	ri**ñe**	él	ri**ña**
nosotros	reñ**imos**	nosotros	ri**ñamos**
vosotros	reñ**ís**	vosotros	ri**ñáis**
ellos	ri**ñen**	ellos	ri**ñan**

FUTURE		CONDITIONAL	
yo	reñi**ré**	yo	reñi**ría**
tú	reñi**rás**	tú	reñi**rías**
él	reñi**rá**	él	reñi**ría**
nosotros	reñi**remos**	nosotros	reñi**ríamos**
vosotros	reñi**réis**	vosotros	reñi**ríais**
ellos	reñi**rán**	ellos	reñi**rían**

IMPERFECT		PRETERITE	
yo	reñ**ía**	yo	reñ**í**
tú	reñ**ías**	tú	reñ**iste**
él	reñ**ía**	él	ri**ñó**
nosotros	reñ**íamos**	nosotros	reñ**imos**
vosotros	reñ**íais**	vosotros	reñ**isteis**
ellos	reñ**ían**	ellos	ri**ñeron**

resolver *to solve*

PAST PARTICIPLE	IMPERATIVE
resuelto	**resuelve**
GERUND	resolve**d**
resolv**iendo**	

PRESENT		PRESENT SUBJUNCTIVE	
yo	**resuelvo**	yo	**resuelva**
tú	**resuelves**	tú	**resuelvas**
él	**resuelve**	él	**resuelva**
nosotros	resolvemos	nosotros	resolvamos
vosotros	resolvéis	vosotros	resolváis
ellos	**resuelven**	ellos	**resuelvan**

FUTURE		CONDITIONAL	
yo	resolveré	yo	resolvería
tú	resolverás	tú	resolverías
él	resolverá	él	resolvería
nosotros	resolveremos	nosotros	resolveríamos
vosotros	resolveréis	vosotros	resolveríais
ellos	resolverán	ellos	resolverían

IMPERFECT		PRETERITE	
yo	resolvía	yo	resolví
tú	resolvías	tú	resolviste
él	resolvía	él	resolvió
nosotros	resolvíamos	nosotros	resolvimos
vosotros	resolvíais	vosotros	resolvisteis
ellos	resolvían	ellos	resolvieron

reunir *to put together, to gather*

PAST PARTICIPLE	IMPERATIVE
reunido	**reúne**
	reunid
GERUND	
reuniendo	

PRESENT		PRESENT SUBJUNCTIVE	
yo	reúno	yo	reúna
tú	reúnes	tú	reúnas
él	reúne	él	reúna
nosotros	reunimos	nosotros	reunamos
vosotros	reunís	vosotros	reunáis
ellos	reúnen	ellos	reúnan

FUTURE		CONDITIONAL	
yo	reuniré	yo	reuniría
tú	reunirás	tú	reunirías
él	reunirá	él	reuniría
nosotros	reuniremos	nosotros	reuniríamos
vosotros	reuniréis	vosotros	reuniríais
ellos	reunirán	ellos	reunirían

IMPERFECT		PRETERITE	
yo	reunía	yo	reuní
tú	reunías	tú	reuniste
él	reunía	él	reunió
nosotros	reuníamos	nosotros	reunimos
vosotros	reuníais	vosotros	reunisteis
ellos	reunían	ellos	reunieron

rogar to beg

PAST PARTICIPLE	IMPERATIVE
rogado	ruega
	rogad
GERUND	
rogando	

PRESENT		PRESENT SUBJUNCTIVE	
yo	ruego	yo	ruegue
tú	ruegas	tú	ruegues
él	ruega	él	ruegue
nosotros	rogamos	nosotros	roguemos
vosotros	rogáis	vosotros	roguéis
ellos	ruegan	ellos	rueguen

FUTURE		CONDITIONAL	
yo	rogaré	yo	rogaría
tú	rogarás	tú	rogarías
él	rogará	él	rogaría
nosotros	rogaremos	nosotros	rogaríamos
vosotros	rogaréis	vosotros	rogaríais
ellos	rogarán	ellos	rogarían

IMPERFECT		PRETERITE	
yo	rogaba	yo	rogué
tú	rogabas	tú	rogaste
él	rogaba	él	rogó
nosotros	rogábamos	nosotros	rogamos
vosotros	rogabais	vosotros	rogasteis
ellos	rogaban	ellos	rogaron

romper *to break*

PAST PARTICIPLE

roto

GERUND

romp**iendo**

IMPERATIVE

romp**e**
romp**ed**

PRESENT		PRESENT SUBJUNCTIVE	
yo	rompo	yo	rompa
tú	rompes	tú	rompas
él	rompe	él	rompa
nosotros	rompemos	nosotros	rompamos
vosotros	rompéis	vosotros	rompáis
ellos	rompen	ellos	rompan

FUTURE		CONDITIONAL	
yo	romperé	yo	rompería
tú	romperás	tú	romperías
él	romperá	él	rompería
nosotros	romperemos	nosotros	romperíamos
vosotros	romperéis	vosotros	romperíais
ellos	romperán	ellos	romperían

IMPERFECT		PRETERITE	
yo	rompía	yo	rompí
tú	rompías	tú	rompiste
él	rompía	él	rompió
nosotros	rompíamos	nosotros	rompimos
vosotros	rompíais	vosotros	rompisteis
ellos	rompían	ellos	rompieron

saber *to know*

PAST PARTICIPLE	IMPERATIVE
sab**ido**	sab**e**
	sab**ed**
GERUND	
sab**iendo**	

PRESENT		PRESENT SUBJUNCTIVE	
yo	sé	yo	sepa
tú	sabes	tú	sepas
él	sabe	él	sepa
nosotros	sabemos	nosotros	sepamos
vosotros	sabéis	vosotros	sepáis
ellos	saben	ellos	sepan

FUTURE		CONDITIONAL	
yo	sabré	yo	sabría
tú	sabrás	tú	sabrías
él	sabrá	él	sabría
nosotros	sabremos	nosotros	sabríamos
vosotros	sabréis	vosotros	sabríais
ellos	sabrán	ellos	sabrían

IMPERFECT		PRETERITE	
yo	sabía	yo	supe
tú	sabías	tú	supiste
él	sabía	él	supo
nosotros	sabíamos	nosotros	supimos
vosotros	sabíais	vosotros	supisteis
ellos	sabían	ellos	supieron

VERB TABLE 146

sacar *to take out*	
PAST PARTICIPLE	IMPERATIVE
sac**ado**	sac**a**
	sac**ad**
GERUND	
sac**ando**	

PRESENT		PRESENT SUBJUNCTIVE	
yo	saco	yo	**saque**
tú	sacas	tú	**saques**
él	saca	él	**saque**
nosotros	sacamos	nosotros	**saquemos**
vosotros	sacáis	vosotros	**saquéis**
ellos	sacan	ellos	**saquen**

FUTURE		CONDITIONAL	
yo	sacaré	yo	sacaría
tú	sacarás	tú	sacarías
él	sacará	él	sacaría
nosotros	sacaremos	nosotros	sacaríamos
vosotros	sacaréis	vosotros	sacaríais
ellos	sacarán	ellos	sacarían

IMPERFECT		PRETERITE	
yo	sacaba	yo	**saqué**
tú	sacabas	tú	sacaste
él	sacaba	él	sacó
nosotros	sacábamos	nosotros	sacamos
vosotros	sacabais	vosotros	sacasteis
ellos	sacaban	ellos	sacaron

salir to go out

PAST PARTICIPLE	IMPERATIVE
salido	**sal**
	salid
GERUND	
saliendo	

PRESENT		PRESENT SUBJUNCTIVE	
yo	salgo	yo	salga
tú	sales	tú	salgas
él	sale	él	salga
nosotros	salimos	nosotros	salgamos
vosotros	salís	vosotros	salgáis
ellos	salen	ellos	salgan

FUTURE		CONDITIONAL	
yo	saldré	yo	saldría
tú	saldrás	tú	saldrías
él	saldrá	él	saldría
nosotros	saldremos	nosotros	saldríamos
vosotros	saldréis	vosotros	saldríais
ellos	saldrán	ellos	saldrían

IMPERFECT		PRETERITE	
yo	salía	yo	salí
tú	salías	tú	saliste
él	salía	él	salió
nosotros	salíamos	nosotros	salimos
vosotros	salíais	vosotros	salisteis
ellos	salían	ellos	salieron

satisfacer *to satisfy*

PAST PARTICIPLE

satisfecho

GERUND

satisfac**iendo**

IMPERATIVE

satisfaz/satisfac**e**
satisfac**ed**

PRESENT		PRESENT SUBJUNCTIVE	
yo	**satisfago**	yo	**satisfaga**
tú	satisfac**es**	tú	**satisfagas**
él	satisfac**e**	él	**satisfaga**
nosotros	satisfac**emos**	nosotros	**satisfagamos**
vosotros	satisfac**éis**	vosotros	**satisfagáis**
ellos	satisfac**en**	ellos	**satisfagan**

FUTURE		CONDITIONAL	
yo	**satisfaré**	yo	**satisfaría**
tú	**satisfarás**	tú	**satisfarías**
él	**satisfará**	él	**satisfaría**
nosotros	**satisfaremos**	nosotros	**satisfaríamos**
vosotros	**satisfaréis**	vosotros	**satisfaríais**
ellos	**satisfarán**	ellos	**satisfarían**

IMPERFECT		PRETERITE	
yo	satisfac**ía**	yo	**satisfice**
tú	satisfac**ías**	tú	**satisficiste**
él	satisfac**ía**	él	**satisfizo**
nosotros	satisfac**íamos**	nosotros	**satisficimos**
vosotros	satisfac**íais**	vosotros	**satisficisteis**
ellos	satisfac**ían**	ellos	**satisficieron**

seguir to follow

PAST PARTICIPLE	IMPERATIVE
segu**ido**	**sigue**
	segu**id**
GERUND	
siguiendo	

PRESENT		PRESENT SUBJUNCTIVE	
yo	**sigo**	yo	**siga**
tú	**sigues**	tú	**sigas**
él	**sigue**	él	**siga**
nosotros	**seguimos**	nosotros	**sigamos**
vosotros	**seguís**	vosotros	**sigáis**
ellos	**siguen**	ellos	**sigan**

FUTURE		CONDITIONAL	
yo	seguiré	yo	seguiría
tú	seguirás	tú	seguirías
él	seguirá	él	seguiría
nosotros	seguiremos	nosotros	seguiríamos
vosotros	seguiréis	vosotros	seguiríais
ellos	seguirán	ellos	seguirían

IMPERFECT		PRETERITE	
yo	seguía	yo	seguí
tú	seguías	tú	segu**iste**
él	seguía	él	**siguió**
nosotros	seguíamos	nosotros	seguimos
vosotros	seguíais	vosotros	segu**isteis**
ellos	seguían	ellos	**siguieron**

sentir *to feel*

PAST PARTICIPLE	IMPERATIVE
sentido	
	siente
GERUND	sentid
sintiendo	

PRESENT		PRESENT SUBJUNCTIVE	
yo	siento	yo	sienta
tú	sientes	tú	sientas
él	siente	él	sienta
nosotros	sentimos	nosotros	sintamos
vosotros	sentís	vosotros	sintáis
ellos	sienten	ellos	sientan

FUTURE		CONDITIONAL	
yo	sentiré	yo	sentiría
tú	sentirás	tú	sentirías
él	sentirá	él	sentiría
nosotros	sentiremos	nosotros	sentiríamos
vosotros	sentiréis	vosotros	sentiríais
ellos	sentirán	ellos	sentirían

IMPERFECT		PRETERITE	
yo	sentía	yo	sentí
tú	sentías	tú	sentiste
él	sentía	él	sintió
nosotros	sentíamos	nosotros	sentimos
vosotros	sentíais	vosotros	sentisteis
ellos	sentían	ellos	sintieron

ser *to be*

PAST PARTICIPLE	IMPERATIVE
sido	**sé**
	sed
GERUND	
siendo	

PRESENT		PRESENT SUBJUNCTIVE	
yo	**soy**	yo	**sea**
tú	**eres**	tú	**seas**
él	**es**	él	**sea**
nosotros	**somos**	nosotros	**seamos**
vosotros	**sois**	vosotros	**seáis**
ellos	**son**	ellos	**sean**

FUTURE		CONDITIONAL	
yo	**seré**	yo	**sería**
tú	**serás**	tú	**serías**
él	**será**	él	**sería**
nosotros	**seremos**	nosotros	**seríamos**
vosotros	**seréis**	vosotros	**seríais**
ellos	**serán**	ellos	**serían**

IMPERFECT		PRETERITE	
yo	**era**	yo	**fui**
tú	**eras**	tú	**fuiste**
él	**era**	él	**fue**
nosotros	**éramos**	nosotros	**fuimos**
vosotros	**erais**	vosotros	**fuisteis**
ellos	**eran**	ellos	**fueron**

tener *to have*

PAST PARTICIPLE	IMPERATIVE
ten**ido**	
	ten
GERUND	tene**d**
ten**iendo**	

PRESENT		PRESENT SUBJUNCTIVE	
yo	tengo	yo	tenga
tú	tienes	tú	tengas
él	tiene	él	tenga
nosotros	tenemos	nosotros	tengamos
vosotros	tenéis	vosotros	tengáis
ellos	tienen	ellos	tengan

FUTURE		CONDITIONAL	
yo	tendré	yo	tendría
tú	tendrás	tú	tendrías
él	tendrá	él	tendría
nosotros	tendremos	nosotros	tendríamos
vosotros	tendréis	vosotros	tendríais
ellos	tendrán	ellos	tendrían

IMPERFECT		PRETERITE	
yo	tenía	yo	tuve
tú	tenías	tú	tuviste
él	tenía	él	tuvo
nosotros	teníamos	nosotros	tuvimos
vosotros	teníais	vosotros	tuvisteis
ellos	tenían	ellos	tuvieron

torcer to twist

PAST PARTICIPLE	IMPERATIVE
torcido	**tuerce**
	torced
GERUND	
torciendo	

PRESENT		PRESENT SUBJUNCTIVE	
yo	tuerzo	yo	tuerza
tú	tuerces	tú	tuerzas
él	tuerce	él	tuerza
nosotros	torcemos	nosotros	torzamos
vosotros	torcéis	vosotros	torzáis
ellos	tuercen	ellos	tuerzan

FUTURE		CONDITIONAL	
yo	torceré	yo	torcería
tú	torcerás	tú	torcerías
él	torcerá	él	torcería
nosotros	torceremos	nosotros	torceríamos
vosotros	torceréis	vosotros	torceríais
ellos	torcerán	ellos	torcerían

IMPERFECT		PRETERITE	
yo	torcía	yo	torcí
tú	torcías	tú	torciste
él	torcía	él	torció
nosotros	torcíamos	nosotros	torcimos
vosotros	torcíais	vosotros	torcisteis
ellos	torcían	ellos	torcieron

traer *to bring*	
PAST PARTICIPLE	IMPERATIVE
traído	tra**e**
	tra**ed**
GERUND	
trayendo	

PRESENT		PRESENT SUBJUNCTIVE	
yo	traigo	yo	traiga
tú	traes	tú	traigas
él	trae	él	traiga
nosotros	traemos	nosotros	traigamos
vosotros	traéis	vosotros	traigáis
ellos	traen	ellos	traigan
FUTURE		CONDITIONAL	
yo	traeré	yo	traería
tú	traerás	tú	traerías
él	traerá	él	traería
nosotros	traeremos	nosotros	traeríamos
vosotros	traeréis	vosotros	traeríais
ellos	traerán	ellos	traerían
IMPERFECT		PRETERITE	
yo	traía	yo	traje
tú	traías	tú	trajiste
él	traía	él	trajo
nosotros	traíamos	nosotros	trajimos
vosotros	traíais	vosotros	trajisteis
ellos	traían	ellos	trajeron

valer *to be worth*	
PAST PARTICIPLE	IMPERATIVE
valido	vale
	valed
GERUND	
valiendo	

PRESENT		PRESENT SUBJUNCTIVE	
yo	valgo	yo	valga
tú	vales	tú	valgas
él	vale	él	valga
nosotros	valemos	nosotros	valgamos
vosotros	valéis	vosotros	valgáis
ellos	valen	ellos	valgan
FUTURE		**CONDITIONAL**	
yo	valdré	yo	valdría
tú	valdrás	tú	valdrías
él	valdrá	él	valdría
nosotros	valdremos	nosotros	valdríamos
vosotros	valdréis	vosotros	valdríais
ellos	valdrán	ellos	valdrían
IMPERFECT		**PRETERITE**	
yo	valía	yo	valí
tú	valías	tú	valiste
él	valía	él	valió
nosotros	valíamos	nosotros	valimos
vosotros	valíais	vosotros	valisteis
ellos	valían	ellos	valieron

vencer *to win*

PAST PARTICIPLE	IMPERATIVE
vencido	
	vence
	venced
GERUND	
venciendo	

PRESENT		PRESENT SUBJUNCTIVE	
yo	venzo	yo	venza
tú	vences	tú	venzas
él	vence	él	venza
nosotros	vencemos	nosotros	venzamos
vosotros	vencéis	vosotros	venzáis
ellos	vencen	ellos	venzan

FUTURE		CONDITIONAL	
yo	venceré	yo	vencería
tú	vencerás	tú	vencerías
él	vencerá	él	vencería
nosotros	venceremos	nosotros	venceríamos
vosotros	venceréis	vosotros	venceríais
ellos	vencerán	ellos	vencerían

IMPERFECT		PRETERITE	
yo	vencía	yo	vencí
tú	vencías	tú	venciste
él	vencía	él	venció
nosotros	vencíamos	nosotros	vencimos
vosotros	vencíais	vosotros	vencisteis
ellos	vencían	ellos	vencieron

VERB TABLE

venir *to come*

PAST PARTICIPLE	IMPERATIVE
ven**ido**	**ven**
GERUND	ven**id**
vin**iendo**	

PRESENT		PRESENT SUBJUNCTIVE	
yo	vengo	yo	venga
tú	vienes	tú	vengas
él	viene	él	venga
nosotros	venimos	nosotros	vengamos
vosotros	venís	vosotros	vengáis
ellos	vienen	ellos	vengan

FUTURE		CONDITIONAL	
yo	vendré	yo	vendría
tú	vendrás	tú	vendrías
él	vendrá	él	vendría
nosotros	vendremos	nosotros	vendríamos
vosotros	vendréis	vosotros	vendríais
ellos	vendrán	ellos	vendrían

IMPERFECT		PRETERITE	
yo	venía	yo	vine
tú	venías	tú	viniste
él	venía	él	vino
nosotros	veníamos	nosotros	vinimos
vosotros	veníais	vosotros	vinisteis
ellos	venían	ellos	vinieron

ver *to see*

PAST PARTICIPLE	IMPERATIVE
visto	ve
	ved
GERUND	
v**iendo**	

PRESENT		PRESENT SUBJUNCTIVE	
yo	veo	yo	vea
tú	ves	tú	veas
él	ve	él	vea
nosotros	vemos	nosotros	veamos
vosotros	veis	vosotros	veáis
ellos	ven	ellos	vean

FUTURE		CONDITIONAL	
yo	veré	yo	vería
tú	verás	tú	verías
él	verá	él	vería
nosotros	veremos	nosotros	veríamos
vosotros	veréis	vosotros	veríais
ellos	verán	ellos	verían

IMPERFECT		PRETERITE	
yo	veía	yo	vi
tú	veías	tú	viste
él	veía	él	vio
nosotros	veíamos	nosotros	vimos
vosotros	veíais	vosotros	visteis
ellos	veían	ellos	vieron

VERB TABLE

volcar *to overturn*

PAST PARTICIPLE	IMPERATIVE
volc**ado**	**vuelca**
	volc**ad**
GERUND	
volc**ando**	

PRESENT		PRESENT SUBJUNCTIVE	
yo	**vuelco**	yo	**vuelque**
tú	**vuelcas**	tú	**vuelques**
él	**vuelca**	él	**vuelque**
nosotros	volc**amos**	nosotros	vol**quemos**
vosotros	volc**áis**	vosotros	vol**quéis**
ellos	**vuelcan**	ellos	**vuelquen**

FUTURE		CONDITIONAL	
yo	volcar**é**	yo	volcar**ía**
tú	volcar**ás**	tú	volcar**ías**
él	volcar**á**	él	volcar**ía**
nosotros	volcar**emos**	nosotros	volcar**íamos**
vosotros	volcar**éis**	vosotros	volcar**íais**
ellos	volcar**án**	ellos	volcar**ían**

IMPERFECT		PRETERITE	
yo	volc**aba**	yo	vol**qué**
tú	volc**abas**	tú	volc**aste**
él	volc**aba**	él	volc**ó**
nosotros	volc**ábamos**	nosotros	volc**amos**
vosotros	volc**abais**	vosotros	volc**asteis**
ellos	volc**aban**	ellos	volc**aron**

volver to return

PAST PARTICIPLE	IMPERATIVE
vuelto	**vuelve**
	volve**d**
GERUND	
volv**iendo**	

PRESENT		PRESENT SUBJUNCTIVE	
yo	**vuelvo**	yo	**vuelva**
tú	**vuelves**	tú	**vuelvas**
él	**vuelve**	él	**vuelva**
nosotros	volv**emos**	nosotros	volv**amos**
vosotros	volv**éis**	vosotros	volv**áis**
ellos	**vuelven**	ellos	**vuelvan**

FUTURE		CONDITIONAL	
yo	volver**é**	yo	volver**ía**
tú	volver**ás**	tú	volver**ías**
él	volver**á**	él	volver**ía**
nosotros	volver**emos**	nosotros	volver**íamos**
vosotros	volver**éis**	vosotros	volver**íais**
ellos	volver**án**	ellos	volver**ían**

IMPERFECT		PRETERITE	
yo	volv**ía**	yo	volv**í**
tú	volv**ías**	tú	volv**iste**
él	volv**ía**	él	volv**ió**
nosotros	volv**íamos**	nosotros	volv**imos**
vosotros	volv**íais**	vosotros	volv**isteis**
ellos	volv**ían**	ellos	volv**ieron**

---

zurcir *to darn*

PAST PARTICIPLE	IMPERATIVE
zurc**ido**	zurc**e**
	zurc**id**
GERUND	
zurc**iendo**	

PRESENT		PRESENT SUBJUNCTIVE	
yo	**zurzo**	yo	**zurza**
tú	**zurces**	tú	**zurzas**
él	**zurce**	él	**zurza**
nosotros	**zurcimos**	nosotros	**zurzamos**
vosotros	**zurcís**	vosotros	**zurzáis**
ellos	**zurcen**	ellos	**zurzan**

FUTURE		CONDITIONAL	
yo	**zurciré**	yo	**zurciría**
tú	**zurcirás**	tú	**zurcirías**
él	**zurcirá**	él	**zurciría**
nosotros	**zurciremos**	nosotros	**zurciríamos**
vosotros	**zurciréis**	vosotros	**zurciríais**
ellos	**zurcirán**	ellos	**zurcirían**

IMPERFECT		PRETERITE	
yo	**zurcía**	yo	**zurcí**
tú	**zurcías**	tú	**zurciste**
él	**zurcía**	él	**zurció**
nosotros	**zurcíamos**	nosotros	**zurcimos**
vosotros	**zurcíais**	vosotros	**zurcisteis**
ellos	**zurcían**	ellos	**zurcieron**

The following pages, 163 to 186, contain an index of over 2,800 commonly used verbs cross-referred to the appropriate conjugation model.

- Regular verbs belonging to the first, second and third conjugation are numbered 1, 2 and 3 respectively. For the regular conjugations see pp 6 to 13.

- Irregular verbs are numerically cross-referred to the appropriate model as conjugated on pp 82 to 161. Thus, **alzar** is cross-referred to p 100 where **cruzar**, the model for this verb group, is conjugated.

- Verbs which are most commonly used in the reflexive form – e.g. **amodorrarse** – have been cross-referred to the appropriate non-reflexive model. For the full conjugation of a reflexive verb, see pp 28 to 31.

- Verbs printed in **bold** – e.g. **abrir** – are themselves models.

- Superior numbers refer you to notes on p 187 which indicate how the verb differs from its model.

Grammar

abalanzar	100	acaecer[1]	99	acostumbrar	1
abandonar	1	acalorarse	1	acrecentar	133
abanicar	146	acampar	1	acreditar	1
abaratar	1	acaparar	1	acribillar	1
abarcar	146	acariciar	1	activar	1
abarrotar	1	acarrear	1	actualizar	100
abastecer	99	acatar	1	**actuar**	84
abatir	3	acatarrarse	1	acuciar	1
abdicar	146	acaudalar	1	acuclillarse	1
abjurar	1	acaudillar	1	acudir	3
ablandar	1	acceder	2	acumular	1
abnegarse	128	accidentarse	1	acuñar	1
abocar	146	accionar	1	acurrucarse	1
abochornar	1	acelerar	1	acusar	1
abofetear	1	acentuar	84	achacar	146
abogar	131	aceptar	1	achicar	146
abolir	82	acercar	146	achicharrar	1
abollar	1	acertar	133	adaptar	1
abombar	1	acicalar	1	adecuar	1
abonar	1	aclamar	1	adelantar	1
abordar	1	aclarar	1	adelgazar	100
aborrecer	99	aclimatar	1	aderezar	100
abortar	1	acobardarse	1	adeudar	1
abotonar	1	acodarse	1	adherirse	150
abrasar	1	acoger	95	adicionar	1
abrazar	100	acolchar	1	adiestrar	1
abreviar	1	acometer	2	adivinar	1
abrigar	131	acomodar	1	adjudicar	146
abrir	83	acompañar	1	adjuntar	1
abrochar	1	acomplejar	1	administrar	1
abrumar	1	acondicionar	1	admirar	1
absolver	160	acongojar	1	admitir	3
absorber	2	aconsejar	1	adoctrinar	1
abstenerse	152	acontecer[1]	99	adolecer	99
abstraer	154	acoplar	1	adoptar	1
abultar	1	acordar	98	adorar	1
abundar	1	acorralar	1	adormecer	99
aburrir	3	acortar	1	adornar	1
abusar	1	acosar	1	adosar	1
acabar	1	acostar	98	**adquirir**	85

adscribir	113	agrietarse	1	alimentar	1
aducir	96	agrupar	1	alinear	1
adueñarse	1	aguantar	1	aliñar	1
adular	1	aguar	90	alisar	1
adulterar	1	aguardar	1	alistar	1
advertir	150	aguijonear	1	aliviar	1
afanarse	1	agujerear	1	almacenar	1
afear	1	aguzar	100	almidonar	1
afectar	1	ahogar	131	**almorzar**	**86**
afeitar	1	ahondar	1	alojar	1
aferrar	1	ahorcar	146	alquilar	1
afianzar	100	ahorrar	1	alterar	1
aficionar	1	ahuecar	146	alternar	1
afilar	1	ahumar	1	alucinar	1
afiliarse	1	ahuyentar	1	aludir	3
afinar	1	airarse	1	alumbrar	1
afirmar	1	airear	1	alunizar	100
afligir	104	aislar	88	alzar	100
aflojar	1	ajar	1	allanar	1
afluir	97	ajustar	1	amaestrar	1
afrentar	1	ajusticiar	1	amagar	131
afrontar	1	alabar	1	amainar	1
agachar	1	alabear	1	amalgamar	1
agarrar	1	alambicar	144	amamantar	1
agarrotar	1	alardear	1	amanecer[1]	99
agasajar	1	alargar	131	amanerarse	1
agitar	1	albergar	131	amansar	1
aglomerarse	1	alborotar	1	amar	1
agobiar	1	alborozar	100	amargar	131
agolparse	1	alcanzar	100	amarrar	1
agonizar	100	aleccionar	1	amartillar	1
agotar	1	alegar	131	ambicionar	1
agraciar	1	alegrar	1	amedrentar	1
agradar	1	alejar	1	amenazar	100
agradecer	99	alentar	133	amenguar	90
agrandar	1	aletargar	131	amerizar	100
agravar	1	aletear	1	amilanar	1
agraviar	1	alfombrar	1	aminorar	1
agregar	131	aliarse	110	amnistiar	110
agriar	110	aligerar	1	amodorrarse	1

Grammar

amoldar	1	apadrinar	1	apremiar	1
amonestar	1	apagar	131	aprender	2
amontonar	1	apalabrar	1	apresar	1
amordazar	100	apalear	1	aprestarse	1
amortajar	1	apañar	1	apresurarse	1
amortiguar	90	aparcar	146	apretar	133
amortizar	100	aparecer	99	aprisionar	1
amotinar	1	aparejar	1	aprobar	98
amparar	1	aparentar	1	apropiar	1
ampliar	110	apartar	1	aprovechar	1
amplificar	146	apasionarse	1	aproximar	1
amputar	1	apearse	1	apuntalar	1
amueblar	1	apedrear	1	apuntar	1
amurallar	1	apegarse	1	apuñalar	1
analizar	100	apelar	1	apurar	1
anclar	1	apellidar	1	aquejar	1
andar	87	apelotonarse	1	aquietar	1
anegar	131	apenar	1	arañar	1
anexionar	1	apercibir	3	arar	1
angustiar	1	apesadumbrar	1	arbitrar	1
anhelar	1	apestar	1	arbolar	1
anidar	1	apetecer	99	archivar	1
animar	1	apiadarse	1	arder	2
aniquilar	1	apiñarse	1	arengar	1
anochecer[1]	199	aplacar	146	argamasar	1
anonadar	1	aplanar	1	argüir	97
anotar	1	aplastar	1	argumentar	1
anquilosarse	1	aplaudir	3	armar	1
ansiar	110	aplazar	100	armonizar	100
anteceder	2	aplicar	146	arquear	1
anteponer	135	apocar	146	arraigar	131
anticipar	1	apodar	1	arrancar	146
antojarse	1	apoderarse	1	arrasar	1
anudar	1	aporrear	1	arrastrar	1
anular	1	aportar	1	arrear	1
anunciar	1	aposentarse	1	arrebatar	1
añadir	3	apostar	98	arreglar	1
apabullar	1	apoyar	1	arremangar	131
apacentar	133	apreciar	1	arremeter	2
apaciguar	90	aprehender	2	arrendar	133

arrepentirse	150	asumir	3	aturdir	3
arrestar	1	asustar	1	augurar	1
arriar	110	atacar	146	aullar	88
arribar	1	atar	1	aumentar	1
arriesgar	131	atañer³	2	**aunar**	88
arrimar	1	atardecer¹	99	ausentarse	1
arrinconar	1	atarear	1	autenticar	146
arrodillarse	1	atascar	146	autentificar	146
arrojar	1	ataviar	110	automatizar	100
arropar	1	atemorizar	100	autorizar	100
arrostrar	1	atender	109	auxiliar	1
arrugar	131	atenerse	152	avanzar	100
arruinar	1	atentar	1	avasallar	1
arrullar	1	atenuar	84	avenirse	157
articular	1	aterrar	1	aventajar	1
asaltar	1	aterrizar	100	aventar	133
asar	1	aterrorizar	100	**avergonzar**	89
ascender	109	atesorar	1	averiarse	110
asear	1	atestar	1	**averiguar**	90
asediar	1	atestiguar	90	avezarse	100
asegurar	1	atiborrar	1	avinagrarse	1
asemejarse	1	atildar	1	avisar	1
asentar	133	atisbar	1	avispar	1
asentir	150	atizar	100	avistar	1
aserrar	133	atollar	1	avituallar	1
asesinar	1	atontar	1	avivar	1
aseverar	1	atormentar	1	ayudar	1
asfixiar	1	atornillar	1	ayunar	1
asignar	1	atracar	146	azorar	1
asimilar	1	atraer	154	azotar	1
asir²	3	atragantarse	1	azuzar	100
asistir	3	atrancar	146	babear	1
asociar	1	atrapar	1	bailar	1
asolar	1	atrasar	1	bajar	1
asolear	1	atravesar	133	balancear	1
asomar	1	atreverse	2	balbucear	1
asombrar	1	atribuir	97	balbucir⁴	3
aspar	1	atribular	1	baldar	1
asquear	1	atrofiar	1	bambolearse	1
astringir	3	atropellar	1	bañar	1

Grammar

barajar	1	bostezar	100	caminar	1
barbotar	1	botar	1	campar	1
barnizar	100	bracear	1	camuflar	1
barrenar	1	bramar	1	canalizar	100
barrer	2	bricolajear	1	cancelar	1
barruntar	1	brillar	1	canjear	1
basar	1	brincar	146	canonizar	100
bascular	1	brindar	1	cansar	1
bastar	1	bromear	1	cantar	1
batallar	1	broncearse	1	canturrear	1
batir	3	brotar	1	capacitar	1
bautizar	100	bruñir	116	capar	1
beber	2	bucear	1	capitalizar	100
bendecir	91	bufar	1	capitanear	1
beneficiar	1	bullir	116	capitular	1
berrear	1	burbujear	1	captar	1
besar	1	burlar	1	capturar	1
besuquear	1	buscar	146	caracolear	1
bifurcarse	146	cabalgar	131	caracterizar	100
birlar	1	cabecear	1	carbonizar	100
biselar	1	**caber**	92	carcomer	2
bizquear	1	cacarear	1	carear	1
blandir	3	cachear	1	carecer	99
blanquear	1	caducar	146	cargar	131
blasfemar	1	**caer**	93	casar	1
blasonar	1	calar	1	cascar	146
blindar	1	calcar	146	castigar	131
bloquear	1	calcinar	1	castrar	1
bobinar	1	calcular	1	catar	1
bocetar	1	caldear	1	caucionar	1
bogar	131	calentar	133	causar	1
boicotear	1	calibrar	1	cautivar	1
bombardear	1	calificar	146	cavar	1
bombear	1	calmar	1	cavilar	1
boquear	1	calumniar	1	cazar	100
borbotear	1	calzar	100	cebar	1
bordar	1	callar	1	cecear	1
bordear	1	callejear	1	ceder	2
borrar	1	cambiar	1	cegar	128
bosquejar	1	camelar	1	cejar	1

celar	1	cobrar	1	compadecer	99
celebrar	1	cocear	1	comparar	1
cementar	1	**cocer**	94	comparecer	99
cenar	1	cocinar	1	compartir	3
censar	1	codear	1	compeler	2
censurar	1	codiciar	1	compendiar	1
centellear	1	codificar	146	compensar	1
centralizar	100	coexistir	3	competer[1]	2
centrar	1	**coger**	95	competir	132
centrifugar	131	cohabitar	1	compilar	1
ceñir	140	cohibir	136	complacer	127
cepillar	1	coincidir	3	completar	1
cercar	146	cojear	1	complicar	146
cerciorarse	1	colaborar	1	componer	135
cerner	109	colar	98	comportarse	1
cerrar	133	colear	1	comprar	1
certificar	146	coleccionar	1	comprender	2
cesar	1	colegir	107	comprimir	3
cicatrizar	100	colgar	143	comprobar	98
cifrar	1	colindar	1	comprometer	2
cimbrear	1	colmar	1	computar	1
cimentar	133	colocar	146	comulgar	131
cincelar	1	colonizar	100	comunicar	146
cinchar	1	colorear	1	concebir	132
circular	1	columbrar	1	conceder	2
circuncidar	1	columpiar	1	concentrar	1
circundar	1	comadrear	1	concernir[5]	3
circunscribir	113	comandar	1	concertar	133
circunvalar	1	comarcar	146	concienciar	1
citar	1	combar	1	conciliar	1
civilizar	100	combatir	3	concluir	97
clamar	1	combinar	1	concordar	98
clamorear	1	comedirse	132	concretar	1
clarear	1	comentar	1	concurrir	3
clarificar	146	comenzar	108	condecorar	1
clasificar	146	comer	2	condenar	1
claudicar	146	comercializar	100	condensar	1
clavar	1	comerciar	1	condescender	109
coartar	1	cometer	2	condolerse	126
cobijar	1	comisionar	1	**conducir**	96

conectar	1	contagiar	1	cortejar	1
confeccionar	1	contaminar	1	cosechar	1
conferir	150	**contar**	98	coser	2
confesar	133	contemplar	1	costar	98
confiar	110	contemporizar	100	cotejar	1
configurar	1	contender	109	cotizar	100
confinar	1	contener	152	crear	1
confirmar	1	contentar	1	**crecer**	99
confiscar	146	contestar	1	creer	122
conformar	1	continuar	84	criar	110
confortar	1	contradecir	103	cribar	1
confrontar	1	contraer	154	crispar	1
confundir	3	contrapesar	1	cristalizar	100
congelar	1	contrariar	110	criticar	146
congeniar	1	contrarrestar	1	crucificar	146
congratular	1	contrastar	1	crujir	3
conjeturar	1	contratar	1	**cruzar**	100
conjugar	131	contravenir	157	cuadrar	1
conllevar	1	contribuir	97	cuajar	1
conmemorar	1	convalecer	99	cuantificar	146
conminar	1	convencer	99	cuartear	1
conmover	126	convenir	157	**cubrir**	101
conocer	99	converger	95	cuchichear	1
conquistar	1	convergir	104	cuidar	1
consagrar	1	conversar	1	culebrear	1
conseguir	149	convertir	150	culpar	1
consentir	150	convidar	1	cultivar	1
conservar	1	convocar	146	cumplimentar	1
considerar	1	cooperar	1	cumplir	3
consistir	3	coordinar	1	curar	1
consolar	98	copiar	1	curiosear	1
consolidar	1	coquetear	1	custodiar	1
conspirar	1	coronar	1	chamuscar	146
constar	1	corregir	107	chantajear	1
constituir	97	correr	2	chapotear	1
constreñir	140	corresponder	2	chapurrear	1
construir	97	corroborar	1	chapuzarse	100
consultar	1	corroer	93	charlar	1
consumar	1	corromper	2	chasquear	1
consumir	3	cortar	1	chequear	1

chiflar	1	dejar	1	desacreditar	1
chillar	1	delatar	1	desafiar	110
chirriar	110	delegar	131	desafilar	1
chisporrotear	1	deleitar	1	desafinar	1
chispear	1	deletrear	1	desagradar	1
chocar	146	deliberar	1	desagraviar	1
chochear	1	delinquir[7]	3	desahogar	131
chorrear	1	delirar	1	desahuciar	1
chupar	1	demandar	1	desairar	1
damnificar	146	demarcar	146	desajustar	1
danzar	100	democratizar	100	desalentar	133
dañar	1	demoler	126	desalojar	1
dar	102	demorar	1	desamarrar	1
datar	1	demostrar	98	desamparar	1
deambular	1	demudarse	1	desandar	87
debatir	3	denegar	128	desanimar	1
deber	2	denigrar	1	desaparecer	99
debilitar	1	denominar	1	desaprobar	98
debutar	1	denotar	1	desaprovechar	1
decaer	93	denunciar	1	desarmar	1
decapitar	1	depender	2	desarraigar	131
decepcionar	1	deplorar	1	desarreglar	1
decidir	3	deponer	135	desarticular	1
decir	103	deportar	1	desasir[8]	3
declamar	1	depositar	1	desasosegar	128
declarar	1	depravarse	1	desatar	1
declinar	1	depreciar	1	desatender	109
decolorarse	1	deprimir	1	desatinar	1
decorar	1	depurar	1	desatornillar	1
decrecer	99	derivar	1	desautorizar	100
decretar	1	derramar	1	desavenir	157
dedicar	146	derretir	132	desayunar	1
deducir	96	derribar	1	desazonar	1
defender	109	derrocar	146	desbandarse	1
definir	3	derrochar	1	desbaratar	1
deformar	1	derrotar	1	desbordar	1
defraudar	1	derrumbar	1	descabalgar	131
degenerar	1	desabotonar	1	descabezar	100
degollar[6]	98	desabrochar	1		
degradar	1	desacertar	133		
deificar	146	desaconsejar	1		

Grammar

descalzar	100	desencajar	1	desmejorar	1
descaminar	1	desengañar	1	desmembrar	133
descansar	1	desenmarañar	1	desmentir	150
descararse	1	desenredar	1	desmenuzar	100
descargar	131	desentenderse	109	desmerecer	99
descarriar	110	desenterrar	133	desmontar	1
descartar	1	desentrañar	1	desmoralizar	100
descender	109	desentumecer	99	desmoronarse	1
descifrar	1	desenvolver	160	desnudar	1
descolgar	143	desertar	1	desobedecer	99
descolorirse	3	desesperar	1	desocupar	1
descolorar	1	desestimar	1	desorganizar	100
descomponer	135	desfallecer	99	desorientar	1
desconcertar	133	desfigurar	1	despabilar	1
desconectar	1	desfilar	1	despachar	1
desconfiar	110	desgajar	1	desparramar	1
desconocer	99	desgañitarse	1	despedazar	100
desconsolar	98	desgarrar	1	despedir	132
descontar	98	desgastar	1	despegar	131
descorazonar	1	desgravar	1	despejar	1
descorchar	1	desguazar	100	despenalizar	100
descorrer	2	deshacer	118	desperezarse	100
descoser	2	deshelar[1]	133	despertar	133
descoyuntar	1	desheredar	1	despistar	1
describir	113	deshilar	1	desplegar	128
descuajar	1	deshinchar	1	despoblar	98
descubrir	101	deshilvanar	1	despojar	1
descuidar	1	deshonrar	1	desposeer	122
desdecirse	103	designar	1	despreciar	1
desdeñar	1	desilusionar	1	desprender	2
desdoblar	1	desinfectar	1	despreocuparse	1
desear	1	desinflar	1	desestabilizar	100
desecar	146	desistir	3	destacar	146
desechar	1	desligar	131	destapar	1
desembalar	1	deslizar	100	desteñir	140
desembarazar	100	deslumbrar	1	desterrar	133
desembarcar	146	desmandarse	1	destilar	1
desembocar	146	desmantelar	1	destinar	1
desempeñar	1	desmayar	1	destituir	97
desencadenar	1	desmedirse	132	destornillar	1

destrozar	100	disimular	1	electrocutar	1
destruir	97	disipar	1	**elegir**	107
desunir	3	disminuir	97	elevar	1
desvanecer	99	disolver	141	eliminar	1
desvariar	110	disparar	1	elogiar	1
desvelar	1	dispensar	1	eludir	3
desviar	110	dispersar	1	emanar	1
desvirtuar	84	disponer	135	emancipar	1
desvivirse	3	disputar	1	embadurnar	1
detallar	1	distanciar	1	embalar	1
detener	152	**distinguir**	105	embarazar	100
deteriorar	1	distraer	154	embarcar	146
determinar	1	distribuir	97	embargar	131
detestar	1	disuadir	3	embaular	88
detonar	1	divagar	131	embeber	2
devastar	1	diversificar	146	embellecer	99
devolver	160	divertir	150	embestir	132
devorar	1	dividir	3	embobar	1
dibujar	1	divorciarse	1	embolsar	1
diferenciar	1	divulgar	131	emborrachar	1
dificultar	1	doblar	1	embotar	1
difundir	3	doblegar	131	embotellar	1
digerir	150	doler	126	embozar	100
dignarse	1	domar	1	embragar	131
dilatar	1	domesticar	146	embravecer	99
dilucidar	1	dominar	1	embriagar	131
diluir	97	**dormir**	106	embrollar	1
dimitir	3	dormitar	1	embromar	1
dirigir	104	dotar	1	embrutecer	99
discernir⁹	3	ducharse	1	embutir	3
disciplinar	1	duplicar	146	emerger	95
discrepar	1	durar	1	emigrar	1
disculpar	1	echar	1	emitir	3
discurrir	3	editar	1	emocionar	1
discutir	3	educar	146	empalmar	1
disecar	146	efectuar	84	empantanarse	1
diseminar	1	ejecutar	1	empañar	1
disfrazar	100	ejercer	156	empapar	1
disfrutar	1	elaborar	1	empapelar	1
disgustar	1	electrizar	100	empaquetar	1

empastar	1	encomendar	133	enjaular	1
empatar	1	encomiar	1	enjuagar	131
empedrar	133	enconar	1	enjugar	131
empeñar	1	encontrar	98	enjuiciar	1
empeorar	1	encorvar	1	enlazar	100
empequeñecer	99	encrespar	1	enlodar	1
empezar	**108**	encuadrar	1	enloquecer	99
empinar	1	encubrir	101	enlutar	1
emplazar	100	encumbrar	1	enmarañar	1
emplear	1	enchufar	1	enmascarar	1
empobrecer	99	enderezar	100	enmendar	133
empotrar	1	endeudarse	1	enmohecerse	99
emprender	2	endomingarse	1	enmudecer	99
empujar	1	endosar	1	ennegrecer	99
empuñar	1	endulzar	100	ennoblecer	99
emular	1	endurecer	99	enojar	1
enajenar	1	enemistar	1	enorgullecerse	99
enamorar	1	enfadar	1	enraizar[10]	100
enardecer	99	enfermar	1	enredar	1
encabezar	100	enflaquecer	99	enriquecer	99
encadenar	1	enfocar	146	enrojecer	99
encajar	1	enfrentar	1	enrollar	1
encajonar	1	enfriar	110	enroscar	146
encaminar	1	enfurecer	99	ensalzar	100
encandilar	1	engalanar	1	ensamblar	1
encantar	1	enganchar	1	ensanchar	1
encaramarse	1	engañar	1	ensangrentar	133
encarcelar	1	engarzar	100	ensañarse	1
encarecer	99	engatusar	1	ensartar	1
encargar	131	engendrar	1	ensayar	1
encarrilar	1	engolfarse	1	enseñar	1
encausar	1	engomar	1	ensillar	1
encauzar	100	engordar	1	ensimismarse	1
enceguecer	99	engranar	1	ensoberbecerse	99
encender	109	engrandecer	99	ensordecer	99
encerrar	133	engrasar	1	ensortijar	1
enclavar	1	engreírse	139	ensuciar	1
encoger	95	engrosar	1	entablar	1
encolar	1	enhebrar	1	entallar	1
encolerizar	100	enjabonar	1	**entender**	**109**

enterarse	1	enzarzar	100	espabilar	1
enternecer	99	equilibrar	1	espaciar	1
enterrar	133	equipar	1	espantar	1
entibiar	1	equivaler	155	esparcir	161
entonar	1	equivocarse	146	especificar	146
entornar	1	**erguir**	111	especular	1
entorpecer	99	erigir	104	esperanzar	100
entrar	1	erizarse	100	esperar	1
entreabrir	83	erradicar	146	espesar	1
entregar	131	**errar**	112	espetar	1
entrelazar	100	eructar	1	espiar	110
entremeter	2	escabullirse	116	espirar	1
entremezclar	1	escalar	1	espolear	1
entrenarse	1	escampar[1]	1	espolvorear	1
entreoír	129	escandalizar	100	esponjarse	1
entresacar	146	escapar	1	esposar	1
entretejer	2	escarbar	1	esquematizar	100
entretener	152	escarmentar	1	esquilar	1
entrever	158	escarnecer	99	esquilmar	1
entrevistar	1	escasear	1	esquivar	1
entristecer	99	escatimar	1	establecer	99
entrometerse	2	esclarecer	99	estacionar	1
entroncar	146	esclavizar	100	estafar	1
entumecer	99	escocer	94	estallar	1
enturbiar	1	escoger	95	estampar	1
entusiasmar	1	escoltar	1	estancarse	146
enumerar	1	esconder	2	estandarizar	100
enunciar	1	**escribir**	113	**estar**	114
envainar	1	escrutar	1	estatificar	146
envalentonar	1	escuchar	1	estatuir	97
envanecer	99	escudarse	1	estereotipar	1
envasar	1	escudriñar	1	esterilizar	100
envejecer	99	esculpir	3	estilarse	1
envenenar	1	escupir	3	estimar	1
enviar	110	escurrir	3	estimular	1
envidiar	1	esforzarse	86	estipular	1
envilecer	99	esfumarse	1	estirar	1
enviudar	1	eslabonar	1	estofar	1
envolver	160	esmaltar	1	estorbar	1
		esmerarse	1	estornudar	1

estrangular	1	exonerar	1	familiarizarse	100
estratificar	146	exorcizar	100	fascinar	1
estrechar	1	expandir	3	fastidiar	1
estrellar	1	expansionar	1	fatigar	131
estremecer	99	expatriarse	110	favorecer	99
estrenar	1	expedir	132	fecundar	1
estreñir	140	experimentar	1	felicitar	1
estribar	1	expiar	110	fermentar	1
estropear	1	expirar	1	fertilizar	100
estructurar	1	explayar	1	festejar	1
estrujar	1	explicar	146	fiar	110
estudiar	1	explorar	1	fichar	1
evacuar	1	explosionar	1	figurar	1
evadir	3	explotar	1	fijar	1
evaluar	84	exponer	135	filmar	1
evaporar	1	exportar	1	filtrar	1
evidenciar	1	expresar	1	financiar	1
evitar	1	exprimir	3	fingir	104
evocar	146	expropiar	1	firmar	1
evolucionar	1	expugnar	1	fisgar	131
exacerbar	1	expulsar	1	flexibilizar	100
exagerar	1	expurgar	131	flirtear	1
exaltar	1	extender	109	florecer	99
examinar	1	extenuar	84	flotar	1
exasperar	1	exterminar	1	fluctuar	84
exceder	2	extinguir	105	fluir	97
exceptuar	84	extirpar	1	fomentar	1
excitar	1	extraer	154	forcejear	1
exclamar	1	extralimitarse	1	forjar	1
excluir	97	extrañar	1	formalizar	100
excomulgar	131	extraviar	110	formar	1
excoriar	1	extremar	1	forrar	1
excusar	1	eyacular	1	fortalecer	99
execrar	1	fabricar	146	forzar	86
exhalar	1	facilitar	1	fotocopiar	1
exhibir	3	facturar	1	fotografiar	110
exhortar	1	falsificar	146	fracasar	1
exigir	104	faltar	1	fraccionar	1
eximir	3	fallar	1	fraguar	90
existir	3	fallecer	99	franquear	1

fregar	128	gravar	1	hinchar	1
freír	115	gravitar	1	hipar	1
frenar	1	graznar	1	hipnotizar	100
frotar	1	gritar	1	hojear	1
fruncir	161	**gruñir**	116	holgar	143
frustrar	1	guadañar	1	hollar	98
fugarse	1	guardar	1	homogeneizar	100
fulminar	1	guarecer	99	honrar	1
fumar	1	guarnecer	99	horadar	1
funcionar	1	guasearse	1	horripilar	1
fundamentar	1	guerrear	1	horrorizar	100
fundar	1	guiar	110	hospedar	1
fundir	3	guiñar	1	hospitalizar	100
galantear	1	guisar	1	hostigar	131
galopar	1	gustar	1	huir	97
galvanizar	100	**haber**	117	humanizar	100
ganar	1	habilitar	1	humear	1
garantizar	100	habitar	1	humedecer	99
gastar	1	habituar	84	humillar	1
gatear	1	hablar	1	hundir	3
gemir	132	**hacer**	118	hurgar	131
generalizar	100	hacinar	1	huronear	1
generar	1	halagar	131	hurtar	1
germinar	1	hallar	1	husmear	1
gestionar	1	haraganear	1	idealizar	100
gimotear	1	hartar	1	idear	1
girar	1	hastiar	110	identificar	146
gloriarse	110	hechizar	100	ignorar	1
glorificar	146	heder	109	igualar	1
glosar	1	helar[1]	133	iluminar	1
gobernar	133	henchir	132	ilustrar	1
golpear	1	hender	109	imaginar	1
gorjear	1	heredar	1	imbuir	97
gotear	1	herir	150	imitar	1
gozar	100	hermanar	1	impartir	3
grabar	1	herrar	133	impedir	132
graduar	84	hervir	150	impeler	2
granizar[1]	100	hilar	1	imperar	1
granjear	1	hilvanar	1	implicar	146
gratificar	146	hincar	146	implorar	1

imponer	135	infestar	1	intentar	1
importar	1	inflamar	1	intercalar	1
importunar	1	inflar	1	interceder	2
imposibilitar	1	infligir	104	interesar	1
imprecar	146	influenciar	1	interferir	150
impregnar	1	influir	97	internar	1
impresionar	1	informatizar	100	interpelar	1
imprimir	3	informar	1	interponer	135
improvisar	1	infringir	104	interpretar	1
impugnar	1	infundir	3	interrogar	131
impulsar	1	ingeniar	1	interrumpir	3
imputar	1	ingerir	150	intervenir	157
inaugurar	1	ingresar	1	intimar	1
incapacitar	1	inhibir	3	intrigar	131
incautarse	1	iniciar	1	introducir	96
incendiar	1	injertar	1	inundar	1
incidir	3	injuriar	1	inutilizar	100
incinerar	1	inmiscuirse	97	invadir	3
incitar	1	inmolar	1	inventar	1
inclinar	1	inmortalizar	100	invertir	150
incluir	97	inmutar	1	investigar	131
incomodar	1	innovar	1	invitar	1
incorporar	1	inquietar	1	invocar	146
increpar	1	inquirir	85	inyectar	1
incrustar	1	inscribir	113	**ir**	120
incubar	1	insertar	1	irrigar	131
inculcar	146	insinuar	84	irritar	1
inculpar	1	insistir	3	irrumpir	3
incurrir	3	insolarse	1	izar	100
indagar	131	insonorizar	100	jabonar	1
indemnizar	100	inspeccionar	1	jactarse	1
indentar	1	inspirar	1	jadear	1
indicar	146	instalar	1	jalar	1
indignar	1	instar	1	jalonar	1
indisponer	135	instigar	131	jubilar	1
inducir	96	instituir	97	**jugar**	121
indultar	1	instruir	97	juguetear	1
industrializar	100	insubordinarse	1	juntar	1
infectar	1	insultar	1	juramentar	1
inferir	150	integrar	1	jurar	1

justificar	146	linchar	1	mancomunar	1
juzgar	131	lindar	1	manchar	1
labrar	1	liquidar	1	mandar	1
lacerar	1	lisiar	1	manejar	1
lacrar	1	lisonjear	1	mangonear	1
lactar	1	litigar	131	maniatar	1
ladear	1	loar	1	manifestar	133
ladrar	1	localizar	100	maniobrar	1
lagrimear	1	lograr	1	manipular	1
lamentar	1	lubricar	146	manosear	1
lamer	2	lubrificar	146	mantener	152
laminar	1	**lucir**	123	maquillar	1
languidecer	99	lucubrar	1	maravillar	1
lanzar	100	luchar	1	marcar	146
lapidar	1	lustrar	1	marchar	1
largar	131	llamar	1	marchitar	1
lastimar	1	llamear	1	marear	1
latir	3	llanear	1	martillear	1
lavar	1	llegar	131	mascar	146
leer	122	llenar	1	mascullar	1
legalizar	100	llevar	1	masticar	146
legar	131	llorar	1	masturbarse	1
legislar	1	lloriquear	1	medicar	146
legitimar	1	**llover**[1]	124	medir	132
lesionar	1	llovizar[1]	1	mentar	133
levantar	1	macerar	1	mentir	150
levar	1	machacar	146	merendar	133
liar	110	madrugar	131	moler	126
libar	1	madurar	1	morder	126
liberar	1	magnetizar	100	**morir**	125
libertar	1	magullar	1	motivar	1
librar	1	maldecir	103	motorizar	100
licenciar	1	malear	1	**mover**	126
licitar	1	malgastar	1	movilizar	100
licuar	84	malograr	1	mudar	1
lidiar	1	maltratar	1	mugir	104
ligar	131	malversar	1	multar	1
limar	1	malvivir	3	multiplicar	146
limitar	1	mamar	1	murmurar	1
limpiar	1	manar	1	musitar	1

mutilar	1	ocurrir	3	oxidar	1
nacer	127	odiar	1	pacer	99
nacionalizar	100	ofender	2	pacificar	146
nadar	1	ofrecer	99	pactar	1
narcotizar	100	ofrendar	1	padecer	99
narrar	1	ofuscar	146	**pagar**	131
naturalizarse	100	**oír**	129	paladear	1
naufragar	131	ojear	1	paliar	1
navegar	131	**oler**	130	palidecer	99
necesitar	1	olfatear	1	palmotear	1
negar	128	olvidar	1	palpar	1
negociar	1	omitir	3	palpitar	1
neutralizar	100	ondear	1	paralizar	100
nevar[1]	133	ondular	1	parar	1
neviscar[1]	146	operar	1	parear	1
niquelar	1	opinar	1	parir	3
nivelar	1	oponer	135	parlamentar	1
nombrar	1	opositar	1	parlotear	1
normalizar	100	oprimir	3	parodiar	1
notar	1	optar	1	parpadear	1
notificar	146	opugnar	1	participar	1
nublarse[1]	1	orar	1	particularizar	100
numerar	1	ordenar	1	partir	3
nutrir	3	ordeñar	1	pasar	1
obcecarse	146	orear	1	pasear	1
obedecer	99	organizar	100	pasmar	1
objetar	1	orientar	1	pastar	1
obligar	131	originar	1	patalear	1
obrar	1	orillar	1	patear	1
observar	1	orinar	1	patentar	1
obsesionar	1	orlar	1	patentizar	100
obstaculizar	100	ornamentar	1	patinar	1
obstar	1	ornar	1	patrocinar	1
obstinarse	1	osar	1	pecar	146
obstruir	97	oscilar	1	pedalear	1
obtener	152	oscurecer	99	**pedir**	132
obviar	1	ostentar	1	pegar	131
ocasionar	1	otear	1	peinar	1
ocultar	1	otorgar	131	pelar	1
ocupar	1	ovillar	1	pelear	1

pellizcar	146	pintar	1	preconizar	100
penar	1	pisar	1	predecir	103
pender	2	pisotear	1	predeterminar	1
penetrar	1	pitar	1	predicar	146
pensar	133	plagar	131	predisponer	135
percatarse	1	planchar	1	predominar	1
percibir	3	planear	1	prefabricar	146
perder	109	planificar	146	preferir	150
perdonar	1	plantar	1	prefigurar	1
perdurar	1	plantear	1	pregonar	1
perecer	99	plañir	116	preguntar	1
perfeccionar	1	plasmar	1	premeditar	1
perforar	1	platicar	146	premiar	1
perjudicar	146	plegar	128	prendarse	1
perjurar	1	poblar	98	prender	2
permanecer	99	podar	1	prensar	1
permitir	3	**poder**	134	preocupar	1
permutar	1	podrir	3	preparar	1
perorar	1	polarizarse	100	prescindir	3
perpetrar	1	politizar	100	prescribir	113
perpetuar	84	ponderar	1	presenciar	1
perseguir	149	**poner**	135	presentar	1
perseverar	1	popularizar	100	presentir	150
persignarse	1	pordiosear	1	preservar	1
persistir	3	porfiar	110	presidir	3
personarse	1	portarse	1	presionar	1
personificar	146	posar	1	prestar	1
persuadir	3	poseer	122	presumir	3
pertenecer	99	posesionarse	1	presuponer	135
perturbar	1	posibilitar	1	pretender	2
pervertir	150	posponer	135	prevalecer	99
pesar	1	postergar	131	prevaricar	146
pescar	146	postrar	1	prevenir	157
pestañear	1	postular	1	prever	158
petrificar	146	practicar	146	primar	1
piar	110	precaver	2	principiar	1
picar	146	preceder	2	privar	1
picotear	1	precintar	1	privilegiar	1
pillar	1	precipitar	1	probar	98
pinchar	1	precisar	1	proceder	2

procesar	1	pulir	3	razonar	1
proclamar	1	pulimentar	1	reabastecer	99
procrear	1	pulsar	1	reabrir	83
procurar	1	pulular	1	reaccionar	1
producir	96	pulverizar	100	reactivar	1
profanar	1	puntear	1	reafirmar	1
proferir	150	puntualizar	100	reagrupar	1
profesar	1	punzar	100	realizar	100
profetizar	100	purgar	131	realzar	100
profundizar	100	purificar	146	reanimar	1
programar	1	quebrantar	1	reanudar	1
progresar	1	quebrar	133	reavivar	1
prohibir	136	quedar	1	rebajar	1
prohijar	138	quejarse	1	rebasar	1
proliferar	1	quemar	1	rebatir	3
prolongar	131	querellarse	1	rebelarse	1
prometer	2	**querer**	137	reblandecer	99
promover	126	quitar	1	rebosar	1
promulgar	131	rabiar	1	rebotar	1
pronosticar	146	racionalizar	100	rebozar	100
pronunciar	1	racionar	1	rebuscar	146
propagar	131	radiar	1	rebuznar	1
proponer	135	radicar	146	recabar	1
proporcionar	1	radiografiar	110	recaer	93
propulsar	1	rajar	1	recalcar	146
prorrogar	131	rallar	1	recalentar	133
prorrumpir	3	ramificarse	146	recapacitar	1
proscribir	113	rapar	1	recargar	131
proseguir	149	raptar	1	recatarse	1
prosperar	1	rasar	1	recelar	1
prostituir	97	rascar	146	recibir	3
proteger	95	rasgar	131	reciclar	1
protestar	1	rasguear	1	recitar	1
proveer	122	rasguñar	1	reclamar	1
provenir	157	raspar	1	reclinar	1
provocar	146	rastrear	1	recluir	97
proyectar	1	rastrillar	1	recobrar	1
publicar	146	rasurarse	1	recoger	95
pudrir[11]	3	ratificar	146	recomendar	133
pugnar	1	rayar	1	recompensar	1

recomponer	135	refrigerar	1	relegar	131
reconciliar	1	refugiarse	1	relevar	1
reconfortar	1	refulgir	104	relinchar	1
reconocer	99	refundir	3	relucir	123
reconstruir	97	refunfuñar	1	relumbrar	1
recopilar	1	refutar	1	rellenar	1
recordar	98	regalar	1	remachar	1
recorrer	2	regañar	1	remar	1
recortar	1	regar	128	rematar	1
recostar	98	regatear	1	remedar	1
recrear	1	regenerar	1	remediar	1
recriminar	1	regentar	1	remendar	133
recrudecer	99	regir	107	remeter	2
rectificar	146	registrar	1	remitir	3
recubrir	83	reglamentar	1	remojar	1
recular	1	regocijar	1	remolinar	1
recuperar	1	regodearse	1	remontar	1
recurrir	3	regresar	1	remorder	126
recusar	1	regular	1	remover	126
rechazar	100	regularizar	100	remozar	100
rechinar	1	rehabilitar	1	remunerar	1
redactar	1	rehacer	118	renacer	127
redescubrir	101	rehogar	131	rendir	132
redimir	3	rehuir[12]	97	renegar	128
redoblar	1	**rehusar**	138	renovar	98
redondear	1	reinar	1	rentar	1
reducir	96	reincidir	3	renunciar	1
reembolsar	1	reincorporarse	1	**reñir**	140
reemplazar	100	reintegrar	1	reorganizar	100
referir	150	**reír**	139	reorientar	1
refinar	1	reinvertir	3	reparar	1
reflejar	1	reiterar	1	repartir	3
reflexionar	1	reivindicar	146	repasar	1
refocilarse	1	rejuvenecer	99	repatriar	110
reformar	1	relacionar	1	repeler	2
reforzar	86	relajar	1	repensar	133
refractar	1	relamer	2	repercutir	3
refrenar	1	relampaguear[1]	1	repetir	132
refrendar	1	relanzar	100	repicar	146
refrescar	146	relatar	1	replegar	128

replicar	146	resplandecer	99	revisar	1
repoblar	98	responder	2	revivir	3
reponer	135	resquebrajar	1	revocar	146
reportar	1	restablecer	99	revolcarse	159
reposar	1	restallar	1	revolotear	1
repostar	1	restar	1	revolucionar	1
reprender	2	restaurar	1	revolver	160
representar	1	restituir	97	rezagar	131
reprimir	3	restregar	131	rezar	100
reprobar	98	restringir	104	rezongar	131
reprochar	1	resucitar	1	rezumar	1
reproducir	96	resultar	1	ribetear	1
repudiar	1	resumir	3	ridiculizar	100
repugnar	1	retar	1	rifar	1
repujar	1	retardar	1	rimar	1
repulgar	131	retener	152	rivalizar	100
reputar	1	retirar	1	rizar	100
requerir	150	retocar	146	robar	1
resaltar	1	retorcer	153	robustecer	99
resarcir	161	retornar	1	rociar	110
resbalar	1	retozar	100	rodar	98
rescatar	1	retractar	1	rodear	1
rescindir	3	retraer	154	roer[13]	2
resecarse	146	retransmitir	3	**rogar**	143
resentirse	150	retrasar	1	**romper**	144
reseñar	1	retratar	1	roncar	146
reservar	1	retribuir	97	rondar	1
resfriarse	110	retroceder	2	ronquear	1
resguardar	1	retumbar	1	ronronear	1
residir	3	reunificar	146	rotular	1
resignarse	1	**reunir**	142	roturar	1
resistir	3	revalidar	1	rozar	100
resolver	141	revalorar	1	ruborizarse	100
resollar	98	revelar	1	rubricar	146
resonar	98	reventar	133	rugir	104
resoplar	1	reverberar	1	rumiar	1
respaldar	1	reverdecer	99	rumorearse	1
respetar	1	reverenciar	1	rutilar	1
respingar	131	revertir	150	**saber**	145
respirar	1	revestir	132	saborear	1

sabotear	1	**ser**	151	someter	2
sacar	146	serenarse	1	sonar	98
saciar	1	serpentear	1	sondear	1
sacrificar	146	serrar	133	sonreír	139
sacudir	3	servir	132	soñar	98
salar	1	significar	146	soplar	1
saldar	1	silbar	1	soportar	1
salir	147	silenciar	1	sorber	2
salpicar	146	simpatizar	100	sorprender	2
saltar	1	simplificar	146	sortear	1
saltear	1	simular	1	sosegar	128
saludar	1	sincronizar	100	sospechar	1
salvaguardar	1	singularizar	100	sostener	152
salvar	1	sintetizar	100	soterrar	1
sanar	1	sisear	1	suavizar	100
sancionar	1	sitiar	1	subastar	1
sanear	1	situar	84	subdividir	3
sangrar	1	sobornar	1	subentender	109
santificar	146	sobrar	1	subestimar	1
santiguar	90	sobrecargar	131	subir	3
saquear	1	sobrellevar	1	subrayar	1
satisfacer	148	sobrepasar	1	subsanar	1
saturar	1	sobreponer	135	subscribir	113
sazonar	1	sobresalir	147	subsistir	3
secar	146	sobresaltar	1	subvencionar	1
secuestrar	1	sobrevivir	3	subvertir	150
secundar	1	socializar	100	subyugar	131
sedimentar	1	socorrer	2	suceder	2
seducir	96	sofocar	146	sucumbir	3
segregar	131	sojuzgar	131	sudar	1
seguir	149	solazarse	100	sufrir	3
seleccionar	1	soldar	98	sugerir	150
sembrar	133	solear	1	sugestionar	1
semejar	1	soler[14]	126	sujetar	1
sentar	133	solicitar	1	sumar	1
sentenciar	1	soliviantar	1	sumergir	104
sentir	150	soltar	98	suministrar	1
señalar	1	solucionar	1	sumir	3
separar	1	solventar	1	supeditar	1
sepultar	1	sollozar	100	superar	1

suplicar	146	**tener**	152	traducir	96
suplir	3	tensar	1	**traer**	154
suponer	135	tentar	133	traficar	146
suprimir	3	teñir	140	tragar	131
surcar	146	teorizar	100	traicionar	1
surgir	104	terciar	1	trajinar	1
surtir	3	tergiversar	1	tramar	1
suscitar	1	terminar	1	tramitar	1
suscribir	113	tersar	1	trampear	1
suspender	2	testar	1	tranquilizar	100
suspirar	1	testificar	146	transar	1
sustentar	1	testimoniar	1	transbordar	1
sustituir	97	tildar	1	transcurrir	3
sustraer	154	timar	1	transferir	150
susurrar	1	timbrar	1	transfigurar	1
tabular	1	tintar	1	transformar	1
tachar	1	tintinear	1	transgredir	3
tajar	1	tirar	1	transigir	104
taladrar	1	tiritar	1	transitar	1
talar	1	tirotear	1	transmitir	3
tallar	1	titilar	1	transparentar	1
tambalearse	1	titubear	1	transpirar	1
tamizar	100	titularse	1	transportar	1
tantear	1	tiznar	1	trascender	109
tapar	1	tocar	146	trasegar	128
tapiar	1	tolerar	1	trasladar	1
tapizar	100	tomar	1	traslucir	123
tararear	1	tonificar	146	trasnochar	1
tardar	1	topar	1	traspasar	1
tartamudear	1	toquetear	1	trasplantar	1
tasar	1	**torcer**	153	trasponer	135
tatuar	84	torear	1	trastocar	146
teclear	1	tornar	1	trastornar	1
tejer	2	torpedear	1	tratar	1
telefonear	1	torturar	1	trazar	100
televisar	1	toser	2	trenzar	100
temblar	133	tostar	98	trepar	1
temer	2	trabajar	1	trepidar	1
templar	1	trabar	1	tributar	1
tender	109	trabucar	146	trillar	1

trincar	146	vadear	1	vindicar	146
trinchar	1	vagar	131	violar	1
tripular	1	**valer**	155	violentar	1
triturar	1	validar	1	virar	1
triunfar	1	valorar	1	visitar	1
trivializar	100	valuar	84	vislumbrar	1
trocar	159	vallar	1	vitalizar	100
tronar[1]	98	vanagloriarse	1	vitorear	1
tronchar	1	vaporizar	100	vituperar	1
tropezar	108	varear	1	vivificar	146
trotar	1	variar	110	vivir	3
truncar	146	vedar	1	vocalizar	100
tullir	116	vejar	1	vocear	1
tumbar	1	velar	1	vociferar	1
turbar	1	**vencer**	156	volar	98
turnarse	1	vendar	1	volatilizar	100
tutear	1	vender	2	**volcar**	159
ubicar	146	venerar	1	voltear	1
ufanarse	1	vengar	131	**volver**	160
ulcerar	1	**venir**	157	vomitar	1
ultimar	1	ventear	1	votar	1
ultrajar	1	ventilar	1	vulgarizar	100
ulular	1	ventosear	1	vulnerar	1
uncir	161	**ver**	158	yacer[15]	2
ungir	104	veranear	1	yuxtaponer	135
unificar	146	verdear[1]	1	zafarse	1
uniformar	1	verdecer[1]	99	zaherir	150
unir	3	verificar	146	zambullirse	116
untar	1	versar	1	zampar	1
urbanizar	100	verter	109	zanjar	1
urdir	3	vestir	132	zapatear	1
urgir	104	vetar	1	zarandear	1
usar	1	viajar	1	zarpar	1
usurpar	1	vibrar	1	zigzaguear	1
utilizar	100	viciar	1	zozobrar	1
vaciar	110	vigilar	1	zumbar	1
vacilar	1	vilipendiar	1	**zurcir**	161
vacunar	1	vincular	1	zurrar	1

◻ Notes

The notes below indicate special peculiarities of individual verbs. When only some forms of a given tense are affected, all these are shown. When all forms of the tense are affected, only the 1st and 2nd persons are shown, followed by *etc*.

1 Gerund *2* Past Participle *3* Present *4* Preterite *5* Present Subjunctive *6* Imperfect Subjunctive

1) **acaecer, acontecer, amanecer, anochecer, atardecer, competer, deshelar, escampar, granizar, helar, llover, lloviznar, nevar, neviscar, nublarse, relampaguear, tronar, verdear, verdecer:** used almost exclusively in infinitive and 3rd person singular

2) **asir** *3* asgo *5* asga, asgas *etc*

3) **atañer** *1* atañendo *4* atañó: see also **1)** above

4) **balbucir** *3* balbuceo *5* balbucee, balbucees *etc*

5) **concernir** *3* concierne, conciernen *5* concierna, conciernan: only used in 3rd person

6) **degollar** *3* degüello, degüellas, degüella, degüellan *5* degüelle, degüelles, degüellen

7) **delinquir** *3* delinco *5* delinca, delincas *etc*

8) **desasir** *3* desasgo *5* desasga, desasgas *etc*

9) **discernir** *3* discierno, disciernes, discierne, disciernen *5* discierna, disciernas, disciernan

10) **enraizar** *3* enraízo, enraízas, enraíza, enraízan *5* enraíce, enraíces, enraícen

11) **pudrir** *2* podrido

12) **rehuir** *3* rehúyo, rehúyes, rehúye, rehúyen *5* rehúya, rehúyas, rehúyan

13) **roer** *4* royó, royeron *6* royera, royeras *etc*

14) **soler:** used only in present and imperfect indicative

15) **yacer** *3* yazgo *or* yazco *or* yago *5* yazga *etc or* yazca *etc or* yaga *etc*

❏ The Gender of Nouns

In Spanish, all nouns are either masculine or feminine, whether denoting people, animals or things. Gender is largely unpredictable and has to be learnt for each noun. However, the following guidelines will help you determine the gender for certain types of nouns.

- Nouns denoting male people and animals are usually – but not always – masculine, e.g.

un hombre	**un toro**
a man	*a bull*
un enfermero	**un semental**
a (male) nurse	*a stallion*

- Nouns denoting female people and animals are usually – but not always – feminine, e.g.

una niña	**una vaca**
a girl	*a cow*
una enfermera	**una yegua**
a nurse	*a mare*

- Some nouns are masculine *or* feminine depending on the sex of the person to whom they refer, e.g.

un camarada	**una camarada**
a (male) comrade	*a (female) comrade*
un belga	**una belga**
a Belgian (man)	*a Belgian (woman)*
un marroquí	**una marroquí**
a Moroccan (man)	*a Moroccan (woman)*

- Other nouns referring to either men or women have only one gender which applies to both, e.g.

una persona	**una visita**
a person	*a visitor*
una víctima	**una estrella**
a victim	*a star*

- Often the ending of a noun indicates its gender. Shown below are some of the most important to guide you.

Masculine endings

o
un clavo *a nail*, un plátano *a banana*
EXCEPTIONS: **mano** *hand*, **foto** *photograph*,
moto(cicleta) *motorbike*

l
un tonel *a barrel*, un hotel *a hotel*
EXCEPTIONS: **cal** *lime*, **cárcel** *prison*, **catedral** *cathedral*,
col *cabbage*, **miel** *honey*, **piel** *skin*, **sal** *salt*, **señal** *sign*

r
un tractor *a tractor*, el altar *the altar*
EXCEPTIONS: **coliflor** *cauliflower*, **flor** *flower*, **labor** *task*

y
el rey *the king*, un buey *an ox*
EXCEPTION: **ley** *law*

Feminine endings

a
una casa *a house*, la cara *the face*
EXCEPTIONS: **día** *day*, **mapa** *map*, **planeta** *planet*,
tranvía *tram*, and most words ending in -ma (**tema**
subject, **problema** *problem*, etc)

ión
una canción *a song*, una procesión *a procession*
EXCEPTIONS: most nouns not ending in -ción or -sión,
e.g. **avión** *aeroplane*, **camión** *lorry*, **gorrión** *sparrow*

dad, -tad,
tud
una ciudad *a town*, la libertad *freedom*, una
multitud *a crowd*

ed
una pared *a wall*, la sed *thirst*
EXCEPTION: **césped** *lawn*

itis
una faringitis *pharyngitis*, la celulitis *cellulitis*

iz
una perdiz *a partridge*, una matriz *a matrix*
EXCEPTIONS: **lápiz** *pencil*, **maíz** *corn*, **tapiz** *tapestry*

sis
una tesis *a thesis*, una dosis *a dose*
EXCEPTIONS: **análisis** *analysis*, **énfasis** *emphasis*,
paréntesis *parenthesis*

umbre
la podredumbre *rot*, la muchedumbre *crowd*

❏ Gender of nouns (Continued)

Some nouns change meaning according to gender. The most common are set out below:

	MASCULINE	FEMININE
capital	capital (money)	capital (city) → [1]
clave	harpsichord	clue
cólera	cholera	anger → [2]
cometa	comet	kite
corriente	current month	current
corte	cut	court (royal) → [3]
coma	coma	comma → [4]
cura	priest	cure → [5]
frente	front (in war)	forehead → [6]
guardia	guard(sman)	guard → [7]
guía	guide (person)	guide(book) → [8]
moral	mulberry tree	morals
orden	order (arrangement)	order (command) → [9]
ordenanza	office boy	ordinance
papa	Pope	potato
parte	dispatch	part → [10]
pendiente	earring	slope
pez	fish	pitch
policía	policeman	police
radio	radius, radium	radio

1 **Invirtieron mucho capital**
They invested a lot of capital
La capital es muy fea
The capital city is very ugly

2 **Es difícil luchar contra el cólera**   **Montó en cólera**
Cholera is difficult to combat   He got angry

3 **Me encanta tu corte de pelo**
I love your haircut
Se trasladó la corte a Madrid
The court was moved to Madrid

4 **Entró en un coma profundo**
He went into a deep coma
Aquí hace falta una coma
You need to put a comma here

5 **¿Quién es? – El cura**   **No tiene cura**
Who is it? – The priest   It's hopeless

6 **Han mandado a su hijo al frente**
Her son has been sent to the front
Tiene la frente muy ancha
She has a very broad forehead

7 **Vino un guardia de tráfico**
A traffic policeman came
Están relevando la guardia ahora
They're changing the guard now

8 **Nuestro guía nos hizo reír a carcajadas**
Our guide had us falling about laughing
Busco una guía turística
I'm looking for a guidebook

9 **Están en orden alfabético**
They're in alphabetical order
No hemos recibido la orden de pago
We haven't had the payment order

10 **Le mandó un parte al general**
He sent a dispatch to the general
En alguna parte debe estar
It must be somewhere or other

❑ Gender: the formation of feminines

As in English, male and female are sometimes differentiated by the use of two quite separate words, e.g.

mi marido	**mi mujer**
my husband	*my wife*
un toro	**una vaca**
a bull	*a cow*

There are, however, some words in Spanish which show this distinction by the form of their ending:

- Nouns ending in **-o** change to **-a** to form the feminine → ①
- If the masculine singular form already ends in **-a**, no further **-a** is added to the feminine → ②
- If the last letter of the masculine singular form is a consonant, an **-a** is normally added in the feminine* → ③

Feminine forms to note

MASCULINE	FEMININE	
el abad	la abadesa	*abbot/abbess*
un actor	una actriz	*actor/actress*
el alcalde	la alcaldesa	*mayor/mayoress*
el conde	la condesa	*count/countess*
el duque	la duquesa	*duke/duchess*
el emperador	la emperatriz	*emperor/empress*
un poeta	una poetisa	*poet/poetess*
el príncipe	la princesa	*prince/princess*
el rey	la reina	*king/queen*
un sacerdote	una sacerdotisa	*priest/priestess*
un tigre	una tigresa	*tiger/tigress*
el zar	la zarina	*tzar/tzarina*

* If the last syllable has an accent, it disappears in the feminine (see p 292) → ④

Examples

1. | | |
   |---|---|
   | **un amigo** | **una amiga** |
   | a (male) friend | a (female) friend |
   | **un empleado** | **una empleada** |
   | a (male) employee | a (female) employee |
   | **un gato** | **una gata** |
   | a cat | a (female) cat |

2. | | |
   |---|---|
   | **un deportista** | **una deportista** |
   | a sportsman | a sportswoman |
   | **un colega** | **una colega** |
   | a (male) colleague | a (female) colleague |
   | **un camarada** | **una camarada** |
   | a (male) comrade | a (female) comrade |

3. | | |
   |---|---|
   | **un español** | **una española** |
   | a Spaniard, a Spanish man | a Spanish woman |
   | **un vendedor** | **una vendedora** |
   | a salesman | a saleswoman |
   | **un jugador** | **una jugadora** |
   | a (male) player | a (female) player |

4. | | |
   |---|---|
   | **un lapón** | **una lapona** |
   | a Laplander (man) | a Laplander (woman) |
   | **un león** | **una leona** |
   | a lion | a lioness |
   | **un neocelandés** | **una neocelandesa** |
   | a New Zealander (man) | a New Zealander (woman) |

▢ The formation of plurals

- Nouns ending in an unstressed vowel add **-s** to the singular form → 1

- Nouns ending in a consonant or a stressed vowel add **-es** to the singular form → 2

⚠️ BUT:

café	*coffee shop*	(plur: **cafés**)
mamá	*mummy*	(plur: **mamás**)
papá	*daddy*	(plur: **papás**)
pie	*foot*	(plur: **pies**)
sofá	*sofa*	(plur: **sofás**)
té	*tea*	(plur: **tes**)

and words of foreign origin ending in a consonant, e.g.:

coñac	*brandy*	(plur: **coñacs**)
jersey	*jumper*	(plur: **jerseys**)

⚠️ NOTE:

— nouns ending in **-n** or **-s** with an accent on the last syllable drop this accent in the plural (see p 292) → 3

— nouns ending in **-n** with the stress on the second-last syllable in the singular add an accent to that syllable in the plural in order to show the correct position for stress (see p 292) → 4

— nouns ending in **-z** change this to **c** in the plural → 5

- Nouns with an unstressed final syllable ending in **-s** do not change in the plural → 6

Examples

1. **la casa**
   the house

   el libro
   the book

   las casas
   the houses

   los libros
   the books

2. **un rumor**
   a rumour

   un jabalí
   a boar

   unos rumores
   (some) rumours

   unos jabalíes
   (some) boars

3. **la canción**
   the song

   el autobús
   the bus

   las canciones
   the songs

   los autobuses
   the buses

4. **un examen**
   an exam

   un crimen
   a crime

   unos exámenes
   (some) exams

   unos crímenes
   (some) crimes

5. **la luz**
   the light

   las luces
   the lights

6. **un paraguas**
   an umbrella

   la dosis
   the dose

   el lunes
   Monday

   unos paraguas
   (some) umbrellas

   las dosis
   the doses

   los lunes
   Mondays

☐ The Definite Article

	WITH MASC NOUN	WITH FEM NOUN	
SING	**el**	**la**	*the*
PLUR	**los**	**las**	*the*

♦ The gender and number of the noun determine the form of the article → ①

⚠ NOTE: However, if the article comes directly before a feminine singular noun which starts with a stressed **a-** or **ha-**, the masculine form **el** is used instead of the feminine **la** → ②

♦ For uses of the definite article see p 199.

♦ **a** + **el** becomes **al** → ③

♦ **de** + **el** becomes **del** → ④

1. **el tren**
   the train

   el actor
   the actor

   los hoteles
   the hotels

   los profesores
   the teachers

   la estación
   the station

   la actriz
   the actress

   las escuelas
   the schools

   las mujeres
   the women

2. **el agua** ⚠ BUT:
   the water

   el hacha ⚠ BUT:
   the axe

   la misma agua
   the same water

   la mejor hacha
   the best axe

3. **al cine**
   to the cinema

   al empleado
   to the employee

   al hospital
   to the hospital

4. **del departamento**
   from/of the department

   del autor
   from/of the author

   del presidente
   from/of the president

❏ Uses of the definite article

While the definite article is used in much the same way in Spanish as it is in English, its use is more widespread in Spanish. Unlike English the definite article is also used:

◆ with abstract nouns, except when following certain prepositions → 1

◆ in generalizations, especially with plural or uncountable* nouns → 2

◆ with parts of the body → 3

   'Ownership' is often indicated by an indirect object pronoun or a reflexive pronoun → 4

◆ with titles/ranks/professions followed by a proper name → 5

   ⚠ EXCEPTIONS: with **Don/Doña, San/Santo(a)** → 6

◆ before nouns of official, academic and religious buildings, and names of meals and games → 7

◆ The definite article is NOT used with nouns in apposition unless those nouns are individualized → 8

* An uncountable noun is one which cannot be used in the plural or with an indefinite article, e.g. **el acero** *steel*, **la leche** *milk*.

1. **Los precios suben**
Prices are rising
El tiempo es oro
Time is money
⚠️ BUT:

con pasión	**sin esperanza**
with passion	without hope

2. **No me gusta el café**
I don't like coffee
Los niños necesitan ser queridos
Children need to be loved

3. **Vuelva la cabeza hacia la izquierda**
Turn your head to the left
No puedo mover las piernas
I can't move my legs

4. **La cabeza me da vueltas**
My head is spinning
Lávate las manos
Wash your hands

5.

El rey Jorge III	**el capitán Menéndez**
King George III	Captain Menéndez
el doctor Ochoa	**el señor Ramírez**
Doctor Ochoa	Mr Ramírez

6.

Don Arturo Ruiz	**Santa Teresa**
Mr Arturo Ruiz	Saint Teresa

7.

en la cárcel	**en la universidad**
in prison	at university
en la iglesia	**la cena**
at church	dinner
el tenis	**el ajedrez**
tennis	chess

8. **Madrid, capital de España, es la ciudad que …**
Madrid, the capital of Spain, is the city which …
⚠️ BUT:

Maria Callas, la famosa cantante de ópera …
Maria Callas, the famous opera singer …

❑ The Indefinite Article

	WITH MASC NOUN	WITH FEM NOUN	
SING	**un**	**una**	*a*
PLUR	**unos**	**unas**	*some*

The indefinite article is used in Spanish largely as it is in English.

⚠️ BUT:

- There is no article when a person's profession is being stated → [1]

  The article is used, however, when the profession is qualified by an adjective → [2]

- The article is not used with the following words:

otro	*another*	→ [3]
cierto	*certain*	→ [4]
semejante	*such (a)*	→ [5]
tal	*such (a)*	→ [6]
cien	*a hundred*	→ [7]
mil	*a thousand*	→ [8]
sin	*without*	→ [9]
qué	*what a*	→ [10]

- There is no article with a noun in apposition → [11]. When an abstract noun is qualified by an adjective, the indefinite article is used, but is not translated in English → [12]

1	**Es profesor** He's a teacher	**Mi madre es enfermera** My mother is a nurse
2	**Es un buen médico** He's a good doctor	
	Se hizo una escritora célebre She became a famous writer	
3	**otro libro** another book	
4	**cierta calle** a certain street	
5	**semejante ruido** such a noise	
6	**tal mentira** such a lie	
7	**cien soldados** a hundred soldiers	
8	**mil años** a thousand years	
9	**sin casa** without a house	
10	**¡Qué sorpresa!** What a surprise!	
11	**Baroja, gran escritor de la Generación del 98** Baroja, a great writer of the 'Generación del 98'	
12	**con una gran sabiduría/un valor admirable** with great wisdom/admirable courage	
	Dieron pruebas de una sangre fría increíble They showed incredible coolness	
	una película de un mal gusto espantoso a film in appallingly bad taste	

☐ The Article 'lo'

This is never used with a noun. Instead, it is used in the following ways:

• As an intensifier before an adjective or adverb in the construction

  lo + adjective/adverb + **que** → 1

  ⚠ NOTE: The adjective agrees with the noun it refers to → 2

• With an adjective or participle to form an abstract noun → 3

• In the phrase **lo de** to refer to a subject of which speaker and listener are already aware. It can often be translated as *the business/affair of/about ...* → 4

• In set expressions, the commonest of which are:

a lo mejor	*maybe, perhaps*	→ 5
a lo lejos	*in the distance*	→ 6
a lo largo de	*along, through*	→ 7
por lo menos	*at least*	→ 8
por lo tanto	*therefore, so*	→ 9
por lo visto	*apparently*	→ 10

1. **No sabíamos lo pequeña que era la casa**
   We didn't know how small the house was

   Sé lo mucho que te gusta la música
   I know how much you like music

2. **No te imaginas lo simpáticos que son**
   You can't imagine how nice they are

   Ya sabes lo buenas que son estas manzanas
   You already know how good these apples are

3. **Lo bueno de eso es que ...**
   The good thing about it is that ...

   Sentimos mucho lo ocurrido
   We are very sorry about what happened

4. **Lo de ayer es mejor que lo olvides**
   It's better if you forget what happened yesterday

   Lo de tu hermano me preocupa mucho
   The business about your brother worries me very much

5. **A lo mejor ha salido**
   Perhaps he's gone out

6. **A lo lejos se veían unas casas**
   Some houses could be seen in the distance

7. **A lo largo de su vida**
   Throughout his life

   A lo largo de la carretera
   Along the road

8. **Hubo por lo menos cincuenta heridos**
   At least fifty people were injured

9. **No hemos recibido ninguna instrucción al respecto, y
   por lo tanto no podemos ...**
   We have not received any instructions about it, therefore we
   cannot ...

10. **Por lo visto, no viene**
    Apparently he's not coming OR: He's not coming, it seems

□ Adjectives

Most adjectives agree in number and in gender with the noun or pronoun.

⚠ NOTE that:

— if the adjective refers to two or more singular nouns of the same gender, a plural ending of that gender is required → [1]

— if the adjective refers to two or more singular nouns of different genders, a masculine plural ending is required → [2]

The formation of feminines

♦ Adjectives ending in **-o** change to **-a** → [3]

♦ Some groups of adjectives add **-a**:

  – adjectives of nationality or geographical origin → [4]

  – adjectives ending in **-or** (except irregular comparatives: see p 210), **-án, -ón, -ín** → [5]

  ⚠ NOTE: When there is an accent on the last syllable, it disappears in the feminine (see p 292).

♦ Other adjectives do not change → [6]

The formation of plurals

♦ Adjectives ending in an unstressed vowel add **-s** → [7]

♦ Adjectives ending in a stressed vowel or a consonant add **-es** → [8]

  ⚠ NOTE:

  – if there is an accent on the last syllable of a word ending in a consonant, it will disappear in the plural (see p 292) → [9]

  – if the last letter is a **z** it will become a **c** in the plural → [10]

1. **la lengua y la literatura españolas**
(the) Spanish language and literature

2. **Me he comprado un abrigo y una camisa rojos**
I bought myself a red coat and shirt

3. **mi hermano pequeño**
my little brother

   mi hermana pequeña
   my little sister

4. **un chico español**
a Spanish boy

   una chica española
   a Spanish girl

   el equipo barcelonés
   the team from Barcelona

   la vida barcelonesa
   the Barcelona way of life

5. **un niño encantador**
a charming little boy

   una niña encantadora
   a charming little girl

   un hombre holgazán
   an idle man

   una mujer holgazana
   an idle woman

   un gesto burlón
   a mocking gesture

   una sonrisa burlona
   a mocking smile

   un chico cantarín
   a boy fond of singing

   una chica cantarina
   a girl fond of singing

6. **un final feliz**
a happy ending

   una infancia feliz
   a happy childhood

   mi amigo belga
   my Belgian (male) friend

   mi amiga belga
   my Belgian (female) friend

   el vestido verde
   the green dress

   la blusa verde
   the green blouse

7. **el último tren**
the last train

   los últimos trenes
   the last trains

   una casa vieja
   an old house

   unas casas viejas
   (some) old houses

8. **un médico iraní**
an Iranian doctor

   unos médicos iraníes
   (some) Iranian doctors

   un examen fácil
   an easy exam

   unos exámenes fáciles
   (some) easy exams

9. **un río francés**
a French river

   unos ríos franceses
   (some) French rivers

10. **un día feliz**
a happy day

   unos días felices
   (some) happy days

▢ Invariable Adjectives

Some adjectives and other parts of speech when used adjectivally never change in the feminine or plural.

The commonest of these are:

— nouns denoting colour → 1

— compound adjectives → 2

— nouns used as adjectives → 3

Shortening of Adjectives

◆ The following drop the final **-o** before a masculine singular noun:

> **bueno** *good* → 4
>
> **malo** *bad*
>
> **alguno*** *some* → 5
>
> **ninguno*** *none*
>
> **uno** *one* → 6
>
> **primero** *first* → 7
>
> **tercero** *third*
>
> **postrero** *last* → 8

> * ⚠ NOTE: An accent is required to show the correct position for stress.

◆ **Grande** *big, great* is usually shortened to **gran** before a masculine or feminine singular noun → 9

◆ **Santo** *Saint* changes to **San** except with saints' names beginning with **Do-** or **To-** → 10

◆ **Ciento** *a hundred* is shortened to **cien** before a masculine or feminine plural noun → 11

◆ **Cualquiera** drops the final **-a** before a masculine or feminine singular noun → 12

№		
1	**los vestidos naranja** the orange dresses	
2	**las chaquetas azul marino** the navy blue jackets	
3	**bebés probeta** test-tube babies	**mujeres soldado** women soldiers
4	**un buen libro** a good book	
5	**algún libro** some book	
6	**un día** one day	
7	**el primer hijo** the first child	
8	**un postrer deseo** a last wish	
9	**un gran actor** a great actor	**una gran decepción** a great disappointment
10	**San Antonio** Saint Anthony	**Santo Tomás** Saint Thomas
11	**cien años** a hundred years **cien millones** a hundred million	
12	**cualquier día** any day	**a cualquier hora** any time

❑ Comparatives and Superlatives

Comparatives

These are formed using the following constructions:

más ... (que)		*more ... (than)*	→ 1
menos ... (que)		*less ... (than)*	→ 2
tanto ... como		*as ... as*	→ 3
tan ... como		*as ... as*	→ 4
tan ... que		*so ... that*	→ 5
demasiado ...		*too ...*	
bastante ... }	**para**	*enough ...* } *to* →	6
suficiente ...		*enough ...*	

• *'Than'* followed by a clause is translated by **de lo que** → 7

Superlatives

These are formed using the following constructions:

el/la/los/las más ... (que)	*the most ... (that)*	→ 8
el/la/los/las menos ... (que)	*the least ... (that)*	→ 9

• After a superlative the preposition **de** is often translated as *in* → 10

• The absolute superlative (*very, most, extremely + adjective*) is expressed in Spanish by **muy** + adjective, or by adding **-ísimo/a/os/as** to the adjective when it ends in a consonant, or to its stem (adjective minus final vowel) when it ends in a vowel → 11

> ⚠ NOTE: It is sometimes necessary to change the spelling of the adjective when **-ísimo** is added, in order to maintain the same sound (see p 296) → 12

1. **una razón más seria**
   a more serious reason
   Es más alto que mi hermano
   He's taller than my brother

2. **una película menos conocida**
   a less well known film
   Luis es menos tímido que tú
   Luis is less shy than you

3. **Pablo tenía tanto miedo como yo**
   Paul was as frightened as I was

4. **No es tan grande como creía**
   It isn't as big as I thought

5. **El examen era tan difícil que nadie aprobó**
   The exam was so difficult that nobody passed

6. **No tengo suficiente dinero para comprarlo**
   I haven't got enough money to buy it

7. **Está más cansada de lo que parece**
   She is more tired than she seems

8. **el caballo más veloz**   **la casa más pequeña**
   the fastest horse   the smallest house
   los días más lluviosos   **las manzanas más maduras**
   the wettest days   the ripest apples

9. **el hombre menos simpático**   **la niña menos habladora**
   the least likeable man   the least talkative girl
   los cuadros menos bonitos   **las camisas menos viejas**
   the least attractive paintings   the least old shirts

10. **la estación más ruidosa de Londres**
    the noisiest station in London

11. **Este libro es muy interesante**   **Tienen un coche rapidísimo**
    This book is very interesting   They have an extremely fast car
    Era facilísimo de hacer
    It was very easy to make

12. **Mi tío era muy rico**   **Se hizo riquísimo**
    My uncle was very rich   He became extremely rich
    un león muy feroz   **un tigre ferocísimo**
    a very ferocious lion   an extremely ferocious tiger

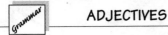

☐ Comparatives and Superlatives *(Continued)*

Adjectives with irregular comparatives/superlatives

ADJECTIVE	COMPARATIVE	SUPERLATIVE
bueno *good*	**mejor** *better*	**el mejor** *the best*
malo *bad*	**peor** *worse*	**el peor** *the worst*
grande *big*	**mayor** OR:	**el mayor** OR:
	más grande *bigger; older*	**el más grande** *the biggest; the oldest*
pequeño *small*	**menor** OR:	**el menor** OR:
	más pequeño *smaller; younger; lesser*	**el más pequeño** *the smallest; the youngest; the least*

- The irregular comparative and superlative forms of **grande** and **pequeño** are used mainly to express:
  — age, in which case they come after the noun → ①
  — abstract size and degrees of importance, in which case they come before the noun → ②

  The regular forms are used mainly to express physical size → ③

- Irregular comparatives and superlatives have one form for both masculine and feminine, but always agree in number with the noun → ①

1. **mis hermanos mayores**
   my older brothers
   la hija menor
   the youngest daughter

2. **el menor ruido**
   the slightest sound
   las mayores dificultades
   the biggest difficulties

3. **Este plato es más grande que aquél**
   This plate is bigger than that one
   Mi casa es más pequeña que la tuya
   My house is smaller than yours

❑ Demonstrative Adjectives

	MASCULINE	FEMININE	
SING	**este**	**esta**	*this*
	ese	**esa**	*that*
	aquel	**aquella**	
PLUR	**estos**	**estas**	*these*
	esos	**esas**	*those*
	aquellos	**aquellas**	

- Demonstrative adjectives normally precede the noun and always agree in number and in gender → ①

- The forms **ese/a/os/as** are used:
    — to indicate distance from the speaker but proximity to the person addressed → ②
    — to indicate a not too remote distance → ③

- The forms **aquel/la/los/las** are used to indicate distance, in space or time → ④

1. **Este bolígrafo no escribe**
   This pen is not working
   Esa revista es muy mala
   That is a very bad magazine
   Aquella montaña es muy alta
   That mountain (over there) is very high
   ¿Conoces a esos señores?
   Do you know those gentlemen?
   Siga Vd hasta aquellos edificios
   Carry on until you come to those buildings
   ¿Ves aquellas personas?
   Can you see those people (over there)?

2. **Ese papel en donde escribes ...**
   That paper you are writing on ...

3. **No me gustan esos cuadros**
   I don't like those pictures

4. **Aquella calle parece muy ancha**
   That street (over there) looks very wide
   Aquellos años sí que fueron felices
   Those were really happy years

◻ Interrogative Adjectives

	MASCULINE	FEMININE	
SING {	¿qué?	¿qué?	what?, which?
	¿cuánto?	¿cuánta?	how much?; how many?
PLUR {	¿qué?	¿qué?	what?, which?
	¿cuántos?	¿cuántas?	how much?; how many?

+ Interrogative adjectives, when not invariable, agree in number and gender with the noun → ①

+ The forms shown above are also used in indirect questions → ②

◻ Exclamatory Adjectives

	MASCULINE	FEMININE	
SING {	¡qué!	¡qué!	what (a)
	¡cuánto!	¡cuánta!	what (a lot of)
PLUR {	¡qué!	¡qué!	what
	¡cuántos!	¡cuántas!	what (a lot of)

+ Exclamatory adjectives, when not invariable, agree in number and gender with the noun → ③

215

Examples

1 **¿Qué libro te gustó más?**
Which book did you like most?

¿Qué clase de hombre es?
What type of man is he?

¿Qué instrumentos toca Vd?
What instruments do you play?

¿Qué ofertas ha recibido Vd?
What offers have you received?

¿Cuánto dinero te queda?
How much money have you got left?

¿Cuánta lluvia ha caído?
How much rain have we had?

¿Cuántos vestidos quieres comprar?
How many dresses do you want to buy?

¿Cuántas personas van a venir?
How many people are coming?

2 **No sé a qué hora llegó**
I don't know at what time she arrived

Dígame cuántas postales quiere
Tell me how many postcards you'd like

3 **¡Qué pena!**
What a pity!

¡Qué tiempo tan/más malo!
What lousy weather!

¡Cuánto tiempo!
What a long time!

¡Cuánta pobreza!
What poverty!

¡Cuántos autobuses!
What a lot of buses!

¡Cuántas mentiras!
What a lot of lies!

□ **Possessive Adjectives**

Weak forms

WITH SING NOUN		WITH PLUR NOUN		
MASC	*FEM*	*MASC*	*FEM*	
mi	mi	mis	mis	*my*
tu	tu	tus	tus	*your*
su	su	sus	sus	*his; her; its; your*
				(of **Vd**)
nuestro	nuestra	nuestros	nuestras	*our*
vuestro	vuestra	vuestros	vuestras	*your*
su	su	sus	sus	*their; your*
				(of **Vds**)

◆ All possessive adjectives agree in number and (when applicable) in gender with the noun, NOT WITH THE OWNER → ①

◆ The weak forms always precede the noun → ①

◆ Since the form **su(s)** can mean *his, her, your (of* **Vd**, **Vds**) or *their*, clarification is often needed. This is done by adding **de él, de ella, de Vds** etc to the noun, and usually (but not always) changing the possessive to a definite article → ②

① **Pilar no ha traído nuestros libros**
Pilar hasn't brought our books

Antonio irá a vuestra casa
Anthony will go to your house

¿Han vendido su coche tus vecinos?
Have your neighbours sold their car?

Mi hermano y tu primo no se llevan bien
My brother and your cousin don't get on

② **su casa → la casa de él**
his house

sus amigos → los amigos de Vd
your friends

sus coches → los coches de ellos
their cars

su abrigo → el abrigo de ella
her coat

❏ **Possessive Adjectives** *(Continued)*

Strong forms

WITH SING NOUN		WITH PLUR NOUN		
MASC	FEM	MASC	FEM	
mío	mía	míos	mías	*my*
tuyo	tuya	tuyos	tuyas	*your*
suyo	suya	suyos	suyas	*his; her; its; your (of Vd)*
nuestro	nuestra	nuestros	nuestras	*our*
vuestro	vuestra	vuestros	vuestras	*your*
suyo	suya	suyos	suyas	*their; your (of Vds)*

+ The strong forms agree in the same way as the weak forms (see p 216).

+ The strong forms always follow the noun, and they are used:
  — to translate the English *of mine, of yours*, etc → [1]
  — to address people → [2]

1   **Es un capricho suyo**
It's a whim of hers
un amigo nuestro
a friend of ours
una revista tuya
a magazine of yours

2   **Muy señor mío** (in letters)
Dear Sir
hija mía
my daughter
¡Dios mío!
My God!
Amor mío
Darling/My love

◻ Indefinite Adjectives

alguno(a)s	*some*
ambos(as)	*both*
cada	*each; every*
cierto(a)s	*certain; definite*
cualquiera, plur **cualesquiera**	*some; any*
los (las) demás	*the others; the remainder*
mismo(a)s	*same; -self*
mucho(a)s	*many; much*
ningún, ninguna	*any; no*
plur **ningunos, ningunas**	
otro(a)s	*other; another*
poco(a)s	*few; little*
tal(es)	*such (a)*
tanto(a)s	*so much; so many*
todo(a)s	*all; every*
varios(as)	*several; various*

Unless invariable, all indefinite adjectives agree in number and gender with the noun → ①

◆ alguno

Before a masculine singular noun it drops the final **-o** and adds an accent to show the correct position for stress → ② (see also p 292)

◆ ambos

Usually it is only used in written Spanish. The spoken language prefers the form **los dos/las dos** → ③

◆ cierto and mismo

They change their meaning according to their position in relation to the noun (see also **Position of Adjectives**, p 224) → ④

◆ cualquiera

It drops the final **-a** before a masculine *or* feminine noun → ⑤

☐ **el mismo día**
the same day

mucha/poca gente
many/few people

las mismas películas
the same films

mucho/poco dinero
much/little money

② **algún día**
some day

alguna razón
some reason

③ **Me gustan los dos cuadros**
I like both pictures

¿Conoces a las dos enfermeras?
Do you know both nurses?

④ **cierto tiempo** ⚠ BUT:
a certain time

el mismo color ⚠ BUT:
the same colour

éxito cierto
sure success

en la iglesia misma
in the church itself

⑤ **cualquier casa** ⚠ BUT:
any house

una revista cualquiera
any magazine

☐ **Indefinite Adjectives** (Continued)

- **ningún** is only used in negative sentences or phrases → [1]

- **otro**

  It is never preceded by an indefinite article → [2]

- **tal**

  It is never followed by an indefinite article → [3]

- **todo**

  It can be followed by a definite article, a demonstrative or possessive adjective or a place name → [4]

   EXCEPTIONS:

  — when **todo** in the singular means *any*, *every*, or *each* → [5]

  — in some set expressions → [6]

1. **No es ninguna tonta**
   She's no fool
   ¿No tienes parientes? – No, ninguno
   Haven't you any relatives? – No, none

2. **¿Me das otra manzana?**
   Will you give me another apple?
   Prefiero estos otros zapatos
   I prefer these other shoes

3. **Nunca dije tal cosa**
   I never said such a thing

4. **Estudian durante toda la noche**
   They study all night
   Ha llovido toda esta semana
   It has rained all this week
   Pondré en orden todos mis libros
   I'll sort out all my books
   Lo sabe todo Madrid
   All Madrid knows it

5. **Podrá entrar toda persona que lo desee**
   Any person who wishes to enter may do so

   ⚠️ BUT:

   Vienen todos los días
   They come every day

6. | | |
   |---|---|
   | **de todos modos**
anyway | **a toda velocidad**
at full/top speed |
   | **por todas partes**
por todos lados
a/en todas partes
a/en todos lados | everywhere |

☐ Position of Adjectives

- Spanish adjectives usually follow the noun → ①, ②

- Note that when used figuratively or to express a quality already inherent in the noun, adjectives can precede the noun → ③

- As in English, demonstrative, possessive (weak forms), numerical, interrogative and exclamatory adjectives precede the noun → ④

- Indefinite adjectives also usually precede the noun → ⑤

  ⚠ NOTE: **alguno** *some* in negative expressions follows the noun → ⑥

- Some adjectives can precede or follow the noun, but their meaning varies according to their position:

	BEFORE NOUN	AFTER NOUN	
antiguo	*former*	*old, ancient*	→ ⑦
diferente	*various*	*different*	→ ⑧
grande	*great*	*big*	→ ⑨
medio	*half*	*average*	→ ⑩
mismo	*same*	*-self, very/precisely*	→ ⑪
nuevo	*new, another, fresh*	*brand new*	→ ⑫
pobre	*poor (wretched)*	*poor (not rich)*	→ ⑬
puro	*sheer, mere*	*pure (clear)*	→ ⑭
varios	*several*	*various, different*	→ ⑮
viejo	*old (long known, etc)*	*old (aged)*	→ ⑯

- Adjectives following the noun are linked by **y** → ⑰

Examples

1. **la página siguiente**
   the following page

   la hora exacta
   the right time

2. **una corbata azul**
   a blue tie

   una palabra española
   a Spanish word

3. **un dulce sueño**
   a sweet dream

   un terrible desastre (all disasters are terrible)
   a terrible disaster

4. **este sombrero**
   this hat

   mi padre
   my father

   ¿qué hombre?
   what man?

5. **cada día**
   every day

   otra vez
   another time

   poco dinero
   little money

6. **sin duda alguna**
   without any doubt

7. **un antiguo colega**
   a former colleague

   la historia antigua
   ancient history

8. **diferentes capítulos**
   various chapters

   personas diferentes
   different people

9. **un gran pintor**
   a great painter

   una casa grande
   a big house

10. **medio melón**
    half a melon

    velocidad media
    average speed

11. **la misma respuesta**
    the same answer

    yo mismo
    myself

    eso mismo
    precisely that

12. **mi nuevo coche**
    my new car

    unos zapatos nuevos
    (some) brand new shoes

13. **esa pobre mujer**
    that poor woman

    un país pobre
    a poor country

14. **la pura verdad**
    the plain truth

    aire puro
    fresh air

15. **varios caminos**
    several ways/paths

    artículos varios
    various items

16. **un viejo amigo**
    an old friend

    esas toallas viejas
    those old towels

17. **una acción cobarde y falsa**
    a cowardly, deceitful act

□ **Personal Pronouns**

	SUBJECT PRONOUNS	
PERSON	SINGULAR	PLURAL
1st	**yo**	**nosotros**
	I	*we* (masc/masc + fem)
		nosotras
		we (all fem)
2nd	**tú**	**vosotros**
	you	*you* (masc/masc + fem)
		vosotras
		you (all fem)
3rd	**él**	**ellos**
	he; it	*they* (masc/masc + fem)
	ella	**ellas**
	she; it	*they* (all fem)
	usted (Vd)	**ustedes (Vds)**
	you	*you*

♦ Subject pronouns have a limited usage in Spanish. Normally they ar
   only used:

   — for emphasis → 1

   — for clarity → 2

   ⚠ BUT: **Vd** and **Vds** should always be used for politeness, whethe
   they are otherwise needed or not → 3

♦ *It* as subject and *they,* referring to things, are never translated int
   Spanish → 4

♦ **tú/usted**

   As a general rule, you should use **tú** (or **vosotros,** if plural) whe
   addressing a friend, a child, a relative, someone you know well, ◀
   when invited to do so. In all other cases, use **usted** (or **ustedes**)

♦ **nosotros/as; vosotros/as; él/ella; ellos/ellas**

   All these forms reflect the number and gender of the noun(s) the
   replace. **Nosotros, vosotros** and **ellos** also replace a combinatio
   of masculine and feminine nouns.

1 **Ellos sí que llegaron tarde**
They really did arrive late
Tú no tienes por qué venir
There is no reason for you to come
Ella jamás creería eso
She would never believe that

2 **Yo estudio español pero él estudia francés**
I study Spanish but he studies French
Ella era muy deportista pero él prefería jugar a las cartas
She was a sporty type but he preferred to play cards
Vosotros saldréis primero y nosotros os seguiremos
You leave first and we will follow you

3 **Pase Vd por aquí**
Please come this way
¿Habían estado Vds antes en esta ciudad?
Had you been to this town before?

4 **¿Qué es? – Es una sorpresa**
What is it? – It's a surprise
¿Qué son? – Son abrelatas
What are they? – They are tin-openers

☐ **Personal Pronouns** (Continued)

DIRECT OBJECT PRONOUNS

PERSON	SINGULAR	PLURAL
1st	**me**	**nos**
	me	*us*
2nd	**te**	**os**
	you	*you*
3rd (masculine)	**lo**	**los**
	him; it; you	*them; you*
	(of **Vd**)	(of **Vds**)
(feminine)	**la**	**las**
	her; it; you	*them; you*
	(of **Vd**)	(of **Vds**)

* **lo** sometimes functions as a 'neuter' pronoun, referring to an idea or information contained in a previous statement or question. It is often not translated → ①

Position of direct object pronouns

* In constructions other than the imperative affirmative, infinitive or gerund, the pronoun always comes before the verb → ②

  In the imperative affirmative, infinitive and gerund, the pronoun follows the verb and is attached to it. An accent is needed in certain cases to show the correct position for stress (see also p 292) → ③

* Where an infinitive or gerund depends on a previous verb, the pronoun may be used either after the infinitive or gerund, or before the main verb → ④

  ⚠ NOTE: see how this applies to reflexive verbs → ④

* For further information, see **Order of Object Pronouns**, p 232.

Reflexive Pronouns

These are dealt with under reflexive verbs, p 24.

1   **¿Va a venir María? – No lo sé**
Is Maria coming? – I don't know

     Hay que regar las plantas – Yo lo haré
The plants need watering – I'll do it

     Habían comido ya pero no nos lo dijeron
They had already eaten, but they didn't tell us

     Yo conduzco de prisa pero él lo hace despacio
I drive fast but he drives slowly

2   **Te quiero**
I love you

     ¿Las ve Vd?
Can you see them?

     ¿No me oyen Vds?
Can't you hear me?

     Tu hija no nos conoce
Your daughter doesn't know us

     No los toques
Don't touch them

3   **Ayúdame**   **Acompáñenos**
Help me   Come with us

     Quiero decirte algo
I want to tell you something

     Estaban persiguiéndonos
They were coming after us

4   **Lo está comiendo** OR: **Está comiéndolo**
She is eating it

     Nos vienen a ver OR: **Vienen a vernos**
They are coming to see us

     No quería levantarse OR: **No se quería levantar**
He didn't want to get up

     Estoy afeitándome OR: **Me estoy afeitando**
I'm shaving

☐ **Personal Pronouns** (Continued)

PERSON	INDIRECT OBJECT PRONOUNS	
	SINGULAR	PLURAL
1st	**me**	**nos**
2nd	**te**	**os**
3rd	**le**	**les**

◆ The pronouns shown in the above table replace the preposition **a** + noun → 1

Position of indirect object pronouns

◆ In constructions other than the imperative affirmative, the infinitive or the gerund, the pronoun comes before the verb → 2

In the imperative affirmative, infinitive and gerund, the pronoun follows the verb and is attached to it. An accent is needed in certain cases to show the correct position for stress (see also p 292) → 3

◆ Where an infinitive or gerund depends on a previous verb, the pronoun may be used either after the infinitive or gerund, or before the main verb → 4

◆ For further information, see **Order of Object Pronouns**, p 232.

Reflexive Pronouns

These are dealt with under reflexive verbs, p 24.

1

Estoy escribiendo a Teresa →   **Le estoy escribiendo**
I am writing to Teresa   I am writing to her

Da de comer al gato →   **Dale de comer**
Give the cat some food   Give it some food

2

Sofía os ha escrito   **¿Os ha escrito Sofía?**
Sophie has written to you   Has Sophie written to you?

Carlos no nos habla
Charles doesn't speak to us

¿Qué te pedían?
What were they asking you for?

No les haga caso Vd
Don't take any notice of them

3

Respóndame Vd   **Díganos Vd la respuesta**
Answer me   Tell us the answer

No quería darte la noticia todavía
I didn't want to tell you the news yet

Llegaron diciéndome que ...
They came telling me that ...

4

Estoy escribiéndole OR: **Le estoy escribiendo**
I am writing to him/her

Les voy a hablar OR: **Voy a hablarles**
I'm going to talk to them

❑ **Personal Pronouns** (Continued)

Order of object pronouns

• When two object pronouns of different persons are combined, the order is: indirect before direct, i.e.

$$
\left.\begin{array}{l} \textbf{me} \\ \textbf{te} \\ \textbf{nos} \\ \textbf{os} \end{array}\right\} \text{ before } \left\{\begin{array}{l} \textbf{lo} \\ \textbf{la} \\ \textbf{los} \\ \textbf{las} \end{array}\right. \rightarrow \boxed{1}
$$

⚠ NOTE: When two 3rd person object pronouns are combined, the first (i.e. the indirect object pronoun) becomes **se** → ②

Points to note on object pronouns

• As **le/les** can refer to either gender, and **se** to either gender, singular or plural, sometimes clarification is needed. This is done by adding **a él** to him, **a ella** to her, **a Vd** to you etc to the phrase, usually after the verb → ③

• When a noun object precedes the verb, the corresponding object pronoun must be used too → ④

• Indirect object pronouns are often used instead of possessive adjectives with parts of the body or clothing to indicate 'ownership', and also in certain common constructions involving reflexive verbs (see also **The Indefinite Article**, p 198) → ⑤

• **Le** and **les** are often used in Spanish instead of **lo** and **los** when referring to people. Equally **la** is sometimes used instead of **le** when referring to a feminine person or animal, although this usage is considered incorrect by some speakers of Spanish → ⑥

Examples

1. **Paloma os lo mandará mañana**
   Paloma is sending it to you tomorrow
   ¿Te los ha enseñado mi hermana?
   Has my sister shown them to you?
   No me lo digas
   Don't tell me (that)
   Todos estaban pidiéndotelo
   They were all asking you for it
   No quiere prestárnosla
   He won't lend it to us

2. **Se lo di ayer**
   I gave it to him/her/them yesterday

3. **Le escriben mucho a ella**
   They write to her often
   Se lo van a mandar pronto a ellos
   They will be sending it to them soon

4. **A tu hermano lo conozco bien**
   I know your brother well
   A María la vemos algunas veces
   We sometimes see Maria

5. **La chaqueta le estaba ancha**
   His jacket was too loose
   Me duele el tobillo
   My ankle is aching
   Se me ha perdido el bolígrafo
   I have lost my pen

6. **Le/lo encontraron en el cine**
   They met him at the cinema
   Les/los oímos llegar
   We heard them coming
   Le/la escribimos una carta
   We wrote a letter to her

☐ Personal Pronouns *(Continued)*

Pronouns after prepositions

- These are the same as the subject pronouns, except for the forms **mí** *me*, **ti** *you* (sing), and the reflexive **sí** *himself, herself, themselves, yourselves* → 1

- **Con** *with* combines with **mí, ti** and **sí** to form

  > **conmigo** *with me* → 2
  > **contigo** *with you*
  > **consigo** *with himself/herself* etc

- The following prepositions always take a subject pronoun:

  > | | |
  > |---|---|
  > | **entre** | *between, among* → 3 |
  > | **hasta** ⎱ | |
  > | **incluso** ⎰ | *even, including* → 4 |
  > | **salvo** ⎱ | |
  > | **menos** ⎰ | *except* → 5 |
  > | **según** | *according to* → 6 |

- These pronouns are used for emphasis, especially where contrast is involved → 7

- **Ello** *it, that* is used after a preposition when referring to an idea already mentioned, but never to a concrete noun → 8

- **A él, de él** NEVER contract → 9

1. **Pienso en ti**
   I think about you

   Es para ella
   This is for her

   Volveréis sin nosotros
   You'll come back without us

   Hablaba para sí
   He was talking to himself

   ¿Son para mí?
   Are they for me?

   Iban hacia ellos
   They were going towards them

   Volaban sobre vosotros
   They were flying above you

2. **Venid conmigo**
   Come with me

   Lo trajeron consigo ⚠ BUT: **¿Hablaron con vosotros?**
   They brought it/him with them   Did they talk to you?

3. **entre tú y ella**
   between you and her

4. **Hasta yo puedo hacerlo**
   Even I can do it

5. **todos menos yo**
   everybody except me

6. **según tú**
   according to you

7. **¿A ti no te escriben?**
   Don't they write to you?

   Me lo manda a mí, no a ti
   She is sending it to me, not to you

8. **Nunca pensaba en ello**
   He never thought about it

   Por todo ello me parece que ...
   For all those reasons it seems to me that ...

9. **A él no lo conozco**
   I don't know him

   No he sabido nada de él
   I haven't heard from him

□ Indefinite Pronouns

algo	*something, anything*	→ 1
alguien	*somebody, anybody*	→ 2
alguno/a/os/as	*some, a few*	→ 3
cada uno/a	*each (one)*	→ 4
	everybody	
cualquiera	*anybody; any*	→ 5
los/las demás	*the others*	
	the rest	→ 6
mucho/a/os/as	*many; much*	→ 7
nada	*nothing*	→ 8
nadie	*nobody*	→ 9
ninguno/a	*none, not any*	→ 10
poco/a/os/as	*few; little*	→ 11
tanto/a/os/as	*so much; so many*	→ 12
todo/a/os/as	*all; everything*	→ 13
uno … (el) otro **una … (la) otra** }	*(the) one … the other*	
unos … (los) otros **unas … (las) otras** }	*some … (the) others*	→ 14
varios/as	*several*	→ 15

- **algo, alguien, alguno**

  They can never be used after a negative. The appropriate negative pronouns are used instead: **nada**, **nadie**, **ninguno** (see also negatives, p 272) → 16

1	**Tengo algo para ti**	**¿Viste algo?**
	I have something for you	Did you see anything?
2	**Alguien me lo ha dicho**	**¿Has visto a alguien?**
	Somebody said it to me	Have you seen anybody?
3	**Algunos de los niños ya sabían leer**	
	Some of the children could read already	
4	**Le dió una manzana a cada uno**	**¡Cada uno a su casa!**
	She gave each of them an apple	Everybody go home!
5	**Cualquiera puede hacerlo**	
	Anybody can do it	
	Cualquiera de las explicaciones vale	
	Any of the explanations is a valid one	
6	**Yo me fui, los demás se quedaron**	
	I went, the others stayed	
7	**Muchas de las casas no tenían jardín**	
	Many of the houses didn't have a garden	
8	**¿Qué tienes en la mano? – Nada**	
	What have you got in your hand? – Nothing	
9	**¿A quién ves? – A nadie**	
	Who can you see? – Nobody	
10	**¿Cuántas tienes? – Ninguna**	
	How many have you got? – None	
11	**Había muchos cuadros, pero vi pocos que me gustaran**	
	There were many pictures, but I saw few I liked	
12	**¿Se oía mucho ruido? – No tanto**	
	Was it very noisy? – Not so very	
13	**Lo ha estropeado todo**	**Todo va bien**
	He has spoiled everything	All is going well
14	**Unos cuestan 300 pesetas, los otros 400 pesetas**	
	Some cost 300 pesetas, the others 400 pesetas	
15	**Varios de ellos me gustaron mucho**	
	I liked several of them very much	
16	**Veo a alguien**	**No veo a nadie**
	I can see somebody	I can't see anybody
	Tengo algo que hacer	**No tengo nada que hacer**
	I have something to do	I don't have anything to do

☐ **Relative Pronouns**

PEOPLE		
SINGULAR	PLURAL	
que	**que**	*who, that* (subject) → ①
que **a quien**	**que** **a quienes**	*who(m), that* (direct object) → ②
a quien	**a quienes**	*to whom, that* → ③
de que **de quien**	**de que** **de quienes**	*of whom, that* → ④
cuyo/a	**cuyos/as**	*whose* → ⑤

THINGS		
SINGULAR AND PLURAL		
que	*which, that* (subject)	→ ⑥
que	*which, that* (direct object)	→ ⑦
a que	*to which, that*	→ ⑧
de que	*of which, that*	→ ⑨
cuyo	*whose*	→ ⑩

⚠ NOTE: These forms can also refer to people.

• **cuyo** agrees with the noun it accompanies, NOT WITH THE OWNER → ⑤/ ⑩

• You cannot omit the relative pronoun in Spanish as you can in English → ②/⑦

1. **Mi hermano, que tiene veinte años, es el más joven**
   My brother, who is twenty, is the youngest

2. **Los amigos que más quiero son ...**
   The friends (that) I like best are ...

   María, a quien Daniel admira tanto, es ...
   Maria, whom Daniel admires so much, is ...

3. **Mis abogados, a quienes he escrito hace poco, están ...**
   My lawyers, to whom I wrote recently, are ...

4. **La chica de que te hablé llega mañana**
   The girl (that) I told you about is coming tomorrow

   los niños de quienes se ocupa Vd
   the children (that) you look after

5. **Vendrá la mujer cuyo hijo está enfermo**
   The woman whose son is ill will be coming

6. **Hay una escalera que lleva a la buhardilla**
   There's a staircase which leads to the loft

7. **La casa que hemos comprado tiene ...**
   The house (which) we've bought has ...

   Este es el regalo que me ha mandado mi amiga
   This is the present (that) my friend has sent to me

8. **la tienda a que siempre va**
   the shop (which) she always goes to

9. **las injusticias de que se quejan**
   the injustices (that) they're complaining about

10. **la ventana cuyas cortinas están corridas**
    the window whose curtains are drawn

❏ Relative Pronouns *(Continued)*

el cual, el que

+ These are used when the relative is separated from the word it refers to, or when it would otherwise be unclear which word it referred to. The pronouns always agree in number and gender with the noun → ☐1

El cual may also be used when the verb in the relative clause is separated from the relative pronoun → ☐2

lo que, lo cual

+ The neuter form **lo** is normally used when referring to an idea, statement or abstract noun. In certain expressions, the form **lo cual** may also be used as the subject of the relative clause → ☐3

Relative pronouns after prepositions

+ **Que** and **quienes** are generally used after the prepositions:

a	*to*	→	☐4
con	*with*	→	☐5
de	*from, about, of*	→	☐6
en	*in, on, into*	→	☐7

It should be noted that **en que** can sometimes be translated by:
— *where*. In this case it can also be replaced by **en donde** or **donde** → ☐8
— *when*. Sometimes here it can be replaced by **cuando** → ☐9

+ **El que** or **el cual** are used after other prepositions, and they always agree → ☐10

Examples

1. **El padre de Elena, el cual tiene mucho dinero, es …**
   Elena's father, who has a lot of money, is …
   (**el cual** is *used here since* **que** *or* **quien** *might equally refer to Elena*)

   Su hermana, a la cual/la que hacía mucho que no veía, estaba también allí
   His sister, whom I hadn't seen for a long time, was also there

2. **Vieron a su tío, el cual, después de levantarse, salió**
   They saw their uncle, who, after having got up, went out

3. **No sabe lo que hace**
   He doesn't know what he is doing

   Lo que dijiste fue una tontería
   What you said was foolish

   Todo estaba en silencio, lo que (*or* lo cual) me pareció muy raro
   All was silent, which I thought most odd

4. **las tiendas a (las) que íbamos**
   the shops we used to go to

5. **la chica con quien (*or* la que) sale**
   the girl he's going out with

6. **el libro de(l) que te hablé**
   the book I told you about

7. **el lío en (el) que te has metido**
   the trouble you've got yourself into

8. **el sitio en que (en donde/donde) se escondía**
   the place where he/she was hiding

9. **el año en que naciste**
   the year (when) you were born

10. **el puente debajo del que/cual pasa el río**
    the bridge under which the river flows

    las obras por las cuales/que es famosa
    the plays for which she is famous

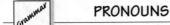

❑ **Relative Pronouns** (Continued)

el que, la que; los que, las que

These mean *the one(s) who/which, those who* → 1

⚠️ NOTE: **quien(es)** can replace **el que** *etc* when used in a general sense → 2

todos los que, todas las que

These mean *all who, all those/the ones which* → 3

todo lo que

This translates *all that, everything that* → 4

el de, la de; los de, las de

These can mean:

— *the one(s) of, that/those of* → 5

— *the one(s) with* → 6

☐1 **Esa película es la que quiero ver**
That film is the one I want to see
¿Te acuerdas de ese amigo? El que te presenté ayer
Do you remember that friend? The one I introduced you to
yesterday
Los que quieran entrar tendrán que pagar
Those who want to go in will have to pay

☐2 **Quien** (*or* **el que**) **llegue antes ganará el premio**
He who arrives first will win the prize

☐3 **Todos los que salían iban de negro**
All those who were coming out were dressed in black
**¿Qué autobuses puedo tomar? – Todos los que pasen
por aquí**
Which buses can I take? – Any (All those) that come this way

☐4 **Quiero saber todo lo que ha pasado**
I want to know all that has happened

☐5 **Trae la foto de tu novio y la de tu hermano**
Bring the photo of your boyfriend and the one of your brother
Viajamos en mi coche y en el de María
We travelled in my car and Maria's
Te doy estos libros y también los de mi hermana
I'll give you these books and my sister's too

☐6 **Tu amigo, el de las gafas, me lo contó**
Your friend, the one with glasses, told me

❑ Interrogative Pronouns

¿qué?	*what?; which?*
¿cuál(es)?	*which?; what?*
¿quién(es)?	*who?*

qué

It always translates *what* → 1

⚠ NOTE: **por** + **qué** is normally translated by *why* → 2

cuál

It normally implies a choice, and translates *which* → 3

⚠ EXCEPT when no choice is implied or more specific information is required → 4

⚠ NOTE: Whilst the pronoun **qué** can also work as an adjective, **cuál** only works as a pronoun → 5

quién

— **quién(es)** (subject or after preposition)	*who*	→ 6
— **a quién(es)** (object)	*whom*	→ 7
— **de quién(es)**	*whose*	→ 8

+ All the forms shown above are also used in indirect questions → 9

grammar

1 **¿Qué estan haciendo?**
What are they doing?
¿Qué dices?
What are you saying?
¿Para qué lo quieres?
What do you want it for?

2 **¿Por qué no llegaron Vds antes?**
Why didn't you arrive earlier?

3 **¿Cuál de estos vestidos te gusta más?**
Which of these dresses do you like best?
¿Cuáles viste?
Which ones did you see?

4 **¿Cuál es la capital de España?**
What is the capital of Spain?
¿Cuál es tu consejo?
What is your advice?
¿Cuál es su fecha de nacimiento?
What is your date of birth?

5 **¿Qué libro es más interesante?**
Which book is more interesting?
¿Cuál (de estos libros) es más interesante?
Which (of these books) is more interesting?

6 **¿Quién ganó la carrera?**
Who won the race?
¿Con quiénes los viste?
Who did you see them with?

7 **¿A quiénes ayudaste?**
Who(m) did you help?
¿A quién se lo diste?
Who did you give it to?

8 **¿De quién es este libro?**
Whose is this book?

9 **Le pregunté para qué lo quería**
I asked him/her what he/she wanted it for
No me dijeron cuáles preferían
They didn't tell me which ones they preferred
No sabía a quién acudir
I didn't know who to turn to

☐ Possessive Pronouns

These are the same as the strong forms of the possessive adjectives, but they are always accompanied by the definite article.

	SINGULAR		
	MASCULINE	FEMININE	
	el mío	**la mía**	*mine*
	el tuyo	**la tuya**	*yours* (of **tú**)
	el suyo	**la suya**	*his; hers; its; yours* (of **Vd**)
	el nuestro	**la nuestra**	*ours*
	el vuestro	**la vuestra**	*yours* (of **vosotros**)
	el suyo	**la suya**	*theirs; yours* (of **Vds**)

	PLURAL		
	MASCULINE	FEMININE	
	los míos	**las mías**	*mine*
	los tuyos	**las tuyas**	*yours* (of **tú**)
	los suyos	**las suyas**	*his; hers; its; yours* (of **Vd**)
	los nuestros	**las nuestras**	*ours*
	los vuestros	**las vuestras**	*yours* (of **vosotros**)
	los suyos	**las suyas**	*theirs; yours* (of **Vds**)

+ The pronoun agrees in number and gender with the noun it replaces, NOT WITH THE OWNER → ①

+ Alternative translations are *my own, your own*, etc → ②

+ After the prepositions **a** and **de** the article **el** is contracted in the normal way (see p 196)

$$a + el\ mío \rightarrow al\ mío \rightarrow ③$$

$$de + el\ mío \rightarrow del\ mío \rightarrow ④$$

① **Pregunta a Cristina si este bolígrafo es el suyo**
Ask Christine if this pen is hers

¿Qué equipo ha ganado, el suyo o el nuestro?
Which team won – theirs or ours?

Mi perro es más joven que el tuyo
My dog is younger than yours

Daniel pensó que esos libros eran los suyos
Daniel thought those books were his

Si no tienes discos, te prestaré los míos
If you don't have any records, I'll lend you mine

Las habitaciones son menos amplias que las vuestras
The rooms are smaller than yours

② **¿Es su familia tan grande como la tuya?**
Is his/her/their family as big as your own?

Sus precios son más bajos que los nuestros
Their prices are lower than our own

③ **¿Por qué prefieres este sombrero al mío?**
Why do you prefer this hat to mine?

Su coche se parece al vuestro
His/her/their car looks like yours

④ **Mi libro está encima del tuyo**
My book is on top of yours

Su padre vive cerca del nuestro
His/her/their father lives near ours

❑ Demonstrative Pronouns

	MASCULINE	FEMININE	NEUTER	
SING	éste	ésta	esto	*this*
	ése	ésa	eso	*that*
	aquél	aquélla	aquello	
PLUR	éstos	éstas		*these*
	ésos	ésas		*those*
	aquéllos	aquéllas		

- The pronoun agrees in number and gender with the noun it replaces → 1

- The difference in meaning between the forms **ése** and **aquél** is the same as between the corresponding adjectives (see p 212)

- The masculine and feminine forms have an accent, which is the only thing that differentiates them from the corresponding adjectives.

- The neuter forms always refer to an idea or a statement or to an object when we want to identify it, etc, but never to specified nouns → 2

- An additional meaning of **aquél** is *the former*, and of **éste** *the latter* → 3

1. **¿Qué abrigo te gusta más? – Este de aquí**
Which coat do you like best? – This one here

   Aquella casa era más grande que ésta
That house was bigger than this one

   estos libros y aquéllos
these books and those (over there)

   Quiero estas sandalias y ésas
I'd like these sandals and those ones

2. **No puedo creer que esto me esté pasando a mí**
I can't believe this is really happening to me

   Eso de madrugar es algo que no le gusta
(This business of) getting up early is something she doesn't like

   Aquello sí que me gustó
I really did like that

   Esto es una bicicleta
This is a bicycle

3. **Hablaban Jaime y Andrés, éste a voces y aquél casi en un susurro**
James and Andrew were talking, the latter in a loud voice and the former almost in a whisper

ADVERBS

◻ Adverbs

Formation

+ Most adverbs are formed by adding **-mente** to the feminine form of the adjective. Accents on the adjective are not affected since the suffix **-mente** is stressed independently → ①

⚠ NOTE: **-mente** is omitted:

— in the first of two or more of these adverbs when joined by a conjunction → ②
— in **recientemente** *recently* when immediately preceding a past participle → ③
An accent is then needed on the last syllable (see p 292)

+ The following adverbs are formed in an irregular way:

> **bueno** → **bien**
> *good*   *well*
> **malo** → **mal**
> *bad*   *badly*

Adjectives used as adverbs

Certain adjectives are used adverbially. These include:
alto, bajo, barato, caro, claro, derecho, fuerte and **rápido** → ④

⚠ NOTE: Other adjectives used as adverbs agree with the subject, and can normally be replaced by the adverb ending in **-mente** or an adverbial phrase → ⑤

Position of Adverbs

+ When the adverb accompanies a verb, it may either immediately follow it or precede it for emphasis → ⑥

⚠ NOTE: The adverb can never be placed between **haber** and the past participle in compound tenses → ⑦

+ When the adverb accompanies an adjective or another adverb, it generally precedes the adjective or adverb → ⑧

① **FEM ADJECTIVE**
lenta slow
franca frank
feliz happy
fácil easy

ADVERB
lentamente slowly
francamente frankly
felizmente happily
fácilmente easily

② **Lo hicieron lenta pero eficazmente**
They did it slowly but efficiently

③ **El pan estaba recién hecho**
The bread had just been baked

④ **hablar alto/bajo**
to speak loudly/softly
costar barato/caro
to be cheap/expensive
ver claro
to see clearly

cortar derecho
to cut (in a) straight (line)
Habla muy fuerte
He talks very loudly
correr rápido
to run fast

⑤ **Esperaban impacientes** (*or* **impacientemente/con impaciencia**)
They were waiting impatiently
Vivieron muy felices (*or* **muy felizmente**)
They lived very happily

⑥ **No conocemos aún al nuevo médico**
We still haven't met the new doctor
Aún estoy esperando
I'm still waiting
Han hablado muy bien
They have spoken very well
Siempre le regalaban flores
They always gave her flowers

⑦ **Lo he hecho ya**
I've already done it
No ha estado nunca en Italia
She's never been to Italy

⑧ **un sombrero muy bonito**
a very nice hat
mañana temprano
early tomorrow

hablar demasiado alto
to talk too loud
hoy mismo
today

☐ Comparatives and Superlatives

Comparatives

These are formed using the following constructions:

más ... (que)	*more ... (than)*	→ 1
menos ... (que)	*less ... (than)*	→ 2
tanto como	*as much as*	→ 3
tan ... como	*as ... as*	→ 4
tan ... que	*so ... that*	→ 5
demasiado ... para	*too ... to*	→ 6
(lo) bastante ... ⎫ (lo) suficientemente ... ⎬ para	*enough to*	→ 7
cada vez más/menos	*more and more/* *less and less*	→ 8

Superlatives

- These are formed by placing **más/menos** *the most/the least* before the adverb → 9

- **lo** is added before a superlative which is qualified → 10

- The absolute superlative (*very, most, extremely* + adverb) is formed by placing **muy** before the adverb. The form **-ísimo** (see also p 292) is also occasionally found → 11

Adverbs with irregular comparatives/superlatives

ADVERB	COMPARATIVE	SUPERLATIVE
bien	**mejor***	**(lo) mejor**
well	*better*	*(the) best*
mal	**peor**	**(lo) peor**
badly	*worse*	*(the) worst*
mucho	**más**	**(lo) más**
a lot	*more*	*(the) most*
poco	**menos**	**(lo) menos**
little	*less*	*(the) least*

* **más bien** also exists, meaning *rather* → 12

Examples

1. **más de prisa** **más abiertamente**
   more quickly   more openly
   Mi hermana canta más fuerte que yo
   My sister sings louder than me

2. **menos fácilmente** **menos a menudo**
   less easily   less often
   Nos vemos menos frecuentemente que antes
   We see each other less frequently than before

3. **Daniel no lee tanto como Andrés**
   Daniel doesn't read as much as Andrew

4. **Hágalo tan rápido como le sea posible**
   Do it as quickly as you can
   Ganan tan poco como nosotros
   They earn as little as we do

5. **Llegaron tan pronto que tuvieron que esperarnos**
   They arrived so early that they had to wait for us

6. **Es demasiado tarde para ir al cine**
   It's too late to go to the cinema

7. **Eres (lo) bastante grande para hacerlo solo**
   You're old enough to do it by yourself

8. **Me gusta el campo cada vez más**
   I like the countryside more and more

9. **María es la que corre más rápido**
   Maria is the one who runs fastest
   El que llegó menos tarde fue Miguel
   Miguel was the one to arrive the least late

10. **Lo hice lo más de prisa que pude**
    I did it as quickly as I could

11. **muy lentamente** **tempranísimo** **muchísimo**
    very slowly   extremely early   very much

12. **Era un hombre más bien bajito**
    He was a rather short man
    Estaba más bien inquieta que impaciente
    I was restless rather than impatient

❑ Common Adverbs and their usage

bastante	*enough; quite*	→ 1
bien	*well*	→ 2
cómo	*how*	→ 3
cuánto	*how much*	→ 4
demasiado	*too much; too*	→ 5
más	*more*	→ 6
menos	*less*	→ 7
mucho	*a lot; much*	→ 8
poco	*little, not much; not very*	→ 9
siempre	*always*	→ 10
también	*also, too*	→ 11
tan	*as*	→ 12
tanto	*as much*	→ 13
todavía/aún	*still; yet; even*	→ 14
ya	*already*	→ 15

- **bastante, cuánto, demasiado, mucho, poco** and **tanto** are also used as adjectives that agree with the noun they qualify (see indefinite adjectives, p 220, and interrogative adjectives, p 214)

1. **Es bastante tarde**
It's quite late

2. **¡Bien hecho!**
Well done!

3. **¡Cómo me ha gustado!**
How I liked it!

4. **¿Cuánto cuesta este libro?**
How much is this book?

5. **He comido demasiado**
I've eaten too much
    Es demasiado caro
It's too expensive

6. **Mi hermano trabaja más ahora**
My brother works more now
    Es más tímida que Sofía
She is shyer than Sophie

7. **Se debe beber menos**
One must drink less
    Estoy menos sorprendida que tú
I'm less surprised than you are

8. **¿Lees mucho?**
Do you read a lot?
    ¿Está mucho más lejos?
Is it much further?

9. **Comen poco**
They don't eat (very) much
    María es poco decidida
Maria is not very daring

10. **Siempre dicen lo mismo**
They always say the same (thing)

11. **A mí también me gusta**
I like it too

12. **Ana es tan alta como yo**
Ana is as tall as I am

13. **Nos aburrimos tanto como vosotros**
We got as bored as you did

14. **Todavía/aún tengo dos**
I've still got two
    Todavía/aún no han llegado
They haven't arrived yet
Mejor aún/todavía
Even better

15. **Ya lo he hecho**
I've done it already

On the following pages you will find some of the most frequent uses of prepositions in Spanish. Particular attention is paid to cases where usage differs markedly from English. It is often difficult to give an English equivalent for Spanish prepositions, since usage *does* vary so much between the two languages. In the list below, the broad meaning of the preposition is given on the left, with examples of usage following. Prepositions are dealt with in alphabetical order, except **a**, **de**, **en** and **por** which are shown first.

a

at	**echar algo a algn**	*to throw sth at sb*
	a 50 pesetas el kilo	*(at) 50 pesetas a kilo*
	a 100 km por hora	*at 100 km per hour*
	sentarse a la mesa	*to sit down at the table*
in	**al sol**	*in the sun*
	a la sombra	*in the shade*
onto	**cayeron al suelo**	*they fell onto the floor*
	pegar una foto al álbum	*to stick a photo into the album*
to	**ir al cine**	*to go to the cinema*
	dar algo a algn	*to give sth to sb*
	venir a hacer	*to come to do*
from	**quitarle algo a algn**	*to take sth from sb*
	robarle algo a algn	*to steal sth from sb*
	arrebatarle algo a algn	*to snatch sth from sb*
	comprarle algo a algn	*to buy sth from/for sb**
	esconderle algo a algn	*to hide sth from sb*
means	**a mano**	*by hand*
	a caballo	*on horseback (but note other forms of transport used with* **en** *and* **por**)
	a pie	*on foot*

* The translation here obviously depends on the context.

manner	**a la inglesa**	*in the English manner*
	a pasos lentos	*with slow steps*
	poco a poco	*little by little*
	a ciegas	*blindly*
time, date: at, on	**a medianoche**	*at midnight*
	a las dos y cuarto	*at quarter past two*
	a tiempo	*on time*
	a final/fines de mes	*at the end of the month*
	a veces	*at times*
distance	**a 8 km de aquí**	*(at a distance of) 8 kms from here*
	a dos pasos de mi casa	*just a step from my house*
	a lo lejos	*in the distance*
with **el** + infin	**al levantarse**	*on getting up*
	al abrir la puerta	*on opening the door*
after certain adjectives	**dispuesto a todo**	*ready for anything*
	parecido a esto	*similar to this*
	obligado a ello	*obliged to (do) that*
after certain verbs	see p 66	

Personal a

When the direct object of a verb is a person or pet animal, **a** must always be placed immediately before it.

EXAMPLES:
    querían mucho a sus hijos
    they loved their children dearly
    el niño miraba a su perro con asombro
    the boy kept looking at his dog in astonishment

⚠ EXCEPTION: **tener**   **tienen dos hijos**
                 to have   *they have two children*

Grammar

de

from	**venir de Londres**	*to come from London*
	un médico de Valencia	*a doctor from Valencia*
	de la mañana a la noche	*from morning till night*
	de 10 a 15	*from 10 to 15*
belonging to,	**el sombrero de mi padre**	*my father's hat*
of	**las lluvias de abril**	*April showers*
contents,	**una caja de cerillas**	*a box of matches*
composition,	**una taza de té**	*a cup of tea; a tea-cup*
material	**un vestido de seda**	*a silk dress*
destined for	**una silla de cocina**	*a kitchen chair*
	un traje de noche	*an evening dress*
descriptive	**la mujer del sombrero verde**	*the woman with the green hat*
	el vecino de al lad/lado	*the next door neighbour*
manner	**de manera irregular**	*in an irregular way*
	de una puñalada	*by stabbing*
quality	**una mujer de edad**	*an aged lady*
	objetos de valor	*valuable items*
comparative + number	**había más/menos de 100 personas**	*there were more/fewer than 100 people*
after superlatives: *in*	**la ciudad más/menos bonita del mundo**	*the most/least beautiful city in the world*
after certain adjectives	**contento de ver**	*pleased to see*
	fácil/difícil de entender	*easy/difficult to understand*
	capaz de hacer	*capable of doing*
after certain verbs	see p 66	

en

in, at	**en el campo**	*in the country*
	en Londres	*in London*
	en la cama	*in bed*
	con un libro en la mano	*with a book in his hand*
	en voz baja	*in a low voice*
	en la escuela	*in/at school*
into	**entra en la casa**	*go into the house*
	metió la mano en su bolso	*she put her hand into her handbag*
on	**un cuadro en la pared**	*a picture on the wall*
	sentado en una silla	*sitting on a chair*
	en la planta baja	*on the ground floor*
time, dates, months: at, in	**en este momento**	*at this moment*
	en 1994	*in 1994*
	en enero	*in January*
transport: by	**en coche**	*by car*
	en avión	*by plane*
	en tren	*by train (but see also **por**)*
language	**en español**	*in Spanish*
duration	**lo haré en una semana**	*I'll do it in one week*
after certain adjectives	**es muy buena/mala en geografía**	*she is very good/bad at geography*
	fueron los primeros/ últimos/únicos en + infin	*they were the first/ last/only ones + infin*
after certain verbs	see p 66	

por

motion: along, through, around	**vaya por ese camino** **por el túnel** **pasear por el campo**	go along that path through the tunnel to walk around the countryside
vague location	**tiene que estar por** **aquí** **le busqué por todas** **partes**	it's got to be somewhere around here I looked for him everywhere
vague time	**por la tarde** **por aquellos días**	in the afternoon in those days
rate	**90 km por hora** **un cinco por ciento** **ganaron por 3 a 0**	90 km per hour five per cent they won by 3 to 0
agent of passive: by	**descubierto por unos** **niños** **odiado por sus** **enemigos**	discovered by some children hated by his enemies
by (means of)	**por barco** **por tren** **por correo aéreo** **llamar por teléfono**	by boat by train (freight) by airmail to telephone
cause, reason: for, because	**¿por qué?** **por todo eso** **por lo que he oído**	why?, for what reason? because of all that judging by what I've heard
+ infinitive: to	**libros por leer** **cuentas por pagar**	books to be read bills to be paid
equivalence	**¿me tienes por tonto?**	do you think I'm stupid?

+ adjective/ + adverb + que: however	por buenos que sean	however good they are
	por mucho que lo quieras	however much you want it
for	¿cuanto me darán por este libro?	how much will they give me for this book?
	te lo cambio por éste	I'll swap you this one for it
	no siento nada por ti	I feel nothing for you
	si no fuera por ti	if it weren't for you
	¡Por Dios!	For God's sake!
for the benefit of, on behalf of	lo hago por ellos	I do it for their benefit
	firma por mí	sign on my behalf

por also combines with other prepositions to form double prepositions usually conveying the idea of movement. The commonest of these are:

over	saltó por encima de la mesa	she jumped over the table
under	nadamos por debajo del puente	we swam under the bridge
past	pasaron por delante de Correos	they went past the post office
behind	por detrás de la puerta	behind the door
through	la luz entraba por entre las cortinas	light was coming in through the curtains
+ donde	¿por dónde has venido?	which way did you come?

ante

faced with, before	lo hicieron ante mis propios ojos	they did it before my very eyes
	ante eso no se puede hacer nada	one can't do anything when faced with that
preference	la salud ante todo	health above all things

antes de

| before (time) | antes de las 5 | before 5 o'clock |

bajo/debajo de

These are usually equivalent, although **bajo** is used more frequently in a figurative sense and with temperatures.

under	**bajo/debajo de la cama**	under the bed
	bajo el dominio romano	under Roman rule
below	**un grado bajo cero**	one degree below zero

con

with	**vino con su amigo**	she came with her friend
after certain adjectives	**enfadado con ellos**	angry with them
	magnánimo con sus súbditos	magnanimous with his subjects

contra

against	**no tengo nada contra ti**	I've nothing against you
	apoyado contra la pared	leaning against the wall

delante de

in front of	**iba delante de mí**	she was walking in front of me

desde

from	**desde aquí se puede ver**	you can see it from here
	llamaban desde España	they were phoning from Spain
	desde otro punto de vista	from a different point of view
	desde la 1 hasta las 6	from 1 till 6
	desde entonces	from then onwards
since	**desde que volvieron**	since they returned
for	**viven en esa casa desde hace 3 años**	they've been living in that house for 3 years

⚠️ (NOTE TENSE)

detrás de

behind	**están detrás de la puerta**	*they are behind the door*

durante

during	**durante la guerra**	*during the war*
for	**anduvieron durante 3 días**	*they walked for 3 days*

entre

between	**entre 8 y 10**	*between 8 and 10*
among	**María y Elena, entre otras**	*Maria and Elena, among others*
reciprocal	**ayudarse entre sí**	*to help each other*

excepto

except (for)	**todos excepto tú**	*everybody except you*

hacia

towards	**van hacia ese edificio**	*they're going towards that building*
around (time)	**hacia las 3**	*at around 3 (o'clock)*
	hacia fines de enero	*around the end of January*

Hacia can also combine with some adverbs to convey a sense of motion in a particular direction:

hacia arriba	*upwards*
hacia abajo	*downwards*
hacia adelante	*forwards*
hacia atrás	*backwards*
hacia adentro	*inwards*
hacia afuera	*outwards*

hasta

until	**hasta la noche**	*until night*
as far as	**viajaron hasta Sevilla**	*they travelled as far as Seville*
up to	**conté hasta 300 ovejas**	*I counted up to 300 lambs*
	hasta ahora no los había visto	*up to now I hadn't seen them*
even	**hasta un tonto lo entendería**	*even an imbecile would understand that*

para

for	**es para ti**	*it's for you*
	es para mañana	*it's for tomorrow*
	una habitación para dos noches	*a room for two nights*
	para ser un niño, lo hace muy bien	*for a child he is very good at it*
	salen para Cádiz	*they are leaving for Cádiz*
	se conserva muy bien para sus años	*he keeps very well for his age*
+ infin: (in order) to	**es demasiado torpe para comprenderlo**	*he's too stupid to understand*
+ sí: to oneself	**hablar para sí**	*to talk to oneself*
	reír para sí	*to laugh to oneself*
with time	**todavía tengo para 1 hora**	*I'll be another hour (at it) yet*

salvo

except (for)	**todos salvo él**	*all except him*
	salvo cuando llueve	*except when it's raining*
barring	**salvo imprevistos**	*barring the unexpected*
	salvo contraorden	*unless you hear to the contrary*

Grammar

según

| according to | según su consejo | according to her advice |
| | según lo que me dijiste | according to what you told me |

sin

without	sin agua/dinero	without water/money
	sin mi marido	without my husband
+ infinitive	sin contar a los otros	without counting the others

sobre

on	sobre la cama	on the bed
	sobre el armario	on (top of) the wardrobe
on (to)	póngalo sobre la mesa	put it on the table
about, on	un libro sobre Eva Perón	a book about Eva Perón
above, over	volábamos sobre el mar	we were flying over the sea
	la nube sobre aquella montaña	the cloud above that mountain
approximately	vendré sobre las 4	I'll come about 4 o'clock
about	Madrid tiene sobre 4 millones de habitantes	Madrid has about 4 million inhabitants

tras

behind	está tras el asiento	it's behind the seat
after	uno tras otro	one after another
	día tras día	day after day
	corrieron tras el ladrón	they ran after the thief

◻ Conjunctions

There are conjunctions which introduce a main clause, such as **y** *and*, **pero** *but*, **si** *if*, **o** *or* etc, and those which introduce subordinate clauses like **porque** *because*, **mientras que** *while*, **después de que** *after* etc. They are used in much the same way as in English, but the following points are of note:

- Some conjunctions in Spanish require a following subjunctive, see pp 60 to 63.

- Some conjunctions are 'split' in Spanish like *both ... and*, *either ... or* in English:

tanto ... como	*both ... and*	→ 1
ni ... ni	*neither ... nor*	→ 2
o (bien) ... o (bien)	*either ... or (else)*	→ 3
sea ... sea	*either ... or,*	→ 4
	whether ... or	

- **y**

 — Before words beginning with **i-** or **hi-** + consonant it becomes **e** → 5

- **o**

 — Before words beginning with **o-** or **ho-** it becomes **u** → 6
 — Between numerals it becomes **ó** → 7

- **que**

 — meaning *that* → 8
 — in comparisons, meaning *than* → 9
 — followed by the subjunctive, see p 58.

- **porque** (Not to be confused with **por qué** *why*)

 — **como** should be used instead at the beginning of a sentence → 10

- **pero, sino**

 — **pero** normally translates *but* → 11
 — **sino** is used when there is a direct contrast after a negative → 12

1. **Estas flores crecen tanto en verano como en invierno**
These flowers grow in both summer and winter

2. **Ni él ni ella vinieron**
Neither he nor she came
No tengo ni dinero ni comida
I have neither money nor food

3. **Debe de ser o ingenua o tonta**
She must be either naïve or stupid
O bien me huyen o bien no me reconocen
Either they're avoiding me or else they don't recognize me

4. **Sea en verano, sea en invierno, siempre me gusta andar**
I always like walking, whether in summer or in winter

5. **Diana e Isabel**
Diana and Isabel
madre e hija   BUT: **árboles y hierba**
mother and daughter   trees and grass

6. **diez u once**   **minutos u horas**
ten or eleven   minutes or hours

7. **37 ó 38**
37 or 38

8. **Dicen que te han visto**
They say (that) they've seen you
¿Sabías que estábamos allí?
Did you know that we were there?

9. **Le gustan más que nunca**
He likes them more than ever
María es menos guapa que su hermana
Maria is less attractive than her sister

10. **Como estaba lloviendo no pudimos salir**
Because/As it was raining we couldn't go out
(Compare with: **No pudimos salir porque estaba lloviendo**)

11. **Me gustaría ir, pero estoy muy cansada**
I'd like to go, but I am very tired

12. **No es escocesa sino irlandesa**
She is not Scottish but Irish

◻ Augmentative, diminutive and pejorative suffixes

These can be used after nouns, adjectives and some adverbs. They are attached to the end of the word after any final vowel has been removed

e.g. **puerta → puertita**

doctor → doctorcito

⚠ NOTE: Further changes sometimes take place (see p 296).

Augmentatives

These are used mainly to imply largeness, but they can also suggest clumsiness, ugliness or grotesqueness. The commonest augmentatives are:

ón/ona	→ 1
azo/a	→ 2
ote/a	→ 3

Diminutives

These are used mainly to suggest smallness or to express a feeling of affection. Occasionally they can be used to express ridicule or contempt. The commonest diminutives are:

ito/a	→ 4
(e)cito/a	→ 5
(ec)illo/a	→ 6
(z)uelo/a	→ 7

Pejoratives

These are used to convey the idea that something is unpleasant or to express contempt. The commonest suffixes are:

ucho/a	→ 8
acho/a	→ 9
uzo/a	→ 10
uco/a	→ 11
astro/a	→ 12

	ORIGINAL WORD	DERIVED FORM
1	**un hombre** a man	**un hombrón** a big man
2	**bueno** good	**buenazo** (person) easily imposed on
	un perro a dog	**un perrazo** a really big dog
	gripe flu	**un gripazo** a really bad bout of flu
3	**grande** big	**grandote** huge
	palabra word	**palabrota** swear word
	amigo friend	**amigote** old pal
4	**una casa** a house	**una casita** a cottage
	un poco a little	**un poquito** a little bit
	un rato a while	**un ratito** a little while
	mi hija my daughter	**mi hijita** my dear sweet daughter
	despacio slowly	**despacito** nice and slowly
5	**un viejo** an old man	**un viejecito** a little old man
	un pueblo a village	**un pueblecito** a small village
	una voz a voice	**una vocecita** a sweet little voice
6	**una ventana** a window	**una ventanilla** a small window (car, train etc)
	un chico a boy	**un chiquillo** a small boy
	una campana a bell	**una campanilla** a small bell
	un palo a stick	**un palillo** a toothpick
	un médico a doctor	**un mediquillo** a quack (doctor)
7	**los pollos** the chickens	**los polluelos** the little chicks
	hoyos hollows	**hoyuelos** dimples
	un ladrón a thief	**un ladronzuelo** a petty thief
	una mujer a woman	**una mujerzuela** a whore
8	**un animal** an animal	**un animalucho** a wretched animal
	un cuarto a room	**un cuartucho** a poky little room
	una casa a house	**una casucha** a shack
9	**rico** rich	**ricacho** nouveau riche
10	**gente** people	**gentuza** scum
11	**una ventana** a window	**un ventanuco** a miserable little window
12	**un político** a politician	**un politicastro** a third-rate politician

◻ Word order

Word order in Spanish is much more flexible than in English. You can often find the subject placed after the verb or the object before the verb, either for emphasis or for stylistic reasons → ①

There are some cases, however, where the order is always different from English. Most of these have already been dealt with under the appropriate part of speech, but are summarized here along with other instances not covered elsewhere.

- Object pronouns nearly always come before the verb → ②

  For details, see pp 228 to 231.

- Qualifying adjectives nearly always come after the noun → ③

  For details, see p 224.

- Following direct speech the subject always follows the verb → ④

For word order in negative sentences, see p 272.

For word order in interrogative sentences, see p 276.

1. **Ese libro te lo di yo**
   I gave you that book
   No nos vio nadie
   Nobody saw us

2. **Ya los veo**   **Me lo dieron ayer**
   I can see them now   They gave it to me yesterday

3. **una ciudad española**   **vino tinto**
   a Spanish town   red wine

4. **– Pienso que sí – dijo María**
   'I think so,' said Maria
   – No importa – replicó Daniel
   'It doesn't matter,' Daniel replied

☐ Negatives

A sentence is made negative by adding **no** between the subject and the verb (and any preceding object pronouns) → ①

There are, however, some points to note:

— in phrases like *not her, not now,* etc the Spanish **no** usually comes after the word it qualifies → ②
— with verbs of saying, hoping, thinking etc *not* is translated by **que no** → ③

Double negatives

no ... nada	nothing	(not ... anything)
no ... nadie	nobody	(not ... anybody)
no ... más	no longer	(not ... any more)
no ... nunca	never	(not ... ever)
no ... jamás	never (stronger)	(not ... ever)
no ... más que	only	(not ... more than)
no ... ningún(o)(a)	no	(not any)
no ... tampoco	not ... either	
no ... ni ... ni	neither ... nor	
no ... ni siquiera	not even	

Word order

- **No** precedes the verb (and any object pronouns) in both simple and compound tenses, and the second element follows the verb → ④

- Sometimes the above negatives are placed before the verb (with the exception of **más** and **más que**), and **no** is then dropped → ⑤

- For use of **nada, nadie** and **ninguno** as pronouns, see p 236.

---

1 AFFIRMATIVE   NEGATIVE

El coche es suyo → **El coche no es suyo**
The car is his   The car is not his

Yo me lo pondré → **Yo no me lo pondré**
I will put it on   I will not put it on

2 **¿Quién lo ha hecho? – Ella no**
Who did it? – Not her

¿Quieres un cigarrillo? – Ahora no
Do you want a cigarette? – Not now

Dame ese libro, el que está a tu lado no, el otro
Give me that book, not the one near you, the other one

3 **Opino que no**   **Dijeron que no**
I think not   They said not

4 **No dicen nada**
They don't say anything

No han visto a nadie
They haven't seen anybody

No me veréis más
You won't see me any more

No te olvidaré nunca/jamás
I'll never forget you

No habían recorrido más que 40 kms cuando …
They hadn't travelled more than 40 kms when …

No se me ha ocurrido ninguna idea
I haven't had any ideas

No les estaban esperando ni mi hijo ni mi hija
Neither my son nor my daughter were waiting for them

No ha venido ni siquiera Juan
Even John hasn't come

5 **Nadie ha venido hoy**
Nobody came today

Nunca me han gustado
I've never liked them

Ni mi hermano ni mi hermana fuman
Neither my brother nor my sister smokes

☐ **Negatives** (Continued)

Negatives in short replies

• **No**, *no* is the usual negative response to a question → ①

⚠ NOTE: It is often translated as *not* → ②
(see also p 272).

• Nearly all the other negatives listed on p 272 may be used without a verb in a short reply → ③

Combinations of negatives

These are the most common combinations of negative particles:

no ... nunca más	→ ④
no ... nunca a nadie	→ ⑤
no ... nunca nada/nada nunca	→ ⑥
no ... nunca más que	→ ⑦
no ... ni ... nunca	→ ⑧

1. **¿Quieres venir con nosotros? – No**
   Do you want to come with us? – No

2. **¿Vienes o no?**
   Are you coming or not?

3. **¿Ha venido alguien? – ¡Nadie!**
   Has anyone come? – Nobody!
   ¿Has ido al Japón alguna vez? – Nunca
   Have you ever been to Japan? – Never

4. **No lo haré nunca más**
   I'll never do it again

5. **No se ve nunca a nadie por allí**
   You never see anybody around there

6. **No cambiaron nada nunca**
   They never changed anything

7. **No he hablado nunca más que con su mujer**
   I've only ever spoken to his wife

8. **No me ha escrito ni llamado por teléfono nunca**
   He/she has never written to me or phoned me

❑ Question forms

Direct

There are two ways of forming direct questions in Spanish:

- by inverting the normal word order so that

  subject + verb → *verb + subject* → ①

- by maintaining the word order *subject + verb*, but by using a rising intonation at the end of the sentence → ②

⚠️ NOTE: In compound tenses the auxiliary may never be separated from the past participle, as happens in English → ③

Indirect

An indirect question is one that is 'reported', e.g. he asked me *what the time was,* tell me *which way to go.* Word order in indirect questions can adopt one of the two following patterns:

- interrogative word + subject + verb → ④

- interrogative word + verb + subject → ⑤

¿verdad?, ¿no?

These are used wherever English would use *isn't it?, don't they?, weren't we?, is it?* etc tagged on to the end of a sentence → ⑥

sí

Sí is the word for *yes* in answer to a question put either in the affirmative or in the negative → ⑦

1. **¿Vendrá tu madre?**
   Will your mother come?
   ¿Es posible eso?
   Is it possible?

   ¿Lo trajo Vd?
   Did you bring it?
   ¿Cuándo volverán Vds?
   When will you come back?

2. **El gato, ¿se bebió toda la leche?**
   Did the cat drink up all his milk?
   Andrés, ¿va a venir?
   Is Andrew coming?

3. **¿Lo ha terminado Vd?**
   Have you finished it?
   ¿Había llegado tu amigo?
   Had your friend arrived?

4. **Dime qué autobuses pasan por aquí**
   Tell me which buses come this way
   No sé cuántas personas vendrán
   I don't know how many people will turn up

5. **Me preguntó dónde trabajaba mi hermano**
   He asked me where my brother worked
   No sabemos a qué hora empieza la película
   We don't know what time the film starts

6. **Hace calor, ¿verdad?**
   It's warm, isn't it?
   No se olvidará Vd, ¿verdad?
   You won't forget, will you?
   Estaréis cansados, ¿no?
   You will be tired, won't you?
   Te lo dijo María, ¿no?
   Maria told you, didn't she?

7. **¿Lo has hecho? – Sí**
   Have you done it? – Yes (I have)
   ¿No lo has hecho? – Sí
   Haven't you done it? – Yes (I have)

Beware of translating word by word. While on occasions this is quite possible, quite often it is not. The need for caution is illustrated by the following:

♦ English phrasal verbs (i.e. verbs followed by a preposition), e.g. *to run away, to fall down*, are often translated by one word in Spanish → ①

♦ English verbal constructions often contain a preposition where none exists in Spanish, or vice versa → ②

♦ Two or more prepositions in English may have a single rendering in Spanish → ③

♦ A word which is singular in English may be plural in Spanish, or vice versa → ④

♦ Spanish has no equivalent of the possessive construction denoted by ...'s/...s' → ⑤

❑ Specific problems

-ing

This is translated in a variety of ways in Spanish:

♦ *to be ... -ing* can sometimes be translated by a simple tense (see also pp 54 to 56) → ⑥

But, when a physical position is denoted, a past participle is used → ⑦

♦ in the construction *to see/hear sb ... -ing*, use an infinitive → ⑧
-ing can also be translated by:

— an infinitive → ⑨
(see p 46)

— a perfect infinitive → ⑩
(see p 50)

— a gerund → ⑪
(see p 52)

— a noun → ⑫

1	**huir**	**caerse**	**ceder**
	to run away	to fall down	to give in
2	**pagar**	**mirar**	**escuchar**
	to pay for	to look at	to listen to
	encontrarse con	**fijarse en**	**servirse de**
	to meet	to notice	to use
3	**extrañarse de**	**harto de**	
	to be surprised at	fed up with	
	soñar con	**contar con**	
	to dream of	to count on	
4	**unas vacaciones**	**sus cabellos**	
	a holiday	his/her hair	
	la gente	**mi pantalón**	
	people	my trousers	

5. **el coche de mi hermano**   **el cuarto de las niñas**
   my brother's car   the children's bedroom
   (literally: ... of my brother)   *(literally: ... of the children)*

6. **Se va mañana**   **¿Qué haces?**
   He/she is leaving tomorrow   What are you doing?

7. **Está sentado ahí**   **Estaba tendida en el suelo**
   He is sitting over there   She was lying on the ground

8. **Les veo venir**   **La he oído cantar**
   I can see them coming   I've heard her singing

9. **Me gusta ir al cine**   **¡Deja de hablar!**
   I like going to the cinema   Stop talking!
   En vez de contestar   **Antes de salir**
   Instead of answering   Before leaving

10. **Después de haber abierto la caja, María ...**
    After opening the box, Maria ...

11. **Pasamos la tarde fumando y charlando**
    We spent the afternoon smoking and chatting

12. **El esquí me mantiene en forma**
    Skiing keeps me fit

to be

(See also **Verbal Idioms**, pp 74 to 76)

- In set expressions, describing physical and emotional conditions, **tener** is used:

tener calor/frío	to be warm/cold
tener hambre/sed	to be hungry/thirsty
tener miedo	to be afraid
tener razón	to be right

- Describing the weather, e.g. *what's the weather like?*, *it's windy/ sunny*, use **hacer** → ①

- For ages, e.g. *he is 6*, use **tener** (see also p 306) → ②

there is/there are

- Both are translated by **hay** → ③

can, be able

- Physical ability is expressed by **poder** → ④

- If the meaning is *to know how to*, use **saber** → ⑤

- *Can* + a 'verb of hearing or seeing etc' in English is not translated in Spanish → ⑥

to

- Generally translated by **a** → ⑦

- In time expressions, e.g. *10 to 6*, use **menos** → ⑧

- When the meaning is *in order to*, use **para** → ⑨

- Following a verb, as in *to try to do*, *to like to do*, see pp 46 and 48.

- *easy/difficult/impossible* etc *to do* are translated by **fácil/difícil/ imposible** etc **de hacer** → ⑩

① **¿Qué tiempo hace?**
What's the weather like?

Hace bueno/malo/viento
It's lovely/miserable/windy

② **¿Cuántos años tienes?**
How old are you?

Tengo quince (años)
I'm fifteen

③ **Hay un señor en la puerta**
There's a gentleman at the door
Hay cinco libros en la mesa
There are five books on the table

④ **No puedo salir contigo**
I can't go out with you

⑤ **¿Sabes nadar?**
Can you swim?

⑥ **No veo nada**
I can't see anything

¿Es que no me oyes?
Can't you hear me?

⑦ **Dale el libro a Isabel**
Give the book to Isabel

⑧ **las diez menos cinco**
five to ten

a las siete menos cuarto
at a quarter to seven

⑨ **Lo hice para ayudaros**
I did it to help you
Se inclinó para atarse el cordón de zapato
He bent down to tie his shoelace

⑩ **Este libro es fácil/difícil de leer**
This book is easy/difficult to read

must

+ When *must* expresses an assumption, **deber de** is often used → 1

⚠️ NOTE: This meaning is also often expressed by **deber** directly followed by the infinitive → 2

+ When it expresses obligation, there are three possible translations:

— **tener que**	→ 3
— **deber**	→ 4
— **hay que** (impersonal)	→ 5

may

+ If *may* expresses possibility, it can be translated by:

— **poder**
— **puede (ser) que** + subjunctive } → 6

+ To express permission, use **poder** → 7

will

+ If *will* expresses willingness or desire rather than the future, the present tense of **querer** is used → 8

would

+ If *would* expresses willingness, use the preterite or imperfect of **querer** → 9

+ When a repeated or habitual action in the past is referred to, use

— the imperfect → 10

— the imperfect of **soler** + infinitive → 11

1. **Ha debido de mentir**
   He must have lied
   Debe de gustarle
   She must like it

2. **Debe estar por aquí cerca**
   It must be near here
   Debo haberlo dejado en el tren
   I must have left it on the train

3. **Tenemos que salir temprano mañana**
   We must leave early tomorrow
   Tengo que irme
   I must go

4. **Debo visitarles**
   I must visit them
   Debéis escuchar lo que se os dice
   You must listen to what is said to you

5. **Hay que entrar por ese lado**
   One (We *etc*) must get in that way

6. **Todavía puede cambiar de opinión**
   He may still change his mind
   Creo que puede llover esta tarde
   I think it may rain this afternoon
   Puede (ser) que no lo sepa
   She may not know

7. **¿Puedo irme?**   **Puede sentarse**
   May I go?   You may sit down

8. **Quiere Vd esperar un momento, por favor?**
   Will you wait a moment, please?
   No quiere ayudarme
   He won't help me

9. **No quisieron venir**
   They wouldn't come

10. **Las miraba hora tras hora**
    She would watch them for hours on end

11. **Últimamente solía comer muy poco**
    Latterly he would eat very little

☐ Pronunciation of Vowels

Spanish vowels are always clearly pronounced and not relaxed in unstressed syllables as happens in English.

	EXAMPLES	HINTS ON PRONUNCIATION
[a]	**ca**sa	Between English *a* as in *hat* and *u* as in *hut*
[e]	**pen**sar	Similar to English *e* in *pet*
[i]	**fi**lo	Between English *i* as in *pin* and *ee* as in *been*
[o]	**lo**co	Similar to English *o* in *hot*
[u]	**lu**na	Between English *ew* as in *few* and *u* as in *put*

☐ Pronunciation of Diphthongs

All these diphthongs are shorter than similar English diphthongs.

[ai]	**bai**le, **hay**	Like *i* in *side*
[au]	**cau**sa	Like *ou* in *sound*
[ei]	**pei**ne, **rey**	Like *ey* in *grey*
[eu]	**deu**da	Like the vowel sounds in English *may you*, but without the sound of the *y*
[oi]	**boi**na, **voy**	Like *oy* in *boy*

☐ Semi-consonants

[j]	**hacia, ya**	**i** following a consonant and preceding a
	tiene, yeso	vowel, and **y** preceding a vowel are
	labio, yo	pronounced as *y* in English *yet*
[w]	**agua, bueno**	**u** following a consonant and preceding a
	arduo, ruido	vowel is pronounced as *w* in English *walk*

⚠ EXCEPTIONS: **gue, gui** (see p 286)

Pronunciation of Consonants

Some consonants are pronounced almost exactly as in English: [l, m, n, f, k, and in some cases g].

Others, listed below, are similar to English, but differences should be noted.

EXAMPLES

[p]	**p**adre	They are not aspirated, unlike
[k]	**c**o**c**o	English *pot*, *cook* and *ten*.
[t]	**t**an	
[t]	**t**odo, **t**ú	Pronounced with the tip of the
[d]	**d**oy, bal**d**e	tongue touching the upper front teeth and not the roof of the mouth as in English.

The following consonants are not heard in English:

EXAMPLES

[β]	la**b**io	This is pronounced between upper and lower lips, which do not touch, unlike English *b* as in *bend*.
[ɣ]	ha**g**a	Similar to English *g* as in *gate*, but tongue does not touch the soft palate.
[ɲ]	a**ñ**o	Similar to *ni* in *onion*
[x]	**j**ota	Like the guttural *ch* in lo*ch*
[r]	pe**r**a	A single trill with the tip of the tongue against the teeth ridge.
[rr]	**r**ojo, pe**rr**o	A multiple trill with the tip of the tongue against the teeth ridge.

❏ From spelling to sounds

Note the pronunciation of the following (groups of) letters.

LETTER	PRONOUNCED	
b, v	[b]	These letters have the same value. At the start of a breath group, and after written **m** and **n**, the sound is similar to English *boy* → 1
	[β]	in all other positions, the sound is unknown in English (see p 285) → 2
c	[k]	Before **a, o, u** or a consonant, like English *keep*, but not aspirated → 3
	[θ/s]	Before **e, i** like English *thin*, or, in Latin America and parts of Spain, like English *same* → 4
ch	[tʃ]	Like English *church* → 5
d	[d]	At the start of the breath group and after **l** or **n**, it is pronounced similar to English *deep* (see p 285) → 6
	[ð]	Between vowels and after consonants (except **l** or **n**), it is pronounced very like English *though* → 7
	[(ð)]	At the end of words, and in the verb ending **-ado**, it is often not pronounced → 8
g	[x]	Before **e, i**, pronounced gutturally, similar to English *loch* → 9
	[g]	At the start of the breath group and after **n**, it is pronounced like English *get* → 10
	[ɣ]	In other positions the sound is unknown in English → 11
gue	[ge/ɣe]	The **u** is silent → 12
gui	[gi/ɣi]	
güe	[gwe/ɣwe]	The **u** is pronounced like English *walk* → 13
güi	[gwi/ɣwi]	

1 **bomba** ['bomba]	**voy** [boi]	**vicio** ['biθjo]
2 **hubo** ['uβo]	**de veras** [de 'βeras]	**lavar** [la'βar]
3 **casa** ['kasa]	**coco** ['koko]	**cumbre** ['kumbre]
4 **cero** ['θero/'sero]	**cinco** ['θiŋko/'siŋko]	
5 **mucho** ['mutʃo]	**chuchería** [tʃutʃe'ria]	
6 **doy** [doi]	**balde** ['balde]	**bondad** [bon'dað]
7 **modo** ['moðo]	**ideal** [iðe'al]	
8 **Madrid** [ma'ðri(ð)]	**comprado** [kom'pra(ð)o]	
9 **gente** ['xente]	**giro** ['xiro]	**general** [xene'ral]
10 **ganar** [ga'nar]	**pongo** ['poŋgo]	
11 **agua** ['aɣwa]	**agrícola** [a'ɣrikola]	
12 **guija** ['gixa]	**guerra** ['gerra]	**pague** ['paɣe]
13 **agüero** [a'ɣwero]	**argüir** [ar'ɣwir]	

❏ **From spelling to sounds** *(Continued)*

h	[-]	This is always silent → 1
j	[x]	Like the guttural sound in English lo*ch*, but often aspirated at the end of a word → 2
ll	[ʎ]	Similar to English *-lli-* in mi*lli*on → 3
	[j/ʒ]	In some parts of Spain and in Latin America, like English *y*et or plea*s*ure → 4
-nv-	[mb]	This combination of letters is pronounced as in English i*mb*ibe → 5
ñ	[ɲ]	As in English o*ni*on → 6
q	[k]	Always followed by silent letter **u**, and pronounced as in English *k*eep, but not aspirated → 7
s	[s]	Except when mentioned below, like English *s*ing → 8
	[z]	When followed by **b, d, g, l, m, n** like English *z*oo → 9
w	[w]	Like English *v, w* → 10
x	[ks]	Between vowels, often like English e*x*it → 11
	[s]	Before a consonant, and, increasingly, even between vowels, like English *s*end → 12
y	[j]	Like English *y*es → 13
	[ʒ]	In some parts of Latin America, like English lei*s*ure → 14
z	[θ]	Like English *th*in → 15
	[s]	In some parts of Spain and in Latin America, like English *s*end → 16

1	**hombre** ['ombre]	**hoja** ['oxa]	**ahorrar** [ao'rrar]
2	**jota** ['xota]	**tejer** [te'xer]	**reloj** [re'lo(h)]
3	**calle** ['kaʎe]	**llamar** [ʎa'mar]	
4	**pillar** [pi'jar/pi'ʒar]	**olla** ['oja/'oʒa]	
5	**enviar** [em'bjar]	**sin valor** ['sim ba'lor]	
6	**uña** ['uɲa]	**bañar** [ba'ɲar]	
7	**aquel** [a'kel]	**querer** [ke'rer]	
8	**está** [es'ta]	**serio** ['serjo]	
9	**desde** ['dezðe]	**mismo** ['mizmo]	**asno** ['azno]
10	**wáter** ['bater]	**Walkman®** [wak'man]	
11	**éxito** ['eksito]	**máximo** ['maksimo]	
12	**extra** ['estra]	**sexto** ['sesto]	
13	**yo** [jo]	**yedra** ['jeðra]	
14	**yeso** ['ʒeso]	**yerno** ['ʒerno]	
15	**zapato** [θa'pato]	**zona** ['θona]	**luz** [luθ]
16	**zaguán** [sa'ɣwan]	**zueco** ['sweko]	**pez** [pes]

❑ Normal Word Stress

There are simple rules to establish which syllable in a Spanish word is stressed. When an exception to these rules occurs an acute accent (stress-mark) is needed (see p 292). These rules are as follows:

— words ending in a vowel or combination of vowels, or with the consonants **-s** or **-n** are stressed on the next to last syllable. The great majority of Spanish words fall into this category → 1

— words ending in a consonant other than **-s** or **-n** bear the stress on the last syllable → 2

— a minority of words bear the stress on the second to last syllable, and these always need an accent → 3

— some nouns change their stress from singular to plural → 4

❑ Stress in diphthongs

In the case of diphthongs there are rules to establish which of the vowels is stressed (see p 284 for pronunciation). These rules are as follows:

— diphthongs formed by the combination of a 'weak' vowel (**i**, **u**) and a 'strong' vowel (**a**, **e** or **o**) bear the stress on the strong vowel → 5

— diphthongs formed by the combination of two 'weak' vowels bear the stress on the second vowel → 6

⚠ NOTE: Two 'strong' vowels don't form a diphthong but are pronounced as two separate vowels. In these cases stress follows the normal rules → 7

1. **ca**se — **ca**sas
   house — houses
   corre — **co**rren
   he runs — they run
   pa**la**bra — pa**la**bras
   word — words
   crisis — **cri**sis
   crisis — crises

2. re**loj**
   watch
   ver**dad**
   truth
   bati**dor**
   beater

3. mur**cié**lago
   bat
   pájaro
   bird

4. ca**rác**ter — carac**te**res
   character — characters
   régimen — re**gí**menes
   regime — regimes

5. **ba**ile
   dance
   boina — **pe**ine
   beret — comb
   causa — **rei**na
   cause — queen

6. **fui** — **viu**do
   I went — widower

7. me ma**re**o — ca**er**
   I feel dizzy — to fall
   caos — co**rre**a
   chaos — leash

☐ The acute accent (´)

This is used in writing to show that a word is stressed contrary to the normal rules for stress (see p 290) →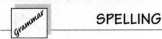

The following points should be noted:

- The same syllable is stressed in the plural form of adjectives and nouns as in the singular. To show this, it is necessary to

  — add an accent in the case of unaccented nouns and adjectives ending in **-n** → 2

  — drop the accent from nouns and adjectives ending in **-n** or **-s** which have an accent on the last syllable → 3

- The feminine form of accented nouns or adjectives does not have an accent → 4

- When object pronouns are added to certain verb forms an accent is required to show that the syllable stressed in the verb form does not change. These verb forms are:

  — the gerund → 5
  — the infinitive, when followed by two pronouns → 6
  — imperative forms, except for the 2nd person plural → 7

- The absolute superlative forms of adjectives are always accented → 8

- Accents on adjectives are not affected by the addition of the adverbial suffix **-mente** → 9

1	**autobús**		**revolución**
	bus		revolution
	relámpago		**árboles**
	lightning		trees
2	**orden**	→	**órdenes**
	order		orders
	examen	→	**exámenes**
	examination		examinations
	joven	→	**jóvenes**
	young		young
3	**revolución**	→	**revoluciones**
	revolution		revolutions
	autobús	→	**autobuses**
	bus		buses
	parlanchín	→	**parlanchines**
	chatty		chatty
4	**marqués**	→	**marquesa**
	marquis		marchioness
	francés	→	**francesa**
	French *(masc)*		French *(fem)*
5	**comprando**	→	**comprándo(se)lo**
	buying		buying it (for him/her/them)
6	**vender**	→	**vendérselas**
	to sell		to sell them to him/her/them
7	**compra**	→	**cómpralo**
	buy		buy it
	hagan	→	**háganselo**
	do		do it for him/her/them
8	**viejo**	→	**viejísimo**
	old		ancient
	caro	→	**carísimo**
	expensive		very expensive
9	**fácil**	→	**fácilmente**
	easy		easily

☐ The acute accent *(Continued)*

It is also used to distinguish between the written forms of words which are pronounced the same but have a different meaning or function. These are as follows:

- Possessive adjectives/personal pronouns → 1

- Demonstrative adjectives/demonstrative pronouns → 2

- Interrogative and exclamatory forms of adverbs, pronouns and adjectives → 3

  ⚠ NOTE: The accent is used in indirect as well as direct questions and exclamations → 4

- The pronoun **él** and the article **el** → 5

- A small group of words which could otherwise be confused. These are:

de	of, from	**dé**	give (pres subj)
mas	but	**más**	more
si	if	**sí**	yes; himself etc → 6
solo/a	alone	**sólo**	only → 7
te	you	**té**	tea

☐ The dieresis (¨)

This is used only in the combinations **güi** or **güe** to show that the **u** is pronounced as a semi-consonant (see p 284) → 8

1. **Han robado mi coche**
They've stolen my car
¿Te gusta tu trabajo?
Do you like your job?

A mí no me vio
He didn't see me
Tú, ¿que opinas?
What do you think?

2. **Me gusta esta casa**
I like this house
¿Ves aquellos edificios?
Can you see those buildings?

Me quedo con ésta
I'll take this one
Aquéllos son más bonitos
Those are prettier

3. **El chico con quien viajé**
The boy I travelled with
Donde quieras
Wherever you want

¿Con quién viajaste?
Who did you travel with?
¿Dónde encontraste eso?
Where did you find that?

4. **¿Cómo se abre?**
How does it open?

No sé cómo se abre
I don't know how it opens

5. **El puerto queda cerca**
The harbour's nearby

Él no quiso hacerlo
HE refused to do it

6. **si no viene**
if he doesn't come

Sí que lo sabe
Yes he DOES know

7. **Vino solo**
He came by himself

Sólo lo sabe él
Only he knows

8. **¡Qué vergüenza!**
How shocking!
En seguida averigüé dónde estaba
I found out straight away where it was

SPELLING

296

❑ Regular spelling changes

The consonants **c**, **g** and **z** are modified by the addition of certain verb or plural endings and by some suffixes. Most of the cases where this occurs have already been dealt with under the appropriate part of speech, but are summarized here along with other instances not covered elsewhere.

Verbs

The changes set out below occur so that the consonant of the verb stem is always pronounced the same as in the infinitive. For verbs affected by these changes see the list of verbs on p 81.

INFINITIVE	CHANGE			TENSES AFFECTED
-car	c + e	→	-que	Present subj, pret → ☐1
-cer, -cir	c + a, o	→	-za, -zo	Present, pres subj → ☐2
-gar	g + e, i	→	-gue, -gui	Present subj, pret → ☐3
-guar	gu + e	→	-güe	Present subj, pret → ☐4
-ger, -gir	g + a, o	→	-ja, -jo	Present, pres subj → ☐5
-guir	gu + a, o	→	-ga, -go	Present, pres subj → ☐6
-zar	z + e	→	-ce	Present subj, pret → ☐7

Noun and adjective plurals

SINGULAR		PLURAL
vowel + z	→	-ces → ☐8

Nouns and adjectives + suffixes

ENDING	SUFFIX	NEW ENDING
vowel + z +	-cito	-cecito → ☐9
-go, -ga +	-ito, -illo	-guito/a, -guillo/a → ☐10
-co, -ca +	-ito, -illo	-quito/a, -quillo/a → ☐11

Adjective absolute superlatives

ENDING	SUPERLATIVE
-co	-quísimo → ☐12
-go	-guísimo → ☐13
vowel + z	-císimo → ☐14

Grammar

1. **Es inútil que lo busques aquí**
   It's no good looking for it here
   Saqué dos entradas
   I got two tickets
2. **Hace falta que venzas tu miedo**
   You must overcome your fear
3. **No creo que lleguemos antes**
   I don't think we'll be there any sooner
   Ya le pagué
   I've already paid her
4. **Averigüé dónde estaba la casa**
   I found out where the house was
5. **Cojo el autobús, es más barato**
   I take the bus, it's cheaper
6. **¿Sigo?**
   Shall I go on?
7. **No permiten que se cruce la frontera**
   They don't allow people to cross the border
   Nunca simpaticé mucho con él
   I never got on very well with him

8. | **voz** | → | **voces** | | **luz** | → | **luces** |
   |---|---|---|---|---|---|---|
   | voice | | voices | | light | | lights |
   | **veloz** | → | **veloces** | | **capaz** | → | **capaces** |
   | quick | | | | capable | | |

9. | **luz** | → | **lucecita** |
   |---|---|---|
   | light | | little light |

10. | **amigo** | → | **amiguito** |
    |---|---|---|
    | friend | | chum |

11. | **chico** | → | **chiquillo** |
    |---|---|---|
    | boy | | little boy |

12. | **rico** | → | **riquísimo** |
    |---|---|---|
    | rich | | extremely rich |

13. | **largo** | → | **larguísimo** |
    |---|---|---|
    | long | | very, very long |

14. | **feroz** | → | **ferocísimo** |
    |---|---|---|
    | fierce | | extremely fierce |

A, a	[a]	**J, j**	['xota]	**R, r**	['erre]
B, b	[be]	**K, k**	[ka]	**S, s**	['ese]
C, c	[θe]	**L, l**	['ele]	**T, t**	[te]
Ch, ch	[tʃe]	**Ll, ll**	['eʎe]	**U, u**	[u]
D, d	[de]	**M, m**	['eme]	**V, v**	['uβe]
E, e	[e]	**N, n**	['ene]	**W, w**	['uβe'doble]
F, f	['efe]	**Ñ, ñ**	['eɲe]	**X, x**	['ekis]
G, g	[xe]	**O, o**	[o]	**Y, y**	[i'γrjeγa]
H, h	['atʃe]	**P, p**	[pe]	**Z, z**	['θeta]
I, i	[i]	**Q, q**	[ku]		

- The letters are feminine and you therefore talk of **una a**, or **la a**.
- Capital letters are used as in English except for the following:
  — adjectives of nationality:

  e.g. **una ciudad alemana**   **un autor español**
         a German town   a Spanish author

  — languages:

  e.g. **¿Habla Vd inglés?**   **Hablan español e italiano**
         Do you speak English?   They speak Spanish and Italian

  — days of the week:

lunes	Monday
martes	Tuesday
miércoles	Wednesday
jueves	Thursday
viernes	Friday
sábado	Saturday
domingo	Sunday

  — months of the year:

enero	January	**julio**	July
febrero	February	**agosto**	August
marzo	March	**se(p)tiembre**	September
abril	April	**octubre**	October
mayo	May	**noviembre**	November
junio	June	**diciembre**	December

Spanish punctuation differs from English in the following ways:

Question marks

There are inverted question marks and exclamation marks at the beginning of a question or exclamation, as well as upright ones at the end.

Indications of dialogue

Dashes are used to indicate dialogue, and are equivalent to the English inverted commas:

– ¿Vendrás conmigo? – le preguntó María
'Will you come with me?' Maria asked him

⚠ NOTE: When no expression of saying, replying etc follows, only one dash is used at the beginning:

– Sí. 'Yes.'

Letter headings

At the beginning of a letter, a colon is used instead of the English comma:

    Querida Cristina: Dear Cristina,   **Muy Sr. mío:** Dear Sir,

Punctuation terms in Spanish

.	punto	!	se cierra admiración
,	coma	" "	comillas (used as '...')
;	punto y coma	"	se abren comillas
:	dos puntos	"	se cierran comillas
...	puntos suspensivos	( )	paréntesis
¿ ?	interrogación	(	se abre paréntesis
¿	se abre interrogación	)	se cierra paréntesis
?	se cierra interrogación	–	guión
¡ !	admiración		
¡	se abre admiración	punto y aparte	new paragraph
		punto final	last full stop

```
4 6 2
8 1 5
9 3 1
```
NUMBERS   300

Cardinal numbers *(one, two, three etc)*

cero	0	setenta	70
uno (un, una)	1	ochenta	80
dos	2	noventa	90
tres	3	cien (ciento)	100
cuatro	4	ciento uno(una)	101
cinco	5	ciento dos	102
seis	6	ciento diez	110
siete	7	ciento cuarenta y dos	142
ocho	8	doscientos(as)	200
nueve	9	doscientos(as) uno(una)	201
diez	10	doscientos(as) dos	202
once	11	trescientos(as)	300
doce	12	cuatrocientos(as)	400
trece	13	quinientos(as)	500
catorce	14	seiscientos(as)	600
quince	15	setecientos(as)	700
dieciséis	16	ochocientos(as)	800
diecisiete	17	novecientos(as)	900
dieciocho	18	mil	1.000
diecinueve	19	mil uno(una)	1.001
veinte	20	mil dos	1.002
veintiuno	21	mil doscientos veinte	1.220
veintidós	22	dos mil	2.000
treinta	30	cien mil	100.000
treinta y uno	31	doscientos(as) mil	200.000
cuarenta	40	un millón	1.000.000
cincuenta	50	dos millones	2.000.000
sesenta	60	un billón	1.000.000.000.000

Fractions

un medio; medio(a)	$\frac{1}{2}$
un tercio	$\frac{1}{3}$
dos tercios	$\frac{2}{3}$
un cuarto	$\frac{1}{4}$
tres cuartos	$\frac{3}{4}$
un quinto	$\frac{1}{5}$
cinco y tres cuartos	$5\frac{3}{4}$

Others

cero coma cinco	0,5
uno coma tres	1,3
(el, un) diez por ciento	10%
dos más/y dos	2 + 2
dos menos dos	2 − 2
dos por dos	2 × 2
dos dividido por dos	2 ÷ 2

```
4 6 2
8 1 5
9 3 1
```

◻ Points to note on cardinals

◆ **uno** drops the **o** before masculine nouns, and the same applies when in compound numerals:

un libro *1 book,* **treinta y un niños** *31 children*

◆ 1, 21, 31 etc and 200, 300, 400 etc have feminine forms:

cuarenta y una pesetas *41 pesetas,* **quinientas libras** *£500*

◆ **ciento** is used before numbers smaller than 100, otherwise **cien** is used:

ciento cuatro *104* but **cien pesetas** *100 pesetas,* **cien mil** *100,000* (see also p 206)

◆ **millón** takes **de** before a noun:

un millón de personas *1,000,000 people*

◆ **mil** is only found in the plural when meaning *thousands of:*

miles de solicitantes *thousands of applicants*

◆ cardinals normally precede ordinals:

los tres primeros pisos *the first three floors*

⚠ NOTE: The full stop is used with numbers over one thousand and the comma with decimals i.e. the opposite of English usage.

❑ **Ordinal numbers** (*first, second, third etc*)

primero (primer, primera)	1°,1ª	undécimo(a)	11°,11ª
segundo(a)	2°,2ª	duodécimo(a)	12°,12ª
tercero (tercer, tercera)	3°,3ª	decimotercer(o)(a)	13°,13ª
cuarto(a)	4°,4ª	decimocuarto(a)	14°,14ª
quinto(a)	5°,5ª	decimoquinto(a)	15°,15ª
sexto(a)	6°,6ª	decimosexto(a)	16°,16ª
séptimo(a)	7°,7ª	decimoséptimo(a)	17°,17ª
octavo(a)	8°,8ª	decimoctavo(a)	18°,18ª
noveno(a)	9°,9ª	decimonoveno(a)	19°,19ª
décimo(a)	10°,10ª	vigésimo(a)	20°,20ª

Points to note on ordinals

• They agree in gender and in number with the noun, which they normally precede, except with royal titles:

> **la primera vez**   **Felipe segundo**
> the first time   Philip II

• **primero** and **tercero** drop the o before a masculine singular noun:

> **el primer premio**   **el tercer día**
> the first prize   the third day

• Beyond **décimo** ordinal numbers are rarely used, and they are replaced by the cardinal number placed immediately after the noun:

> **el siglo diecisiete**   **Alfonso doce**   **en el piso trece**
> the seventeenth century Alfonso XII   on the 13th floor

⚠ BUT: **vigésimo(a)** 20th
(but not with royal titles or centuries)
centésimo(a) 100th
milésimo(a) 1,000th
millonésimo(a) 1,000,000th

```
4 6 2
8 1 5
9 3 1
```

◻ Numbers: Other Uses

- collective numbers:

un par	2, a couple
una decena (de personas)	about 10 (people)
una docena (de niños)	(about) a dozen (children)
una quincena (de hombres)	about fifteen (men)
una veintena* (de coches)	about twenty (cars)
un centenar, una centena (de casas)	about a hundred (houses)
cientos/centenares de personas	hundreds of people
un millar (de soldados)	about a thousand (soldiers)
miles/millares de moscas	thousands of flies

* 30, 40, 50 can also be converted in the same way.

- measurements:

veinte metros cuadrados	20 square metres
veinte metros cúbicos	20 cubic metres
un puente de cuarenta metros de largo/longitud	a bridge 40 metres long

- distance:

De aquí a Madrid hay 400 km	Madrid is 400 km away
a siete km de aquí	7 km from here

◻ Telephone Numbers

Póngame con Madrid, el cuatro, cincuenta y ocho, veintidós, noventa y tres
I would like Madrid 458 22 93

Me da Valencia, el veinte, cincuenta y uno, setenta y tres
Could you get me Valencia 20 51 73

Extensión tres, tres, cinco/trescientos treinta y cinco
Extension number 335

⚠ NOTE: In Spanish telephone numbers may be read out individually, but more frequently they are broken down into groups of two. They are written in groups of two or three numbers (never four).

TIME 304

◻ The Time

¿Qué hora es? *What time is it?*

Es ... *(1 o'clock, midnight, noon)*	*It's ...*
Son las ... *(other times)*	

Es la una y cuarto *It's 1.15*
Son las diez menos cinco *It's 9.55*

00.00	**medianoche; las doce (de la noche)**	*midnight, twelve o'clock*
00.10	**las doce y diez (de la noche)**	
00.15	**las doce y cuarto**	
00.30	**las doce y media**	
00.45	**la una menos cuarto**	
01.00	**la una (de la madrugada)**	*one a.m., one o'clock in the morning*
01.10	**la una y diez (de la madrugada)**	
02.45	**las tres menos cuarto**	
07.00	**las siete (de la mañana)**	
07.50	**las ocho menos diez**	
12.00	**mediodía; las doce (de la mañana)**	*noon, twelve o'clock*
13.00	**la una (de la tarde)**	*one p.m., one o'clock in the afternoon*
19.00	**las siete (de la tarde)**	*seven p.m., seven o'clock in the evening*
21.00	**las nueve (de la noche)**	*nine p.m., nine o'clock at night*

⚠ NOTE: When referring to a timetable, the 24 hour clock is used:

las dieciséis cuarenta y cinco	16.45
las veintiuna quince	21.15

¿A qué hora vas a venir? – A las siete
What time are you coming? – At seven o'clock

Las oficinas cierran de dos a cuatro
The offices are closed from two until four

Vendré a eso de/hacia las siete y media
I'll come at around 7.30

a las seis y pico
just after 6 o'clock

a las cinco en punto
at 5 o'clock sharp

entre las ocho y las nueve
between 8 and 9 o'clock

Son más de las tres y media
It's after half past three

Hay que estar allí lo más tarde a las diez
You have to be there by ten o'clock at the latest

Tiene para media hora
He'll be half an hour (at it)

Estuvo sin conocimiento durante un cuarto de hora
She was unconscious for a quarter of an hour

Les estoy esperando desde hace una hora/desde las dos
I've been waiting for them for an hour/since two o'clock

Se fueron hace unos minutos
They left a few minutes ago

Lo hice en veinte minutos
I did it in twenty minutes

El tren llega dentro de una hora
The train arrives in an hour('s time)

¿Cuánto (tiempo) dura la película?
How long does the film last?

por la mañana/tarde/noche
in the morning/afternoon/evening/at night

mañana por la mañana tomorrow morning	**ayer por la tarde** yesterday afternoon or evening
anoche last night	**anteayer** the day before yesterday	**pasado mañana** the day after tomorrow

□ Dates

¿Qué día es hoy?	
¿A qué día estamos?	What's the date today?
Es (el) ...	
Estamos a ...	It's the ...
uno/primero de mayo	1st of May
dos de mayo	2nd of May
veintiocho de mayo	28th of May
lunes tres de octubre	Monday the 3rd of October
Vienen el siete de marzo	They're coming on the 7th of March

⚠ NOTE: Use cardinal numbers for dates. Only for the first of the month can the ordinal number sometimes be used.

□ Years

Nací en 1970
I was born in 1970
el veinte de enero de mil novecientos setenta
(on) 20th January 1970

□ Other expressions

en los años cincuenta	during the fifties
en el siglo veinte	in the twentieth century
en mayo	in May
lunes (quince)	Monday (the 15th)
el quince de marzo	on March the 15th
el/los lunes	on Monday/Mondays
dentro de diez días	in 10 days' time
hace diez días	10 days ago

□ Age

¿Qué edad tiene?	
¿Cuántos años tiene?	How old is he/she?
Tiene 23 (años)	He/She is 23
Tiene unos 40 años	He/She is around 40
A los 21 años	At the age of 21

grammar

The following index lists comprehensively both grammatical terms and key words in English and Spanish.

a 256, 280
a + el 196
a 200
a governed by verbs 66
personal 257
with infinitives 46, 66
a condición de que 60
a fin de que 60
a lot 252
a menos que 60
a no ser que 60
a que 238
ability 280
abolir 82
about 265
above 265
abrir 83
absolute superlative 208
abstract nouns 202
acabar de 54, 56
accent, acute 290, 292, 294
according to 265
aconsejar 48, 58
acostarse 26
actuar 84
address forms 226
adjectives 204
position 224
used as adverbs 250

shortened forms 206
adquirir 85
adverbs 250
after 265
against 262
age 280, 306
agent 32, 260
ago 306
agreement:
of adjectives 204, 210, 212, 214, 218, 220
of ordinals 302
of past participle 32
al 196
al + infinitive 257
alegrarse 58
algo 236
alguien 236
algún 220
alguno adjective 220
pronoun 236
all 220
almorzar 86
along 260
alphabet 298
amanecer 40
ambos 220
among 263
andar 87
anochecer 40
another 220

ante 261
antes de 261
antes (de) que 60
antiguo 224
any 220
apposition, nouns in 198, 200
approximately 265
aquel 212
aquél 248
aquella 212
aquélla 248
aquellas 212
aquéllas 248
aquello 248
aquellos 212
aquéllos 248
-**ar** verbs 6
around 260, 263
arrepentirse 26
articles 196
as far as 264
as much as 252
as ... as 252
asking, verbs of 58
at 256, 257, 259
atreverse 26
augmentatives 268
aún 254
aunar 88
aunque 64
avergonzar 89
averiguar 90
backwards 263
bad 210, 250

badly 250, 252
bajo 262
barring 264
bastante 254
bastante para, (lo) 252
bastante ... para 208
bastar 42
be, to 280
because 260
before 261
behind 261, 263, 265
belonging to 258
below 262
bendecir 91
best 210, 252
better 210, 252
between 263
bien 250, 252, 254
big 210
both 220
buen 206
bueno 210, 250
by 32, 258, 260
caber 92
cada 220
cada uno 236
cada vez más 252
cada vez menos 252
caer 93
calendar 306
capitals, use of 298
cardinal numbers

300
casarse 26
cause 260
certain 220
cien 206, 301
ciento 301
cierto 220
cocer 94
coger 95
collective numbers 303
colour 224
comer 6
commands 14
como 254, 266
como si 60
comparative of adjectives 208
comparative of adverbs 252
compound tenses 18
con 262
governed by verbs 66
with infinitives 46
con + mí 234
con + sí 234
con + ti 234
con tal (de) que 60
conditional 6
conditional perfect 18, 20
conducir 96
conjunctions 266
conmigo 234
conseguir 48

consigo 234
consonants: pronunciation 285
construir 97
contar 98
contents 258
contigo 234
continuar 52
continuous tenses 52
contra 262
crecer 99
creerse 40
cruzar 100
cual 244
cualesquiera 220
cualquier 206
cualquiera adjective 220 pronoun 236
cuando 64, 240
cuánta 214
cuántas 214
cuánto 214 adjective 214 adverb 254
cuántos 214
cubrir 101
cuyo 238
dar 102
dates 257, 306
days of the week 298
de preposition 32, 258
after superlatives

208
governed by verbs
66
with infinitives 46
dé 294
de + el 196
de forma que 62
de manera que 62
de modo que 62
de que 238
debajo de 262
deber 48
deber (de) 282
decidir 48
decir 103
decirse 40
definite article 196
uses of 198
dejar 48, 58
dejar caer 50
del 196
delante de 262
demás, los 220
demasiado 254
demasiado ...
   para 208, 252
demonstrative
adjectives 212
demonstrative
pronouns 248
desde 262
use of tense
   following 54, 56
desear 48, 58
después (de) que
   64, 266
después de:
   with perfect

infinitive 50
detenerse 26
detrás de 263
dialogue,
   indication of 299
dieresis 294
diferente 224
diminutives 268
diphthongs:
   pronunciation
   284
direct object
pronouns 228
direct questions
   276
direct speech 270
dirigir 104
distance 257, 303
distinguir 105
doler 78
donde 240
dormir 106
dormirse 26
double
   prepositions 261,
   263
downwards 263
dudar que 58
durante 263
duration 258
during 263
e 266
each 220
each other 26
el article 196
él pronoun 226
el cual 240
el de 242

el más ... (que)
   208
el menos ... (que)
   208
el mío 246
el nuestro 246
el que
   relative pronoun
   240, 242
   conjunction 60
el suyo 246
el tuyo 246
el vuestro 246
elegir 107
ella 226
ellas 226
ello 234
ellos 226
emotion, verbs of
   58
empezar 108
emphasis 226
en 259
governed by verbs
   66
with infinitives 46
en cuanto 64
encantar 78
enfadarse 26
enough 252, 254
entender 109
entre 263
enviar 110
-er verbs 6
erguir 111
errar 112
esa 212
ésa 248

esas 212
ésas 248
escribir 113
ese 212
ése 248
eso 248
esos 212
ésos 248
esperar 48
esta 212
ésta 248
estar conjugated 114
 use of 74, 76
 with continuous tenses 52
estas 212
éstas 248
este 212
éste 248
esto 248
estos 212
éstos 248
even 264
every 220
evitar 48
except (for) 263, 264
excepto 263
exclamatory adjectives 214
 faced with 261
faltar 42, 78
feminine:
 endings 189
 formation 192, 204

nouns 188
few 220
first conjugation 6, 8
for 260, 261, 262, 263
 in time expressions 54, 56
for the benefit of 261
former, the 248
forwards 263
fractions 300
freír 115
from 256, 258, 262
future events, use of subjunctive with 64
future perfect 18, 20, 30, 38
 use of 54
future tense 6, 28, 36
 use of 54
gender 188
 and meaning 190
general instructions 16
generalizations 198
gerund 52, 278
good 210, 250
gran 206
grande 210, 224
granizar 40
gruñir 116

gustar 78
gustar más 78
haber 42
 auxiliary 18
 conjugated 117
hablar 6
hacer 48
 conjugated 118
 to express time ago 42
 to express weather 42, 280
hacer entrar 50
hacer falta 44, 48
hacer saber 50
hacer salir 50
hacer venir 50
hacerse 26
hacia 263
hacia abajo 263
hacia adelante 263
hacia adentro 263
hacia afuera 263
hacia arriba 263
hacia atrás 263
hasta 264
hasta que 64
hay 42, 280
 conjugated 119
hay que 42, 48, 282
he 226
hearing, verbs of 48, 278
her adjective 216, 218
 pronoun 228

ners 246
hers, of 218
herself 234
him 228
himself 234
his adjective 216, 218
pronoun 246
his, of 218
how many 214
how much 214
however 62, 260
hypothetical situations 64, 226
impedir 48, 58
imperative 14
imperfect tense 6, 28, 36
use of 56
impersonal constructions 60
impersonal verbs 40
importar 78
in 256, 258, 259
in front of 262
in order to 264
indefinite adjectives 220
indefinite article 200
indefinite pronouns 236
indirect object pronouns 230
indirect questions 276, 294

infinitive 46, 278
intentar 48
interesar 78
interrogative adjectives 214
interrogative pronouns 244
into 259
intonation 276
invariable adjectives 206
inversion 276
inwards 263
ir 120
with gerund 52
ir a buscar 50
ir a to express future 54
-ir verbs 6
irregular comparatives 210, 252
irregular superlatives 210, 252
irregular verbs 80
irse 26
-ísimo 208, 252
it 40, 226, 228
its 216, 246
jactarse 26
jugar 121
la article 196
pronoun 228, 232
la mía 246
la nuestra 246
la suya 246
la tuya 246

la vuestra 246
languages 259, 298
las article 196
pronoun 228
las mías 246
las nuestras 246
las suyas 246
las tuyas 246
las vuestras 246
latter, the 248
lavarse 26, 28, 30
le 230, 232
least 252
least, the 208
leer 122
les 230
less 252, 254
less and less 252
less ... (than) 208, 252
letter headings 299
levantarse 26
little adjective 220
pronoun 252
llamarse 26
llevar in time constructions 52
llover 40, 124
lloviznar 40
lo article 202, 252
pronoun 228, 232
lo cual 240
lo mejor 252
lo peor 252
lo que 240
lograr 48
los article 196

pronoun 228
los demás 236
los míos 246
los nuestros 246
los suyos 246
los tuyos 246
los vuestros 246
lucir 123
mal 250, 252
malo 210, 250
mandar 58
mandar hacer 50
mandar llamar 50
manner 257, 258
many 220
many, so 220
más, lo 252
más 252, 254
más ... (que) 208, 252
más bien 252
más vale 44
masculine endings 189
masculine nouns 188
material 258
may 282
mayor 210
me 24, 228, 230
me 228, 234
means 256
measurements 303
medio 224
mejor 210, 252
menor 210
menos, lo 252
menos 252, 254,

280
menos ... (que) 208, 252
mi 216
mí 234
mía 218
mías 218
mientras 60
mientras que 266
mil 301
miles 301
mine 246
mine, of 218
mío 218
míos 218
mis 216
mismo 220, 224
months 258, 298
more 252, 254
more and more 252
more ... (than) 208, 252
most 252
most, the 208
motion 260
mover 126
much, so 220
mucho adjective 220
mucho pronoun 236
adverb 252, 254
must 44, 282
muy 208, 252
my 216, 218

nacer 127
nada 236
nadie 236
nationality 224, 298
necesitar 48
necessity 60
negar 128
negative
commands 14
negatives 272
in short replies 274
combination of 274
double 272
neuter article 202
neuter pronouns 228, 248
nevar 40
ni ... ni 266
ningún 220
ninguno adjective 220
pronoun 236
no 272, 274, 276
no 274
no creer que 58
no pensar que 58
no sea que 60
no ... jamás 272
no ... más 272
no ... más que 272
no ... nada 272
no ... nadie 272
no ... ni siquiera 272

no ... ni ... ni 272
no ... ninguno 272
no ... nunca 272
no ... tampoco 272
nos 24, 228, 230
nosotras 226
nosotros 226
not 274
nuestra 216
nuestras 216
nuestro 216
nuestros 216
nuevo 224
numbers 300
o 266
ó 266
o (bien) ... o (bien) 266
odiar 48
of 258
oír 48, 129
oír decir que 50
oír hablar de 50
ojalá 60
oler 130
olvidar 48
on 257, 258, 265
on behalf of 261
onto 256
opinion 58
ordenar 58
order of object pronouns 232
ordering, verbs of 58

orders 14
ordinal numbers 302
os 24, 230
other 220
otro 220
our 216, 218
ours 246
ours, of 218
ourselves 25
outwards 263
over 265, 261
pagar 131
para 264
after estar 76
governed by verbs 66
para que 60
para sí 264
parecer 44
parts of the body 198, 232
passive 32
past 261
past anterior 18, 22, 31, 39
use of 56
past participle:
agreement 32
formation 18
pedir 58, 132
pejoratives 268
pensar 48, 133
peor 210, 252
pequeño 210
perfect infinitive 50, 27
perfect tense 18,

20, 30, 38
use of 56
permitir 58
pero 266
personal a 257
personal pronouns 226
phrasal verbs 278
pluperfect tense 18, 20, 30, 38
plurals, formation of 194, 204
pobre 224
poco adjective 220
adverb 252, 254
pronoun 236
poder 48, 134, 280, 282
poderse 42
poner 135
ponerse 26
por 32, 260
after estar 76
governed by verbs 66
with infinitives 46
por debajo de 261
por delante de 261
por detrás de 261
por donde 261
por encima de 261
por entre 261
por qué 244
por ... que 62
porque 266

position: of
adjectives 224
of adverbs 250
of direct object
pronouns 228
of indirect object
pronouns 230
of ordinals 302
positive commands
14
possession 238,
278
possessive
adjectives 216
possessive
pronouns 246
possibility 60, 282
preference 261
preferir 48
prepositions 256
present continuous
54
present participle
52
present tense 6,
28, 36
use of 54
preterite 6, 29, 37
use of 56
primer 206
primero 302
procurar 48
prohibir 48, 58,
136
prometer 48
pronoun objects:
position 14, 228,
230

pronouns 226
after prepositions
234
position 228
pronunciation 284
punctuation 299
punctuation terms
299
puro 224
purpose 62
quality 258
que adjective 214
conjunction 60,
266
pronoun 238
qué 244
quedar 78
quejarse 26
querer 48, 58, 282
conjugated 137
to translate *will,
shall* 54
querer decir 50
question forms
276
question marks
299
quien 238
-quiera 64
rate 260
rather 252
reason 260
reflexive pronouns
24
position 24, 228
reflexive verbs: use
of 24
conjugation 29

regular verbs 6
rehusar 138
reír 139
relative clauses 62
relative pronouns
238
after prepositions
240
reñir 140
resolver 141
result 62
reunir 142
rogar 143
romper 144
saber 48, 145, 280
sacar 146
salir 147
same 220
san 206
satisfacer 148
se 24, 232
se cree 40
se dice 40
se puede 42
se vende 42
sea … sea 266
second conjugation
6, 10
seeing, verbs of 48,
278
seguir with gerund
52
conjugated 149
según 265
-self 220
semi-consonants:
pronunciation

284
entir 58, 150
entirse 26
equence of tenses
4
er 74, 76
onjugated 151
n passive 32
o express time
44
er mejor 44
everal 220
nape 224
ne 226
62, 266, 294
yes 276, 294
oronoun 234, 294
iempre 254
iempre que 60
ince 262
n time
expressions 54,
56
ino 266
mall 210
o ... that 252
obre 265
ome adjective
200, 220
oronoun 236
orprender 58
pelling 286
pelling changes
296

stem 6
stress 290
  in diphthongs 290
su 216
subirse 26
subject pronouns
226
subjunctive:
  imperfect 6, 80
  perfect 18, 22
  pluperfect 18, 22
  present 6
  use of 58
such 220
suffixes 268
suficiente ...
  para 208
suficientemente
  para 252
superlative of
  adjectives 208
superlative of
  adverbs 252
sus 216
suya 218
suyas 218
suyo 218
suyos 218
tal 220
también 254
tan 254
tan pronto como
  64
tan ... como 208,
  252
tan ... que 200,
  252
tanto adjective

220
adverb 254
pronoun 236
tanto como 252
tanto ... como
  208, 266
te 24, 228, 230
telephone numbers
  303
tener 152, 280
tener que 48, 282
tercer 206
tercero 302
than 266
that adjective 212
  conjunction 266
  pronoun 238, 248
the 196
their 216, 218
theirs 246
theirs, of 218
them 228
themselves 234
there is/are 280
these adjective 212
  pronoun 248
they 226
third conjugation
  6, 12
this adjective 212
  pronoun 248
those adjective
  212
  pronoun 248
through 260, 261
ti 234
time 257, 258,
  260, 304

to 256, 264, 280
296
to like 78
to oneself 264
todavía 254
todo adjective 220
pronoun 236
todo lo que 242
todos los que 242
too ... to 252
torcer 153
towards 263
traer 154
transport 259
tras 265
tratarse de 42
tronar 40
tu 216
tú 226
tus 216
tuya 218
tuyas 218
tuyo 218
tuyos 218
u 266
un article 200
una article 200
unas article 200
uncertainty 58
under 261, 262
uno ... (el) otro 236
unos article 200
until 264
up to 264
upwards 263
us 228
usted 226

ustedes 226
valer 155
valer más 44, 48
varios 224
adjective 220
pronoun 236
vencer 156
venderse 42
venir 157
ver 48, 158
verb endings 6
verbal idioms 78
verdad 276
very 208
vestirse 26
viejo 224
vivir 6
volcar 159
volver 160
volverse 26
vosotras 226
vosotros 226
vowels:
pronunciation
284
vuestra 216
vuestras 216
vuestro 216, 218
vuestros 216, 218
we 226
weather 42, 280
well 250, 252
what adjective 214
interrogative
pronoun 244
what a ... 200,
214
when 240

where 240
which adjective
214
interrogative
pronoun 244
relative
pronoun 238
who 238, 244
whom 238, 244
whose 238, 244
why 244
wishing, verbs of
58
with 262
without 265
word order 270,
272
direct questions
276
indirect questions
276
negatives 274
worse 210, 252
worst 210, 252
y 266
ya 254
years 306
yo 226
you 226
your 216, 218
yours 246
yours, of 218
yourselves 234
zurcir 161